MESSEDESIGN
JAHRBUCH

**TRADE FAIR
DESIGN ANNUAL**
2016/17

Sabine Marinescu
Janina Poesch

**MESSEDESIGN
JAHRBUCH**

TRADE FAIR DESIGN ANNUAL
2016/17

avedition

INHALT
CONTENTS

8   **Hand in Hand**
    Hand in hand

→ ARCHITECTURE AND MATERIAL

12 **Unsichtbares sichtbar machen**
    Making the invisible visible
    atelier 522 GmbH, Markdorf
    Roto Frank AG, Leinfelden-Echterdingen
    FENSTERBAU FRONTALE 2016, Nuremberg

16 **Wohnfühlszenarien**
    Feel-good scenarios
    D'art Design Gruppe GmbH, Neuss
    Schüco International KG, Bielefeld
    FENSTERBAU FRONTALE 2016, Nuremberg

20 **Laut und leise**
    Loud and quiet
    Dobas AG, Lucerne
    Argolite AG, Willisau
    Swissbau 2016, Basle

24 **Papierwolke**
    Paper cloud
    hw.design GmbH, Munich
    Munksjö Decor, Aalen
    interzum 2015, Cologne

28 **Der Elefant im Farbenladen**
    Elephant in the room
    MIKS GmbH, Hamburg
    CAPAROL Farben Lacke Bautenschutz GmbH, Ober-Ramstadt
    FARBE, AUSBAU & FASSADE 2016, Munich

32 **Alt und neu**
    Something old, something new
    Paolo Cesaretti, Milan
    Kale Group, Istanbul
    UNICERA 2016, Istanbul

38 **Königliche Lobby**
    Royal lobby
    Paolo Cesaretti, Milan
    Royal Ceramica, El Obour City
    CERSAIE 2015, Bologna

42 **Schlicht und ergreifend**
    Plain and simple
    raumbar Partnerschaftsgesellschaft für Gestaltung, Essen
    Zanders GmbH, Bergisch Gladbach
    BrauBeviale 2015, Nuremberg

→ AUTOMOBILE AND TRANSPORTATION

48 **Wanderlust**
    Wanderlust
    atelier 522 GmbH, Markdorf
    Mercedes-Benz Schweiz AG, Schlieren
    Suisse Caravan Salon 2015, Berne

52 **Offene Begegnung**
    Open encounter
    Braunwagner GmbH, Aachen
    Daimler AG, Stuttgart
    Internationale Automobil-Ausstellung (IAA) 2015, Frankfurt a. Main

56 **Erstklassige Verbindung**
    First-class connection
    Buero Philipp Moeller, Munich
    Flughafen München GmbH, Munich
    ITB 2016, Berlin

60 **Digital und analog**
    Digital and analogue
    jangled nerves GmbH, Stuttgart
    Daimler AG, Stuttgart
    CES 2016, Las Vegas

64 **Echtzeit**
    Realtime
    Atelier Markgraph GmbH, Frankfurt a. Main;
    jangled nerves, Stuttgart
    Daimler AG, Stuttgart
    Internationale Automobil-Ausstellung (IAA) 2015, Frankfurt a. Main

70 **Neu vernetzt**
    Newly connected
    KMS BLACKSPACE GmbH, Munich
    Volkswagen AG, Wolfsburg
    CES 2016, Las Vegas

74 **Urbaner Luxus**
    Urban luxury
    Meiré und Meiré GmbH & Co. KG, Cologne
    BMW AG, Munich
    Internationale Automobil-Ausstellung (IAA) 2015, Frankfurt a. Main

80 **Kinetischer Kompass**
    Kinetic compass
    Schmidhuber Brand Experience GmbH, Munich;
    Mutabor Design GmbH, Hamburg
    AUDI AG, Ingolstadt
    Internationale Automobil-Ausstellung (IAA) 2015,
    Frankfurt a. Main

86 **Gespür für Schnee**
    Sense of snow
    sons GmbH, Kempten
    Kässbohrer Geländefahrzeug AG, Laupheim
    INTERALPIN 2015, Innsbruck

    →   INTERVIEW
    →   INTERVIEW

92 **Geordnetes Chaos**
    Organised chaos
    tisch13 GmbH, Munich
    AUDI AG, Ingolstadt
    CES 2016, Las Vegas

→ **ELECTRONICS, TECHNOLOGY, AND SCIENCE**

98 **Leuchttürme des Wandels**
    Lighthouses of change
    Atelier Markgraph GmbH, Frankfurt a. Main
    Viessmann Werke GmbH & Co. KG, Allendorf (Eder)
    ISH 2015, Frankfurt a. Main

102 **Sauber zu Tisch**
    Clean taste
    D'art Design Gruppe GmbH, Neuss
    Electrolux Hausgeräte GmbH, Nuremberg
    IFA 2015, Berlin

106 **Der Takt der Bilder**
    The rhythm of the images
    D'art Design Gruppe GmbH, Neuss
    NEC Display Solutions Europe GmbH, Munich
    ISE 2016, Amsterdam

110 **Stadterholungsgebiet**
    Urban recreational area
    eins:33 GmbH, Munich
    BEKO Deutschland GmbH, Neu-Isenburg
    IFA 2015, Berlin

114 **Gestern, heute, morgen**
    Yesterday, today, tomorrow
    eins:33 GmbH, Munich
    Gaggenau Hausgeräte GmbH, Munich
    EuroCucina 2016, Milan

    →   INTERVIEW
    →   INTERVIEW

122 **Richtig verbunden!**
    Well connected!
    Heckhaus GmbH & Co. KG, Munich
    NFON AG, Munich
    CeBIT 2016, Hanover

126 **Frühlingsboten**
    Heralds of spring
    q~bus Mediatektur GmbH, Berlin
    Deutsche Telekom AG, Bonn
    CeBIT 2016, Hanover

130 **Magenta-Welle**
    Magenta wave
    q~bus Mediatektur GmbH, Berlin
    Deutsche Telekom AG, Bonn
    IFA 2015, Berlin

134 **Bewegung im Stand**
    Stand in motion
    raumkontakt GmbH, Karlsruhe
    TechnologieRegion Karlsruhe GbR, Karlsruhe
    EXPO REAL 2015, Munich

138 **Auf digitaler Ebene**
    On a digital level
    TRIAD Berlin Projektgesellschaft mbH, Berlin
    Siemens AG, Munich
    HANNOVER MESSE 2015, Hanover

142 **Eine runde Sache**
    Well-rounded
    VAVE GmbH, Offenbach a. Main
    Shanghai United Imaging Healthcare Co., Ltd.,
    Shanghai
    China International Medical Equipment Fair 2015,
    Shanghai

146 **Netzbeleuchter**
    Network illuminator
    WHITEvoid GmbH, Berlin
    Vodafone GmbH, Dusseldorf
    CeBIT 2016, Hanover

→ IN- AND EXTERIOR

152 **Wohlfühloasen**
Feel-good oasises
Architekturbüro Wörner, Stuttgart
Willi SCHILLIG Polstermöbelwerke GmbH & Co. KG, Ebersdorf-Frohnlach
imm cologne 2016, Cologne

156 **Never change a winning team**
Never change a winning team
dan pearlman Markenarchitektur GmbH, Berlin
ROCA SANITARIO S. A., Barcelona
ISH 2015, Frankfurt a. Main

160 **Puristisch und aussagekräftig**
Puristic and expressive
Heine/Lenz/Zizka Projekte GmbH, Frankfurt a. Main
Alape GmbH, Goslar
ISH 2015, Frankfurt a. Main

164 **Gesellschaftskritisches Bällebad**
Sozio-critical ball pool
Interior Architecture and Furniture Design-Programme / Oslo National Academy of the Arts, Oslo
Oslo National Academy of the Arts, Oslo
Stockholm Furniture & Light Fair 2016, Stockholm

→ INTERVIEW
→ INTERVIEW

170 **Panoptikum der Eigenheiten**
Composition of singularities
raumkontor Innenarchitektur, Dusseldorf
Deutsches Tapeten-Institut GmbH, Dusseldorf
imm cologne 2016, Cologne

176 **Polygonales Orchideenwunder**
Polygonal orchid delight
Schmidhuber Brand Experience GmbH, Munich
Franz Kaldewei GmbH & Co. KG, Ahlen
ISH 2015, Frankfurt a. Main

180 **Bühnenreif**
Stage worthy
spek DESIGN GbR, Stuttgart
Gerriets GmbH, Umkirch
Stage|Set|Scenery 2015, Berlin

184 **Neue (Ausstellungs-)Räume**
New (exhibition) rooms
Stefan Zwicky Architekt, Zurich
NR Neue Räume AG, Zurich
neue räume 2015, Zurich

188 **Welcome to the jungle …**
Welcome to the jungle …
Studio Aisslinger, Berlin
DEDON GmbH, Lüneburg
Salone del Mobile 2016, Milan

192 **Textile Architektur**
Textile architecture
Studio Aisslinger, Berlin
Kvadrat A/S, Ebeltoft
imm cologne 2016, Cologne

196 **Fadenspiel**
Cat's cradle
TRIAD Berlin Projektgesellschaft mbH, Berlin
hülsta-werke Hüls GmbH & Co. KG, Stadtlohn
imm cologne 2016, Cologne

200 **Sinn-stiftend**
Making sense of wood
Ueberholz GmbH, Wuppertal
Fachverband Tischler Nordrhein-Westfalen, Dortmund
imm cologne 2016, Cologne

→ INTERVIEW
→ INTERVIEW

→ LIFESTYLE

208 **Farbhygiene**
Colourful hygiene
,simple GmbH, Cologne
Curaden AG, Kriens
Internationale Dental-Schau (IDS) 2015, Cologne

212 **Eleganz und Exotik**
Elegance and exoticism
ARNO Design GmbH, Munich
Messe München GmbH, Munich
INHORGENTA MUNICH 2016, Munich

216 **Ab auf die Piste**
Take to the ski lopes
atelier 522 GmbH, Markdorf
Atomic Austria GmbH, Altenmarkt i. Pongau
ISPO MUNICH 2016, Munich

220 **Ladungsimpuls**
Charged impulses
b&z | Benz & Ziegler GbR, Munich
Spotify GmbH, Berlin
dmexco 2015, Cologne

224 **Moderne Tradition**
Modern tradition
DFROST GmbH & Co. KG, Stuttgart
neubau eyewear / Silhouette International
Schmied AG, Linz
opti 2016, Munich

228 **Messegaudi**
Aprés-ski fun at the fair
m|b|co Messe Bauer & Companions GmbH, Munich
K2 Sports Europe GmbH, Penzberg
ISPO MUNICH 2016, Munich

232 **Gut sortiert**
Well structured
m|b|co Messe Bauer & Companions GmbH, Munich
Marker Völkl (International) GmbH, Baar
ISPO MUNICH 2016, Munich

236 **Kraftpaket**
Powerhouse
Ozon. Büro für integrale Kommunikation., Munich
SRAM Europe Sales & Services BV, Nijkerk
EUROBIKE 2015, Friedrichshafen

240 **Wachsen und gedeihen**
Growing and flourishing
Schmidhuber Brand Experience GmbH, Stuttgart;
Milla & Partner GmbH, Stuttgart
Bundesministerium für Wirtschaft und Energie, Berlin
Expo Milano 2015, Milan

→ LIGHTING

248 **(Im-)Provisorium**
Improvised
Atelier Bernd Steinhuber, Vienna
Wever & Ducré bvba, Roeselare
Light + Building 2016, Frankfurt a. Main

INTERVIEW
INTERVIEW

254 **Strahlkraft**
Radiance
Atelier Bernd Steinhuber, Vienna
XAL GmbH, Graz
Light + Building 2016, Frankfurt a. Main

258 **In Form gefaltet**
Folded into shape
BachmannKern & Partner, Solingen
OSRAM Opto Semiconductors GmbH, Regensburg
Light + Building 2016, Frankfurt a. Main

262 **Licht und Linsen**
Light and candy
ERCO GmbH, Lüdenscheid
ERCO GmbH, Lüdenscheid
Light + Building 2016, Frankfurt a. Main

266 **Universum des Lichts**
Universe of light
Martin et Karczinski GmbH, Munich
Occhio GmbH, Munich
Light + Building 2016, Frankfurt a. Main

270 **Licht und Schatten**
Light and shadow
Meiré und Meiré GmbH & Co. KG, Cologne
BÄRO GmbH & Co. KG, Cologne
Light + Building 2016, Frankfurt a. Main

274 **Kabellos glücklich**
Light unleashed
OCKERTUNDPARTNER, Stuttgart
Nimbus Group GmbH, Stuttgart
Light + Building 2016, Frankfurt a. Main

278 **Stadt, Licht, Netz**
City, light, network
Schmidhuber Brand Experience GmbH, Munich
OSRAM GmbH, Munich
Light + Building 2016, Frankfurt a. Main

282 **Lichtschimmer**
Shimmer of light
VASKU & KLUG, Vienna
Preciosa Lighting, Kamenický Šenov
Euroluce 2015, Milan

HAND IN HAND

⟶ Editorial

„Industrie 4.0": die vollständig vernetzte Industrie, bei der Daten über den gesamten Planeten ausgetauscht werden, Roboter mit Menschen zusammenarbeiten und autonom kommunizierende Maschinen sowie riesige Datenmengen existieren, mit denen Lieferketten perfektioniert werden können. Die Verschmelzung der klassischen Industrie mit der IT hat Einzug in unsere Arbeitswelt gehalten und wirkt sich dementsprechend auch auf unsere (räumliche) Kommunikation aus – egal ob physisch oder digital.

Zu Zeiten von „Industrie 4.0" ist unser Leben geprägt von einer kompletten und weltweiten Vernetzung. Der Megatrend der Konnektivität dominiert den gesellschaftlichen Wandel und verändert nicht nur das Alltagsverhalten eines jeden Einzelnen, sondern auch die allgemeine Kommunikation und Mediennutzung: Internet und Digitalisierung durchdringen alle Bereiche unseres Lebens und beeinflussen Gesellschaft, Ökonomie und Kultur. Die Vernetzung von Gegenständen und Produkten hat sich bereits in den Massenmarkt eingeschlichen, und das mobile Netz ist längst zum täglichen Kommunikationswerkzeug sowie zum selbstverständlichen Begleiter geworden, mit dem sich Inhalte immer, überall und am besten in Echtzeit teilen lassen. Diese Beschleunigung ist mittlerweile sogar so weit vorangeschritten, dass wir Zeit oft als desynchron empfinden und sich das Gefühl der Überforderung und Informationsflut einstellt. Momentan befinden wir uns also noch in der Lernphase, wie mit diesen komplexen Entwicklungen der Mediensysteme umzugehen ist. Laut einer Prognose des amerikanischen Unternehmens Cisco Systems sollen bis zum Jahr 2020 50 Milliarden Geräte vernetzt sein. Das bedeutet, dass auf jeden Menschen weltweit circa 6,5 vernetzte Geräte kommen: „In den nächsten Jahren wird jedes Gerät ans Netz gehen. Der Trend wird jede Branche und jeden Lebensbereich erfassen", ist sich Dave Evans, Chief Futurist bei Cisco Systems, sicher. „Alles wird smart: von der Bildung über das Gesundheitssystem bis hin zur smarten Energie oder smarten Wohnräumen."

Natürlich macht diese Tendenz auch vor dem Messewesen nicht Halt: Wo sich auf der einen Seite ganze Messen den Themen Konnektivität und Autonomie widmen, rücken auf der anderen Seite Aussteller ihre innovativen Produkte in den Mittelpunkt, die uns das digitale und vernetzte Leben vereinfachen sollen. Selbstverständlich findet dies auch in der Gestaltung der Unternehmensauftritte seinen Ausdruck: Reale Welten werden durch Augmented Reality digital erweitert oder verschmelzen mit virtuellen Räumen zu neuen, immersiven Markenerlebnissen.

Für das diesjährige Messedesign Jahrbuch konnten wir viele spannende Konzepte ausfindig machen, bei denen sich Aussteller vernetzt präsentieren und ihre diesbezügliche Kompetenz auch räumlich inszenieren – wie zum Beispiel Mercedes-Benz auf der IAA in Frankfurt am Main 2015, deren Auftritt von der Show „Mercedes Live!" wesentlich geprägt war und das Thema Digitalisierung dank des einzigartigen Bühnenbilds in ein spannendes Raumerlebnis übersetzt werden konnte. Wo sich Megatrends finden lassen, sind aber auch Gegentrends zu verzeichnen. Dementsprechend haben wir auch Projekte entdeckt, die sich dadurch hervortun, dass die „gute alte" Fertigung von Hand im Mittelpunkt der Kommunikation steht. Hier haben wir noch ein bisschen genauer hingeschaut und mit fünf Gestaltern gesprochen, die uns verraten haben, wie durch perfektes Arbeiten Hand in Hand ein Messestand aufgebaut werden kann, auf dem Großexponate mit zwölf Tonnen Nutzlast ausgestellt werden; wie sich Stände und Raumeindruck während der Messezeit durch kunstvolle Handarbeit stetig verändern; wie Aussteller ihre eigene handwerkliche Präzisionsarbeit präsentieren können; und wie die Fertigung von Hand selbst zum Exponat werden kann – ganz ohne digitales Beiwerk. Damit möchten wir nicht nur eine Lanze für all jene Menschen brechen, die einen Messeauftritt unvergesslich machen, sondern auch darauf hinweisen, dass trotz zunehmender Digitalisierung Messen nach wie vor Orte sind, um persönliche Verbindungen zu schaffen, Netzwerke auszubauen sowie Innovationen mit dem Markt zu verknüpfen.

Aber egal, ob digital oder real: Wir wünschen Ihnen nun viel Spaß beim Schmökern, Lesen und Entdecken sowohl physischer als auch digitaler (Marken-)Welten!

Sabine Marinescu und Janina Poesch

HAND IN HAND

⟶ Editorial

"**Industry 4.0**"**: a fully connected industrial world in which data can be exchanged across the entire planet, robots work together with people while autonomously communicating machines and the huge data volumes that exist can be used to optimise supply chains. The merger of conventional industry with IT has already found its way into our working world and is starting to have an affect on our (spatial) communication as well—be it physical or digital.**

In these times of "Industry 4.0" our lives are shaped by a complete and worldwide network. The megatrend connectivity dominates the change in society and is changing not only the everyday behaviour of each individual, but also the general communication and use of media: internet and digitalisation have penetrated every area of our lives and are influencing society, economy and culture. The networking of objects and products has already crept into the mass market and the mobile network has long since become our daily communication tool and natural companion with which content can be shared at all times, everywhere and ideally in real time. This acceleration is meanwhile so far advanced that time sometimes seems to be out of sync and we start to feel overwhelmed by the flood of information. We are currently still in a learning phase about how to handle these complex developments of the media systems. According to a forecast by the US American company Cisco Systems, 50 billion devices will be connected by the year 2020. That is around 6.5 connected devices per person in the world: "In the next few years every device will be connected. The trend will affect every industry and every area of our lives", of that Dave Evans, Chief Futurist at Cisco Systems, is certain. "Everything will become smart: from education to the healthcare system through to smart energy and smart living spaces."

And of course this trend has not left trade fairs untouched: While on the one hand, whole trade fairs are devoted to the topics connectivity and autonomy, on the other exhibitors are turning the spotlight on innovative products which are designed to simplify our digital and networked lives. It therefore goes almost without saying that this is also reflected in the design of the stands: real worlds are extended digitally by augmented reality or merge with virtual spaces to form new, all-engulfing brand experiences.

For this year's Trade Fair Design Annual we have tracked down lots of exciting concepts in which exhibitors present their connectivity and also give the competencies this involves a spatial expression—for instance Mercedes-Benz at the IAA in Frankfurt am Main 2015, whose appearance was largely shaped by the "Mercedes Live!" show and whose unique stage set translated the theme digitalisation into an exciting spatial experience. However, where there are megatrends, there are also counter-trends. We therefore also discovered projects which set themselves apart by putting "good old" manual production at the heart of the communication. We took a closer look here and spoke to five designers who revealed how everyone worked hand in hand to construct a booth which had to bear the weight of huge twelve-tonne exhibits; how trade fair stands and the spatial impression change constantly during the trade fair through artistic handiwork; how exhibitors can present their own precision craftsmanship; and how production by hand becomes an exhibit itself—without any kind of digital accessories. In this way, we do not only want to applaud all those people who make a trade fair appearance unforgettable, but also point out that despite increasing digitalisation trade exhibitions are still places where personal links are made, networks enlarged and innovations connected with the market.

But regardless of whether digital or real: As you browse through the Annual, we wish you an enjoyable read and lots of fun discovering both physical and digital (brand) worlds!

Sabine Marinescu and Janina Poesch

ARCHITECTURE AND MATERIAL

→ Materialien bilden die Basis für unser gesamtes gestaltetes und gebautes Umfeld – und unterliegen damit logischerweise einem sich ständig wandelnden Prozess. Um diesem gerecht zu werden, müssen sich Produzenten von Roh-, Werk- und Baustoffen daher auf immer wieder neue und innovative Art und Weise präsentieren – gerade auf Messen. Und so entstehen Stände, bei denen die Materialien selbst zu Exponaten, zu raumgreifenden Skulpturen geformt oder in eine abstrahierte neue Architektur transformiert werden, um mit diesem Einsatz ihren Nutzen sowie ihre Vielseitigkeit zu demonstrieren.

→ Materials form the basis for our entire designed and built environment—and as such are logically subject to a process of constant change. To do justice to this, producers of raw, technical and building materials have to present themselves again and again in new and innovative ways—particularly at trade fairs. In the resulting stands, the materials are made into exhibits themselves, formed into huge sculptures or transformed into a new abstract architecture in order to demonstrate their benefits and their versatility.

→ 32

→ 24

→ 20

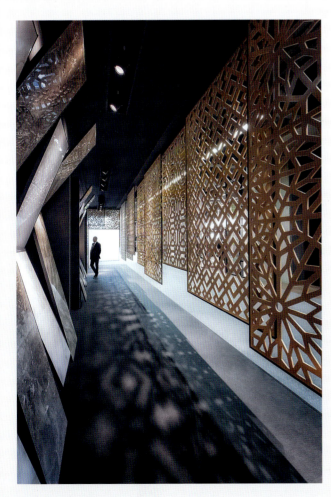
→ 38

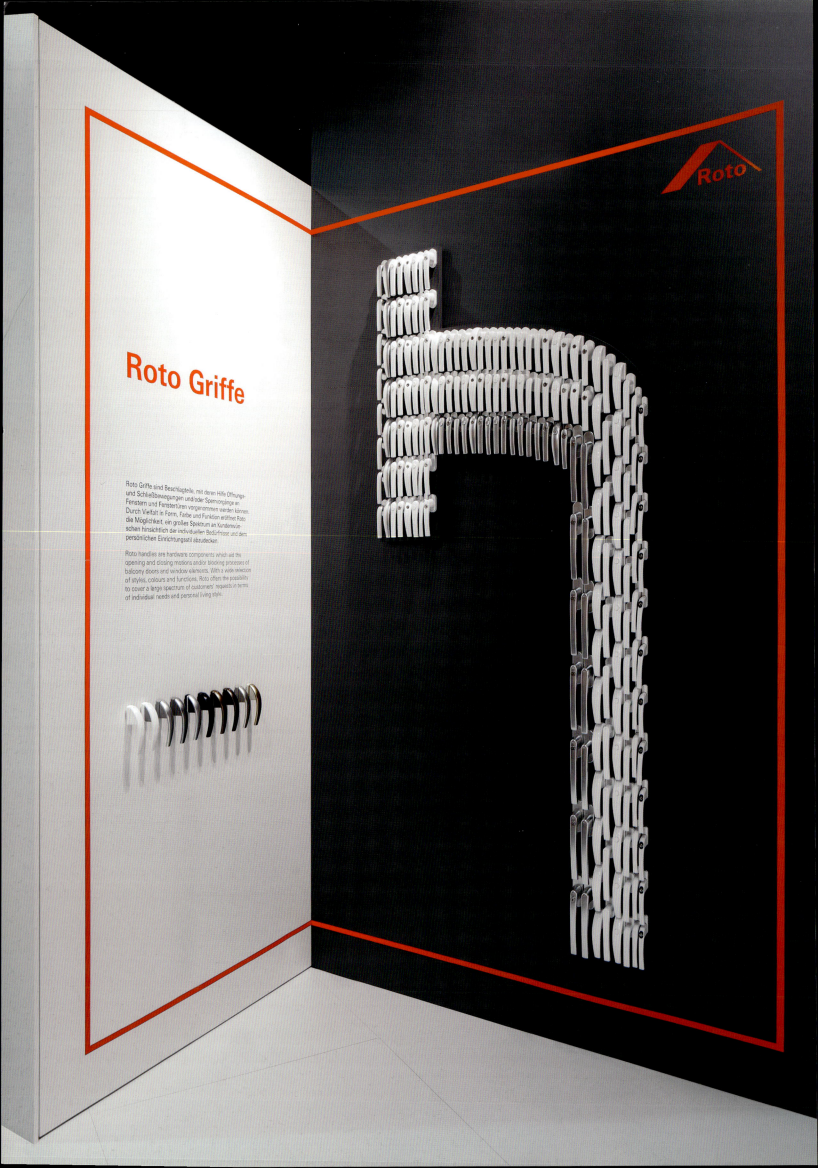

atelier 522 GmbH, Markdorf
Roto Frank AG, Leinfelden-Echterdingen
FENSTERBAU FRONTALE 2016, Nuremberg

UNSICHTBARES SICHTBAR MACHEN

Für die FENSTERBAU FRONTALE 2016 in Nürnberg präsentierte das Markdorfer atelier 522 die Produktpalette der Roto Frank AG in einer minimalistischen, rot-weißen Marktplatzsituation. Unter dem Motto „Stabilität verbindet" entstanden anlässlich der Weltleitmesse für Fenster, Türen und Fassaden 21 verschiedene Gebäude, anhand derer die zurückhaltenden Produkte des weltweit größten Fenster- und Türbeschlagherstellers nicht nur in ihrem alltäglichen Umfeld gezeigt, sondern vor allem aus der Unsichtbarkeit gelöst wurden. Der Marktplatz im Zentrum des 1.205 Quadratmeter großen Auftritts entstand dank der Anordnung dieser Exponathäuser und ermöglichte den Besuchern damit eine offene Begehung. Durchzogen von einem roten Band wurde den Messegästen und Mitarbeitern nicht nur die Orientierung erleichtert, mit der Wahl der Farbe bezogen sich die Gestalter zudem auf das Corporate Design des Leinfeldener Unternehmens. Mithilfe unterschiedlicher Piktogramme wurde der Messestand des Weiteren in fünf Kategorien gegliedert sowie durch Installationen ergänzt, die zwei- mit dreidimensionalem Raum verbanden. Produkte wie Dichtungsbänder und Fenstergriffe wurden so zu wandfüllenden Exponaten angeordnet, welche die konkreten Möglichkeiten und Optimierungen des Herstellers aufgriffen und dem Publikum demonstrierten.

MAKING THE INVISIBLE VISIBLE

For the FENSTERBAU FRONTALE 2016 in Nuremberg, Markdorf's atelier 522 presented the product range of Roto Frank AG in a minimalist, red-and-white market square situation. Themed "stability connects", the stand at the world's leading fair for windows, doors and façades contained 21 different buildings in which the undemonstrative products of the world's biggest producer of window and door fittings could be shown not only in their day-to-day environment, but above all released from their invisibility. The market square created by the arrangement of these exhibit houses at the heart of the 1,205 m² stand allowed visitors easy access. The red strip that ran through the booth not only provided orientation for fairgoers and staff, the choice of colour was also the designers' reference to the corporate design of the company headquartered in Leindfelden near Stuttgart. In addition, the stand was subdivided into categories with the help of pictograms and supplemented by installations which connected the two-dimensional to the three-dimensional space. In this way, products such as sealing tapes and window handles were arranged as wall-to-wall exhibits, demonstrating to the public what specific possibilities and optimisations the manufacturer has to offer.

Dank der minimalistischen Gestaltung der 21 gut strukturierten Häuser sowie der künstlerischen Verwendung der Produkte wurden diese aus ihrer alltäglichen Unsichtbarkeit gelöst.

Thanks to the minimalist design of the 21 well-structured houses and the artistic way the products were presented, the latter were teased out of their day-to-day invisibility.

Der gesamte Auftritt war von den Farben Rot, Weiß und Schwarz geprägt, wodurch die schlichte Inszenierung gewahrt wurde, jedoch spielerisch mit dem Corporate Design des Herstellers umgegangen werden konnte.

The whole stand was dominated by the colours red, white and black. This kept the presentation simple, but at the same time offered opportunities to play with the corporate design of the manufacturer.

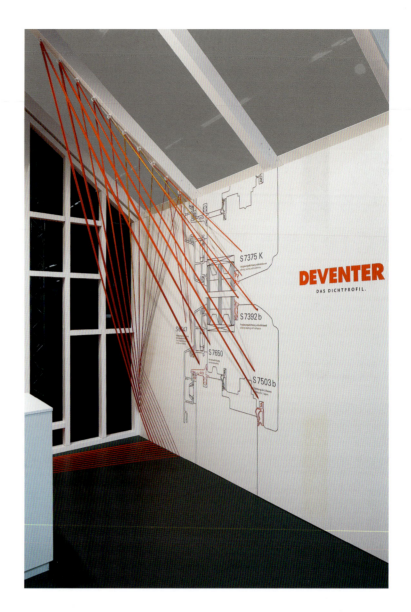

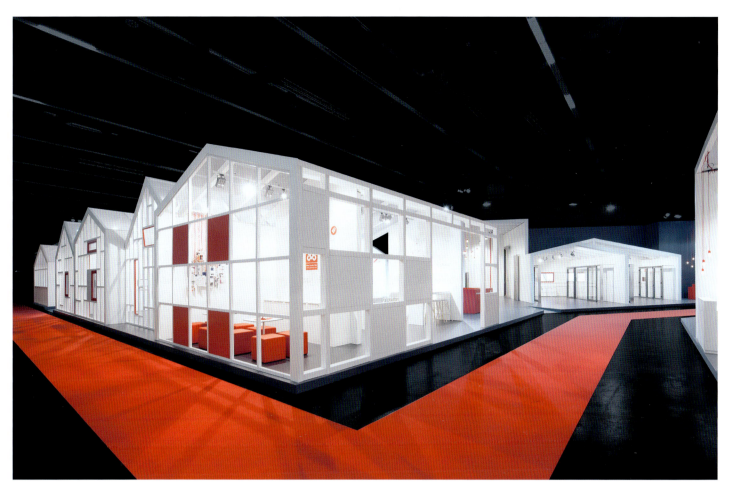

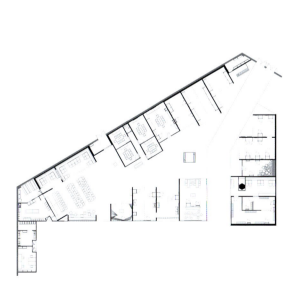

Size 1,205 m² | **Exhibitor** Roto Frank AG, Leinfelden-Echterdingen | **Photos** Benedikt Decker / atelier 522 GmbH, Markdorf | **Architecture / Design / Graphics** atelier 522 GmbH, Markdorf | **Lighting / Media / Construction** Raumtechnik Messebau & Event Services GmbH, Ostfildern

D'art Design Gruppe GmbH, Neuss
Schüco International KG, Bielefeld
FENSTERBAU FRONTALE 2016, Nuremberg

WOHNFÜHL-SZENARIEN

Für den 500 Quadratmeter großen Auftritt der Schüco Polymer Technologies KG (Tochtergesellschaft der Schüco International KG aus Bielefeld) auf der FENSTERBAU FRONTALE 2016 in Nürnberg diente der Neusser D'art Design Gruppe das prämierte Messekonzept der Münchner BAU 2015 als visuelle Klammer – wobei die neue Kunststoff-Systemgeneration „Schüco LivIng" des Bielefelder Bauzulieferers hier in einem zentralen, begehbaren Kubus präsentiert wurde. Durch Hervorheben der wichtigsten Systemeigenschaften wurden hier zwei Zielgruppen inhaltlich überzeugend angesprochen: Im Innenraum des Kubus fanden Geschäftskunden Schlagworte wie „Dichtungstechnologie", „Flexibilität", „Funktionalität" oder „Effizienz", und an den Außenwänden der „LivIng"-Inszenierung wurden mit Aspekten wie Energieeffizienz, Sicherheit, Komfort und Design die Anforderungen der Endverbraucher aufgegriffen. Mittels einer stringenten grafischen sowie architektonischen Gestaltung wurde den Besuchern zudem eine wohnliche und designorientierte Gesamtatmosphäre vermittelt: Großformatige Aufnahmen von Menschen in gemütlicher Umgebung und entsprechendes (Wohn-)Mobiliar komplettierten den Auftritt, der zudem durch offene Bereiche und halbhohe, bepflanzte Raumelemente bestimmt wurde. Hinter der Bar waren in einem standhohen offenen Regalsystem farblich ausgewählte Accessoires angeordnet, um den Cateringbereich zum einen optisch von der benachbarten Ausstellungsfläche abzugrenzen und zum anderen die Gäste auf einen atmosphärischen Besuch einzustimmen.

Rund um die neue Kunststoff-Systemgeneration „Schüco LivIng" gestaltete die D'art Design Gruppe auf der FENSTERBAU FRONTALE eine wohnliche und designorientierte Markenarchitektur für Schüco.

At the FENSTERBAU FRONTALE, D'art Design Gruppe designed a homely and design-oriented brand architecture for Schüco based around the new PVC-U system generation "Schüco LivIng".

FEEL-GOOD SCENARIOS

For the 500 m² exhibition stand of Schüco Polymer Technologies KG (subsidiary company of Schüco International KG from Bielefeld) at the FENSTERBAU FRONTALE 2016 in Nuremberg, Neuss-based D'art Design Gruppe used the prize-winning trade fair concept from the Munich BAU 2015 as visual framework, this time presenting the new PVC-U system generation "Schüco LivIng" of the construction materials supplier from Bielefeld in a central, walk-in cube. By emphasising the most important characteristics of the system, the interests of the two target groups were convincingly addressed: in the interior of the cube, business customers found key words like "Sealing technology", "Flexibility", "Functionality" or "Efficiency", while the outside walls of the "LivIng" production aspects targeted the needs of the end consumer such as energy efficiency, safety, comfort and design. Moreover, by using a stringent graphic and architectural design, the visitors were conveyed a homely and design-oriented overall atmosphere: large-scale photos of people in cosy surroundings and (homely) furnishings and fittings rounded off the booth that was also shaped by open areas and split-level planted room dividers. Behind the bar, colour coordinated accessories were arranged in a floor-to-ceiling open shelving system. This not only separated the catering zone optically from the adjacent exhibition area, it also got the guests in the right mood for the visit.

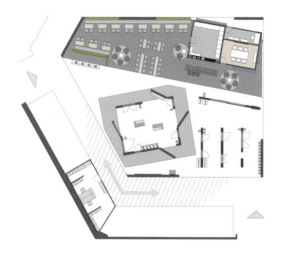

Geschäfts- und Privatkunden konnten sich im zweigeschossigen Kubus von Schüco gleichermaßen wohlfühlen, da hier klar aufgeteilte Informationen für beide Zielgruppen zu finden waren.

Business and private customers felt equally at ease in Schüco's two-storey cube because the information for the two target groups was clearly divided up.

Size 500 m² | **Exhibitor** Schüco International KG, Bielefeld | **Photos** Lukas Palik Fotografie, Dusseldorf | **Architecture / Design** D'art Design Gruppe GmbH, Neuss | **Construction** kohlhaas messebau GmbH & Co. KG, Germering

Dobas AG, Lucerne
Argolite AG, Willisau
Swissbau 2016, Basle

LAUT UND LEISE

Gestaltet von der Luzerner Dobas AG lud der 216 Quadratmeter große Messestand des Willisauer Unternehmens Argolite die Besucher der Swissbau 2016 in Basel ein, sich intensiv mit dem Einfluss von Licht auf die Erscheinung von Oberflächen und Farben auseinanderzusetzen. So wurde veranschaulicht, wie Lichtfarben, -einfallswinkel und -bündelung die Empfindung der hier ausgestellten Produkte prägen. Um das Thema „Licht" besonders eindrücklich zu inszenieren, musste dementsprechend möglichst viel Fremdlicht ausgeschlossen und mit kontrolliertem Licht Akzente geschaffen werden. So betraten die Messegäste einen dunkel bespannten Kubus durch einen niedrigen, aber breiten Eingang, der sich schließlich eng zuspitzte und sie in zwei thematische Räume entließ. Jene Passage war in allen Belangen „laut" gestaltet: einerseits durch das intensive Rot, andererseits durch die harten Oberflächen, die den Schall transportierten. Die beiden angrenzenden Räume erzeugten hingegen ein konträres Raumgefühl: Beide Bereiche waren in Schwarz gehalten und verfügten über vorwiegend weiche Oberflächen, die den Schall absorbierten und eine dumpfe Umgebung generierten. Im rechten dieser beiden Teile wurden dabei die Neuheiten des Herstellers von HPL-Schichtstoffplatten auf großen Schiebewänden präsentiert, die ins rechte Licht gerückt werden konnten, während die Besucher im linken Bereich einen emotional ausgerichteten Raum betraten, in dem sie auf spielerische Art und Weise die Produkteigenschaften des Schichtstoffs HPL kennenlernen konnten.

Durch die stark reduzierte Einsicht in den Stand sollte bei den Besuchern Neugierde geweckt und ein Großteil des Hallenlichts ausgeblendet werden, was zudem eine genaue Betrachtung der Lichtwirkung auf die hier ausgestellten Produkte ermöglichte.

LOUD AND QUIET

Designed by the Lucerne agency Dobas AG, the 216 m² exhibition stand of Argolite from Willisau in Switzerland invited visitors to the Swissbau 2016 in Basle to look more closely at the influence of light on the appearance of surfaces and colours. The stand demonstrated how light colours, the angle of light incidence and light concentration affect the perception of the products on display. To present the topic "light" particularly meaningfully, it was necessary to exclude as much extraneous light as possible so that aspects could be emphasized with controlled light. As fairgoers entered a dark-covered cube through a low, but wide entrance, which tapered off towards the end, they were guided into two themed rooms at the narrower end. This passage was designed to be "loud" in every sense: on the one hand through the vibrant red colour scheme, and on the other through the hard surfaces which transported sounds. The two adjacent rooms, by contrast, generated a completely different spatial feeling: both black spaces were mainly made up of soft surfaces which absorbed sound and created a muffled environment. In the room on the right, the manufacturer of HPL panels presented their innovative new products on large sliding walls which could be moved into the "best" light. Visitors to the left-hand room entered a more emotional space in which they were able to playfully find out more about the product characteristics of HPL.

Reducing the view into the stand was intended on the one hand to arouse the curiosity of the visitors and on the other to shut out most of the hall light, allowing a precise inspection of the effect of light on the products on display.

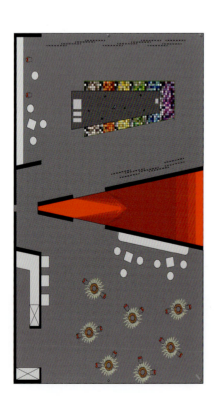

Im Inneren wurden unter anderem sieben Lichtsäulen aus HPL im Kern beleuchtet. Die daraus resultierenden Lichtrosen an Boden und Decke sollten dabei das Gefühl eines Märchenwalds wecken. Die Stelen widmeten sich jeweils einem Thema und verfügten über zwei „Viewmaster", die Bilder von realisierten Projekten zeigten.

Inside, seven light columns made of HPL were illuminated from the core. The resulting light roses on the floor and ceiling conjured up a fairytale forest. Each devoted to a specific topic, the pillars were equipped with two "viewmasters" which showed projects realized with the material.

Size 216 m² | **Exhibitor** Argolite AG, Willisau | **Photos** Kuster Frey Fotografie, Horw | **Architecture / Design / Graphics / Lighting / Construction** Dobas AG, Lucerne

hw.design gmbh, Munich
Munksjö Decor, Aalen
interzum 2015, Cologne

PAPIERWOLKE

2015 konzipierte die Münchner Agentur hw.design bereits zum neunten Mal den Messeauftritt des weltweit führenden Herstellers von Dekorpapieren, dem Unternehmen Munksjö Decor aus Aalen, auf der interzum. Unter dem Motto „Infinite Inspiration" wurden hierfür die High-End-Dekorpapiere mittels einer über der 200 Quadratmeter großen Standfläche scheinbar schwebenden Papierwolke inszeniert. Wobei jene durch eine Lichtinstallation in unterschiedlichen Farben illuminiert wurde, um auf die erweiterte Farbkollektion des Herstellers zu verweisen. Mit der so betonten Vielfalt entstand ein weit sichtbarer Blickfang auf der Kölner Messe, während der übrige Auftritt eher zurückhaltend gestaltet war: Das ruhige Weiß diente sowohl als visuelle Konstante der Marke, als auch als Gegenpol zur Farbigkeit der Wolke. So formte sich ein Ort der Kontemplation, an dem in entspannter Lounge-Atmosphäre inspirierende Gespräche mit Kunden aus aller Welt geführt werden konnten. Eine im Vorfeld verschickte Einladungskarte in Form der Forex-Paneele gehörte ebenfalls zur Standgestaltung. So konnte die Verbindung der farbenprächtigen Wolke zur bunten Vielfalt des Produktkatalogs betont und ein persönlicher Berührungspunkt zum Messestand geschaffen werden.

PAPER CLOUD

In 2015, the Munich-based agency hw.design was commissioned for the ninth time in a row to design the trade fair appearance of the world's leading manufacturer of décor paper, Munksjö Decor from Aalen, at the interzum. Themed "Infinite Inspiration", the premium décor papers were presented by means of a paper cloud that seemed to be floating over the 200 m² stand. Illuminated in various colours by a light installation, it also drew attention to the extended colour collection offered by the manufacturer. The thus emphasised variety created an eye-catcher at the Cologne fair that could be easily seen from a distance. The design of the rest of the stand was fairly low-key by comparison: the peaceful white setting served not only as a visual constant of the brand, but also as counterpoint to the colourful cloud. The result was a place for contemplation in which inspiring consultations could be held with customers from all over the world in a relaxed lounge atmosphere. An invitation card sent out beforehand in the form of forex panels was likewise part of the booth design. It emphasised the link between the richly coloured cloud and the colourful variety of the product catalogue and provided a personal point of contact to the exhibition stand.

Die „Paper Cloud" sollte das neue Portfolio von Munksjö Decor mit schier unerschöpflichen Farbtönen symbolisieren. Dabei wurde die Standarchitektur bewusst diesem Farbspektakel untergeordnet und in betont zurückhaltendem Weiß gehalten.

The "Paper Cloud" was designed to symbolise the new portfolio of Munksjö Decor with a seemingly endless number of colours. The architecture of the stand was deliberately subordinated to this brightly coloured spectacle and was a restrained tone of white throughout.

In den Fokus des Messestands gerückt war die Lichtinszenierung unter minimiertem Materialeinsatz durch Forex-Paneele. Eine logistische Herausforderung stellte jedoch die Verortung dieser Paneele sowie LED-Leuchten nach Größen und XY-Position im Rigging dar.

Using a minimal amount of material in the form of forex panels, the focus was very much on the light production. However, arranging these panels and the LED lights by size and XY position in the rigging turned out to be a logistical challenge.

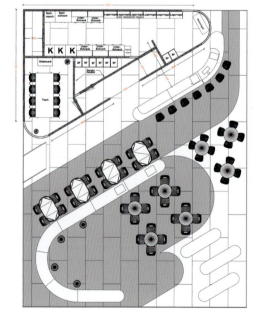

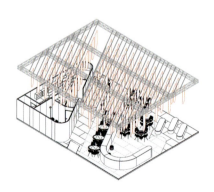

Size 200 m² | **Exhibitor** Munksjö Decor, Aalen | **Photos** Erik Chmil / CHMIL. FOTOGRAFIE. GbR, Cologne |
Architecture / Design hw.design gmbh, Munich | **Construction** i.xpo GmbH & Co. KG, Kaarst

MIKS GmbH, Hamburg
CAPAROL Farben Lacke Bautenschutz GmbH, Ober-Ramstadt
FARBE, AUSBAU & FASSADE 2016, Munich

DER ELEFANT IM FARBENLADEN

Für CAPAROL, den führenden Hersteller von Bautenanstrichmitteln, inszenierte die Hamburger Kreativagentur für Brand Space Design MIKS anlässlich der Münchner Messe FARBE, AUSBAU & FASSADE 2016 einen Auftritt ganz unter dem Motto „Haus des Handwerks". Als Hommage huldigten sie damit diesem Erwerbszweig und machten ihn zum Dreh- und Angelpunkt des 700 Quadratmeter großen Auftritts. Dabei wurde die Produktpalette von CAPAROL in unterschiedlichen, nachgebildeten Wohnbereichen real präsentiert. In jenen konnten die Besucher die facettenreichen Einsatzgebiete des Portfolios des Ober-Ramstädter Unternehmens erkunden. Eine logisch strukturierte Aufteilung in verschiedene Abschnitte verdeutlichte zudem die unterschiedlichen Sparten der Marke und lud zum Entdecken ein, während parallel Informationen über Fassaden, Dekoration, Dämmung oder Akustik vermittelt wurden. Der gesamte Messeauftritt wurde zudem von einer Kampagne in den sozialen Medien, einer Fotoaktion sowie einem virtuellen 360°-Rundgang auf der Internetpräsenz des Herstellers begleitet. So konnte nicht nur die Vielschichtigkeit des Unternehmens betont werden, sondern in Verbindung mit der direkten Kundenansprache auf dem Messestand in den Besuchern der Handwerker und somit die Lust mit CAPAROL zu arbeiten geweckt werden.

Mit einem facettenreichen Auftritt inszenierte MIKS erstmals den führenden Anbieter von Bautenanstrichmitteln CAPAROL auf der FARBE, AUSBAU & FASSADE 2016 in München. Der 700 Quadratmeter große Messeauftritt war dabei eine Hommage an das Handwerk.

With a multifaceted booth, MIKS presented the leading supplier of architectural paints CAPAROL at the FARBE, AUSBAU & FASSADE 2016 in Munich for the first time. The stand with a footprint of 700 m² paid tribute to craftsmanship and craftsmen.

ELEPHANT IN THE ROOM

For CAPAROL, the leading manufacturer of architectural paints, the Hamburg-based creative agency for brand space design MIKS designed a stand for the FARBE, AUSBAU & FASSADE 2016 fair in Munich that was closely aligned with the slogan "House of craft". It was designed as a tribute to this sector and made it the lynchpin of the 700 m² stand. The product spectrum of CAPAROL was presented tangibly in several, replica living spaces where visitors could explore the multifaceted areas in which the portfolio of the company from Ober-Ramstadt is put to use. A logically structured division into various zones also illustrated the different segments of the brand and invited visitors to embark on a journey of discovery, while at the same time information was provided on façades, decoration, insulation and acoustics. The whole trade fair appearance was accompanied by a social media campaign, a photo campaign and a virtual 360° tour of the manufacturer's website. This emphasised not only the many layers and facets of the company, but in conjunction with the direct customer contact on the stand awoke the handiman in the visitors and thus also a desire to work with CAPAROL.

Unter dem Signet des Herstellerlogos, einem farbig gestreiften Elefanten, betraten die Besucher verschiedene Wohnbereiche und konnten angeregt die vielfältigen Produkte und Einsatzgebiete von CAPAROL erkunden.

Under the signet of the manufacturer's logo, a stripy elephant, visitors entered various living areas where they could explore the different products and CAPAROL's wide range of applications.

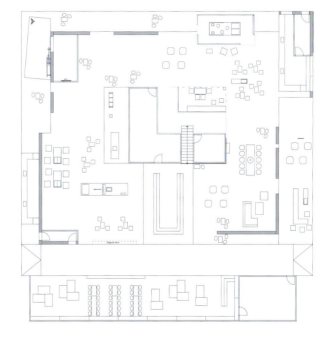

Size 700 m² | **Exhibitor** CAPAROL Farben Lacke Bautenschutz GmbH, Ober-Ramstadt | **Photos** MIKS GmbH / Martin Hasse, Hamburg | **Architecture / Design / Graphics** MIKS GmbH, Hamburg | **Construction** KALLE KRAUSE GmbH, Essen

Paolo Cesaretti, Milan
Kale Group, Istanbul
UNICERA 2016, Istanbul

ALT UND NEU

Auf einer Fläche von 750 Quadratmetern entwarf der Mailänder Architekt Paolo Cesaretti für die Istanbuler Kale Group – Hersteller von Keramik – einen Messestand unter dem Titel „Monochrome". In der Gestaltung vermischten sich archaische sowie zeitgenössische Elemente und verkörperten damit den Istanbuler Standort der Fachmesse für Keramik, Bad und Küche UNICERA 2016. Alle Komponenten des Auftritts folgten dabei klaren geometrischen Strukturen, wobei einzelne Formen andere kontrastierten. Anhand der monochrom und linear gestalteten Umgebung wurde den Besuchern ein Gefühl von Tiefe vermittelt, das sich in den jeweilgen Produktpräsentationen fortsetzte. Hier fanden sich sowohl Abschnitte in Weiß, als auch in vier Grautönen, die vom warmen Ton der Eichenholzelemente gerahmt wurden. Das Gegenstück zum modern-schlichten Charakter wurde somit in einem soliden und nachhaltigen Werkstoff gefunden. Abgerundet wurde der Pavillon nicht nur durch wohnlich inszenierte Lebensräume, sondern auch durch Slogans sowie wandfüllende Bildschirme.

SOMETHING OLD, SOMETHING NEW

On an ground plan measuring 750 m², Milan-based architect Paolo Cesaretti designed an exhibition stand for Istanbul's Kale Group—ceramics manufacturer—entitled "Monochrome". The design blended archaic and contemporary elements, thus embodying the location of the UNICERA 2016 in Istanbul, specialist fair for ceramics, bathrooms and kitchens. All the components of the stand followed clear geometrical structures, with some shapes contrasting with others. The monochrome and linear design of the space conveyed to the visitors a feeling of depth which was continued in the product presentations. Here white sections were to be found next to others in four different shades of grey, all framed by warm oak wood elements. The counterpart to the modern and minimalist character was thus provided by a solid and sustainable material. The pavilion was rounded off not only by cosily presented living spaces, but also by slogans and wall-to-wall screens.

Die Hauptthemen der Kale Group – Forschung, Innovation, Qualität und Stil – spiegelten sich im Messestand des türkischen Unternehmens wider und wurden in der Gestaltung sichtbar.

The core themes of the Kale Group— research, innovation, quality and style—were reflected in the exhibition stand of the Turkish company and visualised in the design.

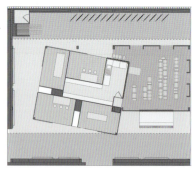
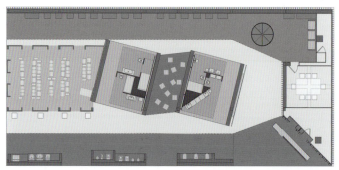

Kontraste boten sowohl die Werkstoffe als auch die verschiedenen geometrischen Formen, wobei der Auftritt weiterhin wie aus einem Guss erschien.

Contrasts were provided both by the materials used as well as the various geometrical forms, while nevertheless presenting a uniform appearance.

Trotz der Vielfalt wahrte der Stand des Mailänder Gestalters Paolo Cesaretti eine stringente, einfache Linie, während die Produkte stets im Vordergrund standen.

Despite the many different elements, the booth by Milan's designer Paolo Cesaretti had a stringent, simple line and the focus was always on the products.

Size 750 m² | **Exhibitor** Kale Group, Istanbul | **Photos** Luca Rotondo Photography, Milan | **Architecture / Design** Paolo Cesaretti, Milan | **Graphics / Media** Modiki, Istanbul | **Lighting** Baccarani e Torri s.r.l., Sassuolo | **Construction** Studio / Nakışçı, Istanbul

Paolo Cesaretti, Milan
Royal Ceramica, El Obour City
CERSAIE 2015, Bologna

KÖNIGLICHE LOBBY

Für den Messestand von Royal Ceramica – Ägyptens größtem Keramik- und Sanitär-Händler – kombinierte der Mailänder Gestalter Paolo Cesaretti anlässlich der CERSAIE 2015 in Bologna die Ästhetik eines geschäftigen wie auch geschäftlichen Orts mit dekorativen Elementen, die der 260 Quadratmeter großen Ausstellungsfläche eine mystische Note verliehen. Um in den zentralen Bereich, die sogenannte Lobby, zu gelangen, mussten die Besucher zunächst zwei Galerien durchqueren: In der ersten wurden ihnen sowohl horizontal als auch vertikal angeordnete Keramikpaneele präsentiert, die eine enorme Vielfalt an Kombinationsmöglichkeiten demonstrieren sollten, während in der zweiten Galerie bei den Messegästen vor gekippten und verspiegelten Flächen die Vision erzeugt werden sollte, selbst mit der gefliesten Paneele zu verschmelzen. So wurde ein Gefühl der Überwältigung generiert, das den Besuchern die Dekorationen und Details in großen Arrangements noch näher brachte. Sowohl durch diese Komponenten als auch mittels der kompletten Abschirmung des Innenraums anhand perforierter Verkleidungen stellte sich zudem ein Empfinden von Luxus, Intimität und Exklusivität ein, das bei einem Besuch eines royalen Marktplatzes schließlich selbstverständlich sein sollte.

ROYAL LOBBY

For the trade fair stand at the CERSAIE 2015 in Bologna of Royal Ceramica—Egypt's largest dealer for ceramic and sanitary products—Milan-based designer Paolo Cesaretti combined the aesthetics of a busy place of business with decorative elements which gave the 260 m² exhibition space a mystical flair. To reach the central area, referred to as the lobby, visitors had to pass through two galleries: in the first, they found vertically and horizontally arranged ceramic panels which were intended to demonstrate the huge variety of combination possibilities. In the second, fairgoers found themselves in front of mirrored and tilted surfaces in order to create the vision that they were becoming one with the tiled panels. The overwhelming feeling this generated brought the visitors closer to the decorations and details in large-scale arrangements. These components combined with the way the entire interior space was closed off by perforated cladding transported a sense of luxury, intimacy and exclusivity that one would expect of a visit to a royal market square.

Verschieden gemusterte Verkleidungen umgaben den gesamten Messestand auf der CERSAIE 2015 in Bologna und boten einen Vorgeschmack auf die elegante Produktpräsentation im Inneren.

Ornamental screens surrounded the entire booth at the CERSAIE 2015 in Bologna, offering a foretaste of the elegant product presentations within.

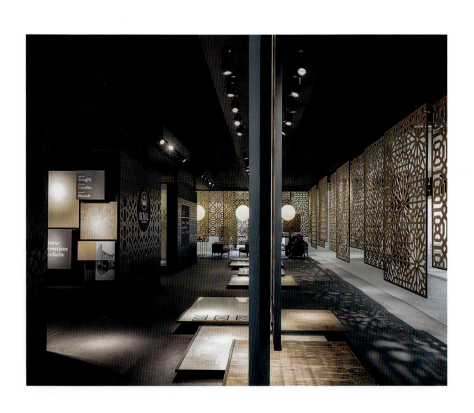

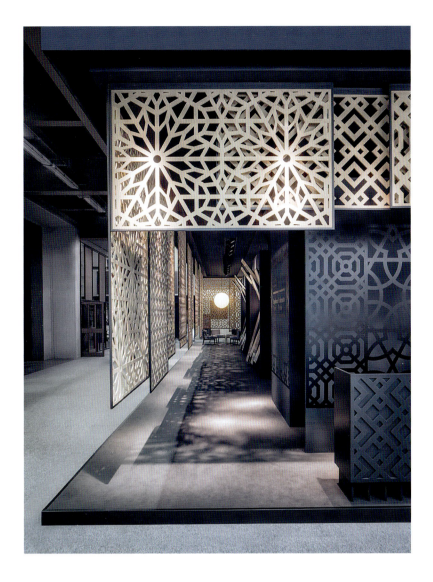

In der zweiten Galerie tauchten die Besucher mittels schräg gestellter, verspiegelter Flächen tief in die filigranen Details der Fabrikate des ägyptischen Herstellers ein.

Thanks to the mirrored surfaces arranged at an angle in the second gallery visitors were submersed in the delicate details of the products of the Egyptian manufacturer.

Size 260 m² | **Exhibitor** Royal Ceramica, El Obour City | **Photos** Lorenzo Pennati, Milan; Stefano Stagni, Bologna | **Architecture / Design** Paolo Cesaretti, Milan | **Graphics** Claudia Astarita, Florence | **Construction** Veneta Allestimenti, Verona

raumbar Partnerschaftsgesellschaft für Gestaltung, Essen
Zanders GmbH, Bergisch Gladbach
BrauBeviale 2015, Nuremberg

SCHLICHT UND ERGREIFEND

Als wichtiger Produzent von hochwertigen Spezialpapieren und -kartons blickt Zanders auf eine fast 200-jährige Papiermachertradition zurück. Nach diversen Umfirmierungen in den letzten Jahren war es nun das erklärte Ziel, sich zur BrauBeviale 2015 in Nürnberg eindrucksvoll und selbstbewusst unter dem Namen Zanders GmbH und dem Claim „the papermakers" zurückzumelden. Dementsprechend entwickelte die Essener Kreativschmiede raumbar Partnerschaftsgesellschaft für Gestaltung auf einer Standfläche von gerade einmal 42 Quadratmetern ein deutliches Produktstatement: Orientiert an gefaltetem Papier entstand ein räumliches Gebilde, aus dem sowohl Wand- und Decken- als auch Tischflächen generiert werden konnten. Ergänzt wurde diese auffallende Architektur durch eine markante Farbkombination aus Weiß, Grau und Schwarz – kontrastiert mit intensivem Hellblau. In jeweils eigenen Bereichen wurden dabei die beiden Papiergattungen CHROMOLUX und Zanlabel präsentiert, die sich optimal in das schlichte Gesamtbild einfügten.

PLAIN AND SIMPLE

An important producer of high-quality special papers and card, Zanders looks back on almost 200 years of paper-making tradition. Renamed several times in the last few years, it was the declared goal to put in an impressive and self-assured appearance at the BrauBeviale 2015 in Nuremberg under the name Zanders GmbH and with the claim "the papermakers". To reflect this return in the design of the stand, the creative minds from raumbar Partnerschaftsgesellschaft für Gestaltung came up with a clear product statement on the footprint of just 42 m²: inspired by folded paper, a spatial structure evolved that was used to generate both walls, ceilings and table tops. This striking architecture was supported by a strong colour combination of white, grey and black—contrasted with a vibrant light blue. The two paper categories CHROMOLUX and Zanlabel each had their own section which were perfectly integrated into the simple overall optic.

Wie aus Papier gefaltet entstand zur BrauBeviale 2015 ein räumliches Gebilde mit Wand-, Decken- und Tischflächen, das durch seine auffallende Architektur sowie Farbkombination die Neugier der Besucher wecken sollte.

As if folded from paper, a spatial structure was developed for the BrauBeviale 2015 which created wall, ceiling and table surfaces whose conspicuous architecture and colour combinations were designed to arouse the curiosity of the visitors.

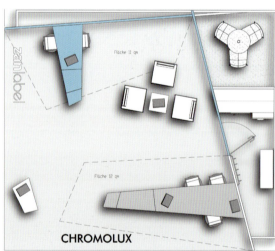

Sowohl als Verweis auf die 200-jährige Tradition des Unternehmens als auch als feiner Bruch mit der modernen Gestaltung dienten unter anderem die Filament-Lampen, die den Messestand in angenehmes Licht tauchten.

Filament lamps that bathed the exhibition stand in a pleasant light were a reference to the 200-year history of the company and created a nice break with the modern design.

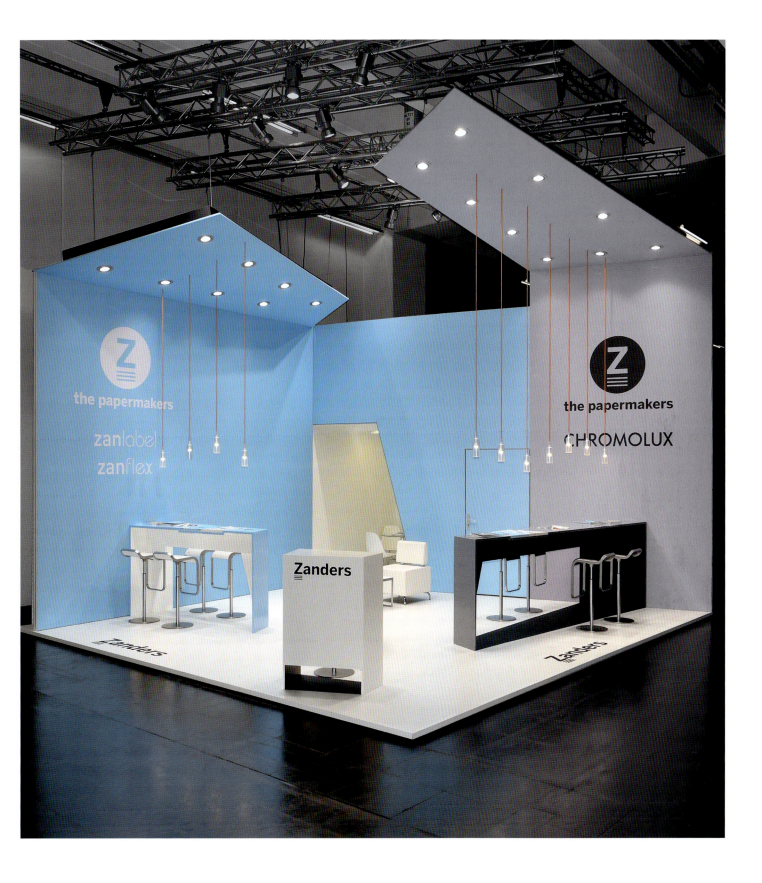

Size 42 m² | **Exhibitor** Zanders GmbH, Bergisch Gladbach | **Photos** Olaf Schiemann / Fotodesign Schiemann, Erkrath | **Architecture / Design / Graphics** raumbar Partnerschaftsgesellschaft für Gestaltung / Michael Lengner, Peter Stark, Essen | **Construction** M.D.C. International GmbH, Cologne

AUTOMOBILE AND TRANSPORTATION

→ Die Messestände der Automobilkonzerne, Flughafenbetreiber und Hersteller von Nutzfahrzeugen gehören zu den größten und aufwendigsten der Branche. Kein Wunder, dass die hier realisierten Projekte oft zur Königsdisziplin des Messedesigns gezählt werden: Dank raumfüllender Bauten oder des Einsatzes innovativer Technologien und Medien heben sie sich stark von anderen Unternehmenspräsentationen ab. Doch neben den beeindruckenden Shows und gewinnbringenden Großinszenierungen entstehen ebenso kleine, feine und handwerklich präzise ausgeführte Auftritte, deren Charme sich die Besucher nur schwer entziehen können.

→ The trade fair stands of the car makers, airport operators and manufacturers of commercial vehicles are among the biggest and most extravagant in the business. Not surprisingly, the projects realised here are considered to be the supreme discipline of booth design: the huge dimensions of the structures or the use of innovative technologies and media set them clearly apart from other corporate presentations. And yet, alongside the impressive shows and large-scale, profitable productions, there are also small, fine and precisely crafted stands whose charm is not lost on the visitors.

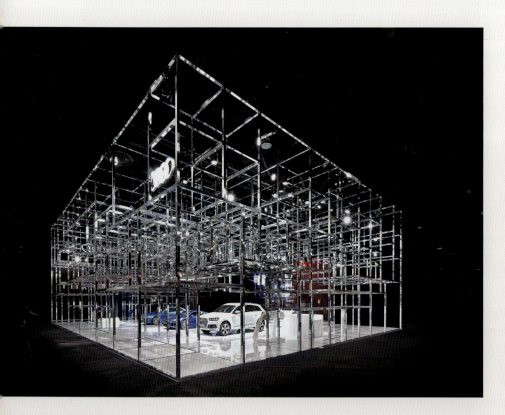

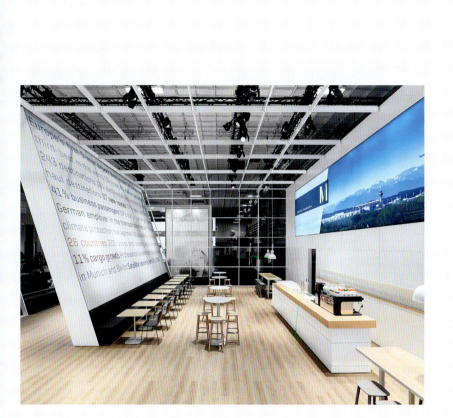

→ 56

→ 70

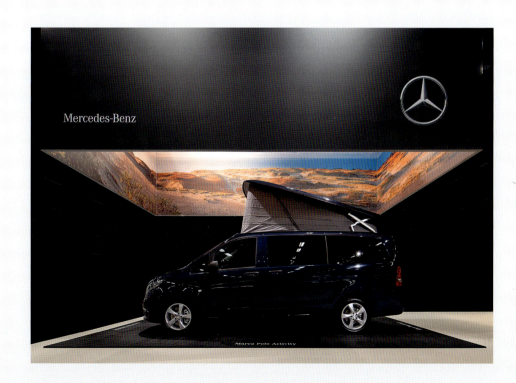

→ 48

Mercedes-Benz

atelier 522 GmbH, Markdorf
Mercedes-Benz Schweiz AG, Schlieren
Suisse Caravan Salon 2015, Berne

WANDERLUST

Ganz schlicht und mit Betonung der wichtigsten Funktion eines Caravans konzipierte das atelier 522 den Messestand der Mercedes-Benz Schweiz AG auf dem Suisse Caravan Salon 2015 in Bern. Auf 407 Quadratmetern inszenierten die Markdorfer Gestalter hier das Erlebnis, mit einem Caravan auf Tour zu gehen. Mittels großer Panoramen wurde die Flexibilität betont, die es den Reiselustigen ermöglicht, an beliebigen Orten zu kochen, zu essen und zu schlafen – mitten in der Natur. Von der Hallendecke abgehängt, flankierten zwei große, rechteckige Kuben direkt über den Fahrzeugen die beiden Seiten des Auftritts. Während die Außenseiten in Schwarz gehalten und mit einem Mercedes-Stern versehen waren, fanden sich auf der Innenseite illuminierte Panoramen von beeindruckenden Landschaften. So blieben die Wagen einerseits leicht begehbar, beförderten die Messegäste andererseits jedoch direkt in eine andere Welt. Hinter den Exponaten befanden sich des Weiteren Besprechungstische mit möglichen Routen durch die Schweizer Regionen, wodurch das Motto „Der Weg ist das Ziel" zudem verdeutlicht wurde. Wie die Außenseiten der Kuben war auch der Informations- und Accessoiresbereich schwarz gestaltet – bis auf ein seitlich angebrachtes Panorama, das den Besuchern den Blick in die Ferne auch auf Augenhöhe ermöglichte.

Das Reisefieber der Besucher wurde mittels großformatiger 360°-Panoramen geweckt, die über den zu begutachtenden Wagen scheinbar schwebten und sie mitten in die Natur beförderten.

The urge of visitors to travel was aroused by means of large-scale 360° panoramas which appeared to be floating above the vehicles on display, transporting them out into the countryside.

WANDERLUST

For the trade fair stand of Mercedes-Benz Schweiz AG at the Suisse Caravan Salon 2015 in Berne, atelier 522 came up with a simple design which placed the emphasis on the most important function of a camper van. On a footprint of 407 m², the designers from Markdorf presented the experience of going on tour in a camper van. Large panoramas were used in order to stress the flexibility which allows travellers to cook, eat and sleep wherever they want—in the great outdoors. Suspended from the hall ceiling, two large rectangular cubes positioned directly above the vehicles flanked the two sides of the booth. While the black exterior bore the Mercedes star, the interior contained illuminated panoramas of breathtaking landscapes. Thus while on the one hand the vehicles remained easy to access, on the other fairgoers were transported directly into another world. Behind the exhibits, consultation tables were inscribed with possible routes through the Swiss regions, explaining the slogan of the stand "The journey is the reward". Like the outside of the cubes, the information and accessories section was black in colour—apart from a panorama attached to the sides which allowed visitors a further faraway view, in this case at eye-level.

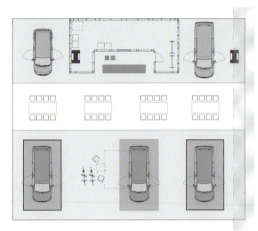

Grafische Elemente verweisen auf mögliche Routen durch die unterschiedlichen Schweizer Regionen – alles frei nach dem Motto: „Der Weg ist das Ziel." Der Messestand sollte dabei den Startpunkt der Erlebnisreise markieren.

Graphic elements make reference to possible routes through the different regions of Switzerland—loosely following the slogan: "The journey is the reward." The exhibition stand was intended to be the starting point of a journey of discovery.

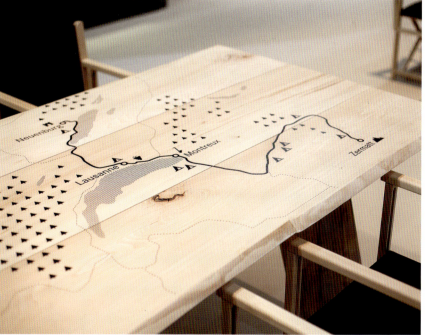

Size 407 m² | **Exhibitor** Mercedes-Benz Schweiz AG, Schlieren | **Photos** Benedikt Decker / atelier 522 GmbH, Markdorf | **Architecture / Design / Graphics** atelier 522 GmbH, Markdorf | **Construction** RUN Retail United AG, Hünenberg

Braunwagner GmbH, Aachen
Daimler AG, Stuttgart
Internationale Automobil-Ausstellung (IAA) 2015, Frankfurt a. Main

OFFENE BEGEGNUNG

Unter dem Motto „Let your city in" wurde auf der IAA 2015 in Frankfurt die Weltpremiere des smart fortwo cabrio gefeiert. Anlässlich dieser Präsentation entwickelte Braunwagner einen Messestand, mit dem das Sondermodell „smart BRABUS tailor made" – die perfekte Symbiose aus Individualisierung und urbaner smart-DNA – ins Zentrum der Betrachtungen gerückt wurde. Unterstützt wurde diese proklamierte urbane Lebensfreude durch den bewussten Einsatz von Sonnenlicht, das durch die große Glasfassade des Forums einfiel. Architektonisch wurde mit „smart extension" der Auftritt der letzten Jahre weiterentwickelt und damit der Fokus auf die Neuausrichtung des Produktportfolios gelegt. Basierend auf der Extension des smart fortwo zum smart forfour nutzten die Aachener Gestalter die Tridionzelle als raumbildende Metapher. Einzelne Standbereiche zu unterschiedlichen Themen wurden dementsprechend an das visuell prägnante Gestaltungselement angelehnt. So entstand unter anderem ein urbaner Platz, der mit einer farbigen Lichtinstallation zur markanten Bühne für die neuen Modelle wurde. Interaktive Stationen in den vier Themenbereichen dienten zudem zur Vermittlung des Mobilitätskonzepts, während ein Baum im Zentrum den Raum für das Zusammenkommen der Besucher definierte. Abgerundet wurde der 3.350 Quadratmeter große Messestand durch diverse Möglichkeiten, die Fahrzeuge im Außenbereich selbst zu testen.

Die Themengebiete Individuality, Mobility, Technology und Design wurden in eigenen Bereichen inszeniert. Sogenannte Design-Spycases sowie interaktive Exponate luden die Besucher dabei ein, die Marke smart und ihr Mobilitätskonzept näher kennenzulernen.

The themes individuality, mobility, technology and design were presented in separate sections. Design spycases as well as interactive exhibits invited visitors to find out more about the smart brand and its mobility concept.

OPEN ENCOUNTER

Themed "Let your city in", the smart fortwo cabrio celebrated its the world début at the IAA 2015 in Frankfurt. To mark this occasion, Braunwagner developed an exhibition stand which turned the spotlight on the special model "smart BRABUS tailor made" the perfect symbiosis of individuality and urban smart-DNA. This commitment to loving life in an urban environment was supported by the deliberate use of sunlight that poured in through the large glass façade of the forum. Architecturally, the "smart extension" was a further development of the booth of recent years, in this way placing the focus on the realignment of the product portfolio. To visualise the extension of the smart fortwo to the smart forfour, the designers from Aachen used the tridion cell as spatial metaphor. Some sections of the stand on a number of different topics were therefore based on this visually striking design element. What evolved was an city square which, thanks to a colourful light installation, became a striking stage for the new models. Interactive stations in the four themed areas helped convey the mobility concept, while a tree in the centre marked out a place of encounter for visitors to the stand. The 3,350 m² of the exhibition booth were rounded off by various possibilities for fairgoers to test the vehicles for themselves in the outside area.

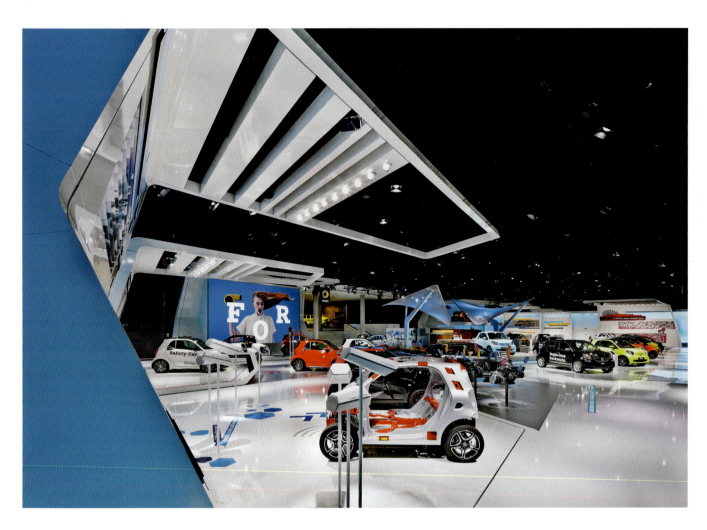

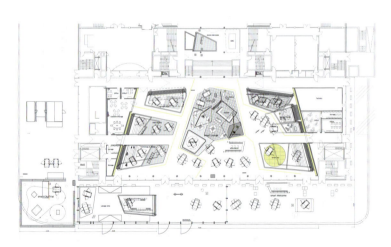

Den architektonischen Rahmen für den Messestand bildete die Tridionzelle. So wurde unter anderem ein urban geprägter Platz geschaffen, der Innovationsanspruch und Vielseitigkeit des Böblinger Unternehmens widerspiegeln sollte.

The tridion cell provided the architectural frame for the stand. The market square that it created, for instance, reflected the innovative aspirations and multiple facets of the company from Böblingen.

Size 3,350 m² | **Exhibitor** Daimler AG, Stuttgart | **Photos** Andreas Keller Fotografie, Altdorf | **Architecture / Design / Graphics** Braunwagner GmbH, Aachen | **Lighting** trussco GmbH, Neuss | **Media** [mu:d] GmbH, Büro für Ereignisse, Cologne | **Construction** Klartext, #### | **Grafik** Messe Event GmbH, Willich

Buero Philipp Moeller, Munich
Flughafen München GmbH, Munich
ITB 2016, Berlin

ERSTKLASSIGE VERBINDUNG

Seit mehreren Jahrzehnten ist der Flughafen München regelmäßig mit einem umfangreichen Informationsangebot auf der ITB Berlin vertreten – seit 2016 in neuem Gewand. Denn für die Internationale Tourismusbörse – die Weltleitmesse der Reisebranche – konzeptionierte das Münchner Buero Philipp Moeller für den global agierenden Konzern einen Auftritt, der sowohl das neue Erscheinungsbild als auch die neue Markenbotschaft „Verbindung leben" in den Raum überträgt. Da der Münchner Flughafen auf einem architektonisch klaren Grundraster von 1,20 auf 1,20 Meter über alle Terminals aufgebaut ist, wurden auch Grundriss und Kubatur des Messestands durch ein strenges Raster strukturiert, das jedoch vom sogenannten Connector – dem akzentuierten Schrägstrich des neuen Logos – räumlich durchbrochen ist. So entstanden zentrale Begegnungszonen, anhand derer die gewünschten Verbindungen auch persönlich mit Kunden und Partnern intensiviert werden konnten. Eine modulare sowie flexible Bauweise ermöglichte zudem eine vielseitige und nachhaltige Verwendung des neuen Messestandkonzepts, das auf der ITB Berlin in der Version 15 auf 15 Meter zum Einsatz kam und durch natürliche sowie hochwertige Materialien auf 225 Quadratmetern offen und modern wirkte. Ebenso lässt sich das System aber auch für Auftritte auf 40 Quadratmetern für regionale Messen als auch auf 350 Quadratmetern – wie zum Beispiel auf der Münchner Messe transport logistic – nutzen.

Der Münchner Flughafen gilt als zentraler Knotenpunkt in einer sich stetig verändernden Welt. Da heißt es, Verbindungen zu schaffen, die nicht nur zuverlässig, sondern auch durch Partnerschaft, Verantwortung, Innovation sowie Kompetenz gekennzeichnet sind …

Munich Airport is a central hub in a constantly changing world. The goal is therefore to create connections which are not only reliable but also characterised by partnership, responsibility, innovation and competence …

FIRST-CLASS CONNECTION

For some decades, Munich Airport has regularly been represented at the ITB Berlin with an extensive information package—since 2016 in a new guise. For the leading international travel trade fair, Munich-based Buero Philipp Moeller designed a stand for the globally operating group which gives a spatial dimension to the new look and also the new brand message "living ideas—connecting lives". As Munich Airport is built on an architecturally clear basic grid of 1.20 by 1.20 m across all terminals, the ground plan and cubage of the booth was structured by a strict grid, interrupted spatially only by the so-called connector—the accentuated forward slash of the new logo. The result were central places of encounter in which the desired connections could be intensified through personal contact to customers and partners. The modular and flexible construction also allowed the new booth concept to be used in many different ways and again and again. At the ITB Berlin the 15 by 15 m version was chosen and the natural and high-quality materials in use throughout made the 225 m² stand appear modern and open. The system can, however, also be adapted for booths of 40 m² at regional fairs or of 350 m², such as at the Munich exhibition transport logistic.

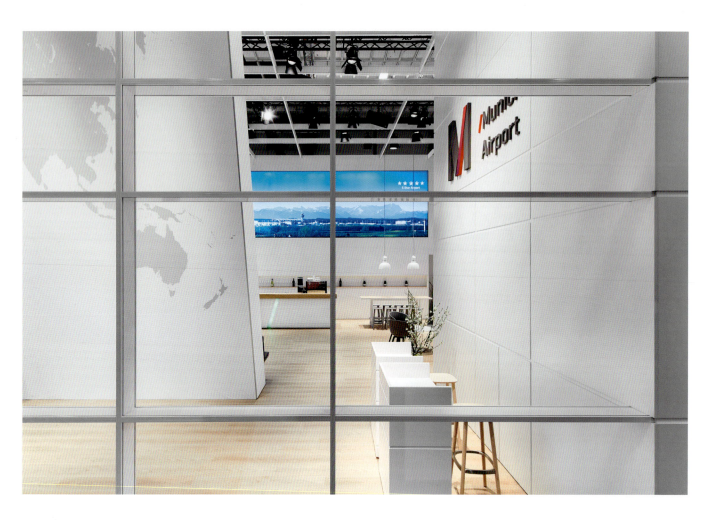

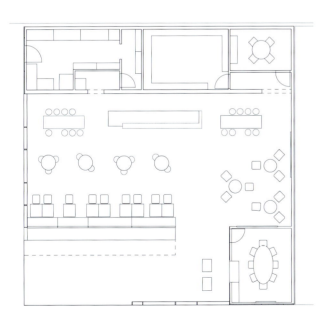

... Markenwerte, die das Buero Philipp Moeller mit einem neuen Messestandkonzept für die Flughafen München GmbH auf der ITB Berlin 2016 visualisierte.

... brand values which Buero Philipp Moeller visualised with a new trade fair stand concept for Flughafen München GmbH at the ITB Berlin 2016.

Size 225 m² | **Exhibitor** Flughafen München GmbH, Munich | **Photos** Olaf Becker / BECKER LACOUR, Munich | **Architecture / Design** Buero Philipp Moeller, Munich | **Construction** Zweiplan DAS PRODUKTIONSBÜRO GmbH, Munich

jangled nerves GmbH, Stuttgart
Daimler AG, Stuttgart
CES 2016, Las Vegas

DIGITAL UND ANALOG

Der 500 Quadratmeter große Messeauftritt von Mercedes-Benz auf der CES 2016 in Las Vegas, gestaltet von jangled nerves, stand ganz im Zeichen von „Mercedes me" und widmete sich damit der Verbindung von moderner Mobilität und digitalem Alltag. Der Messestand verband Gegenwart, Zukunftsvision, analoge sowie digitale Welt und war als Bühne, Präsentations- und Interaktionsfläche vielfältig nutzbar. Mit großzügiger LED-Wand bot der Bühnenraum nicht nur Platz für Exponate wie das Showcar „Concept IAA", sondern auch für Fachvorträge sowie ausreichend Steh- und Sitzfläche für das Publikum. Die angrenzenden Flächen ermöglichten den Gästen informative Gespräche sowie im Bereich der Zukunftsvision einen exklusiven Blick auf das innovative Infotainmentsystem der neuen E-Klasse – noch vor ihrer Weltpremiere. Direkt daneben wurde das Thema der Gegenwart anhand der Modelle AMG GT S und C 63 AMG Coupé präsentiert. Trotz der klar gesteckten Bereiche war der Stand sehr offen gestaltet und wirkte mittels Lounge sowie bequemen Sesseln, Bar und warmem Holzboden einladend. Mit einem dreidimensionalen me-Schriftzug sowie der dynamischen „Silver Flow"-Konstruktion, die anhand von wechselnden Lichtbespielungen inszeniert wurde, setzte man zudem optische Akzente, während Besucher dank iPads und Multitouch-Tischen in der „me Lounge" tiefergehende Informationen erhalten konnten.

DIGITAL AND ANALOGUE

The 500 m² stand of Mercedes-Benz at the CES 2016 in Las Vegas, designed by jangled nerves, was all about "Mercedes me" and as such was devoted to the connection between modern mobility and everyday digital life. The booth combined the present, a vision of the future, the analogue and the digital world and could be used in diverse ways as stage, presentation space and interaction area. With its generously dimensioned LED wall, the stage area not only offered space for exhibits like the showcar "Concept IAA", but also for specialist presentations as well as adequate seating and standing room for the audience. The adjacent areas allowed guests to enter into informative talks and in the future vision section take an exclusive look at the infotainment system of the new E-class—even before its world première. Next to that, the present was on display in the form of the models AMG GT S and C 63 AMG coupé. Despite the clearly zoned areas, the exhibition stand was very open and inviting thanks to the lounge area with comfy armchairs, bar and warm-coloured wooded floor. Optical highlights included a three-dimensional me-logo as well as the dynamic "Silver Flow" structure which was set off by changing light projections while visitors could obtain more in-depth information on iPads and multitouch tables located in the "me Lounge".

Durch individuelle Lichtbespielungen des „Silver Flow" wurden themenbezogene Stimmungen erzeugt. Die Großkonstruktion diente gleichzeitig als Fernzeichen sowie als Dach des 500 Quadratmeter großen Messestands.

The individual light projections on the "Silver Flow" created themed moods. The large-scale structure served as eyecatcher and also as the roof of the 500 m² stand.

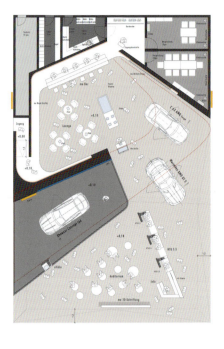

Der dynamische Schwung des „Silver Flow" führte die Besucher von der Plaza in die „Mercedes me"-Welt, wobei der rückgelagerte, offene Raum durch seine hohe Aufenthaltsqualität bestach und einen Rückzugsort vom turbulenten Messetreiben darstellte.

The dynamic sweep of the "Silver Flow" led visitors from the plaza into the "Mercedes me" world where the comfortable open space to the rear of the stand offered visitors a refuge from the hustle and bustle of the fair.

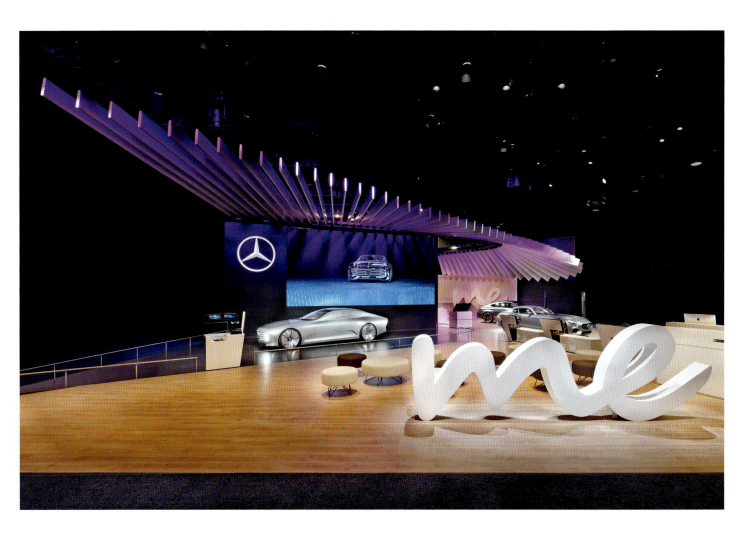

Size 500 m² | **Exhibitor** Daimler AG, Stuttgart | **Photos** Andreas Keller Fotografie, Altdorf | **Architecture / Design / Graphics** jangled nerves GmbH, Stuttgart | **Lighting / Media** trussco GmbH, Neuss | **Construction** Klartext Grafik Messe Event GmbH, Willich

Atelier Markgraph GmbH, Frankfurt a. Main; jangled nerves GmbH, Stuttgart
Daimler AG, Stuttgart
Internationale Automobil-Ausstellung (IAA) 2015, Frankfurt a. Main

ECHTZEIT

Für die Gestaltung des Kuppelbaus der Frankfurter Festhalle, die anlässlich der IAA 2015 zum Markenraum von Mercedes-Benz umfunktioniert wurde, engagierte der Automobilkonzern die Stuttgarter Kreativen von jangled nerves sowie das Frankfurter Atelier Markgraph. Gemeinsam entwickelte das Team ein Ausstellungskonzept auf drei Ebenen und über insgesamt 9.000 Quadratmetern, das die Festhalle in einen Bühnenraum für die Themen Digitalisierung und Design verwandelte. Auf Rolltreppen glitten die Besucher 13 Meter in die Höhe, wo sich ihnen bereits erste Einblicke sowohl in die verschiedenen Themenbereiche als auch auf die Show boten – architektonisch gerahmt vom „Silver Flow", einer dynamisch geformten Großskulptur aus silbernen Lamellen, die nahtlos in die digitale Medienfläche überging. Das Herzstück des Messestands bildete jedoch die 450 Quadratmeter große Bühne, auf der eine Echtzeitinszenierung real fahrende Automobile, Film, Livebild, Musik und Moderationen zu einer Gesamtchoreografie verschmelzen ließ. Im Hintergrund befand sich dabei ein kinetischer LED-Lamellenvorhang, mit dessen Öffnen und Schließen die Blicke der Besucher gezielt auf das aktuelle Produktportfolio – das in einem dreigeschossigen Regal nur auf seinen Bühneneinsatz wartete – gelenkt werden konnte. Zudem wurden Aufnahmen von einer Spider-Cam live eingefangen, die auf die Medienflächen übertragen und mit Augmented-Reality-Ebenen überlagert wurden. So traten das Moderatorenteam sowie die Musiker gemeinsam mit den präsentierten Fahrzeugen in eine Sphäre zwischen Realem und Digitalem.

REALTIME

For the design of the dome of the Frankfurt Festival Hall, which was transformed into a brand space for Mercedes-Benz on the occasion of the IAA 2015, the car maker commissioned the creative minds from Stuttgart-based jangled nerves and Atelier Markgraph from Frankfurt. Together, the joint team developed an exhibition concept on three levels and more than 9,000 m², that turned the festival hall into a stage area for the topics digitisation and design. Escalators transported visitors up to a height of 13 metres. From here, they were able to get a first overview of the various themed areas and also take in the show—architecturally framed by the "Silver Flow", a giant, dynamically-shaped sculpture constructed of silver slats which transitioned seamlessly into the digital media surface. However, the heart of the booth was without a doubt the 450 m² stage on which a real-time performance of real cars, film, live images, music and presentations blended into an holistic choreography. The stage backdrop took the form of a kinetic LED slatted curtain that opened and closed, guiding the eyes of the visitors towards the current product portfolio that awaited its stage appearance on a three-storey shelf. Live recordings captured by a spider cam were broadcast on the media screens, supplemented by layers of augmented reality. The team of compères and musicians who appeared together with the vehicles were located in spheres somewhere between real and digital.

Auf der IAA 2015 präsentierte sich Mercedes-Benz in neuartiger Liveatmosphäre: Für elf Tage verwandelte sich der ehrwürdige Kuppelbau der Frankfurter Festhalle in einen lebendigen Bühnenraum.

At the IAA 2015, Mercedes-Benz presented itself in an innovative new live atmosphere: For eleven days, the venerable dome of the Frankfurt Festival Hall was transformed into a lively stage.

Die Show ließ die Besucher in Echtzeit in die Welt des Automobils eintauchen und machte sie interaktiv zu Mitwirkenden der raumgreifenden Inszenierung. Mercedes-Benz setzte damit das Motto der IAA 2015 „Mobilität verbindet" in ein unmittelbares Erlebnis um.

The spectacle allowed visitors to submerge in real time into the world of the automobile, making them interactive participants of the all-engulfing production. Mercedes-Benz translated the slogan of the IAA 2015 "Mobility connects" into a live experience.

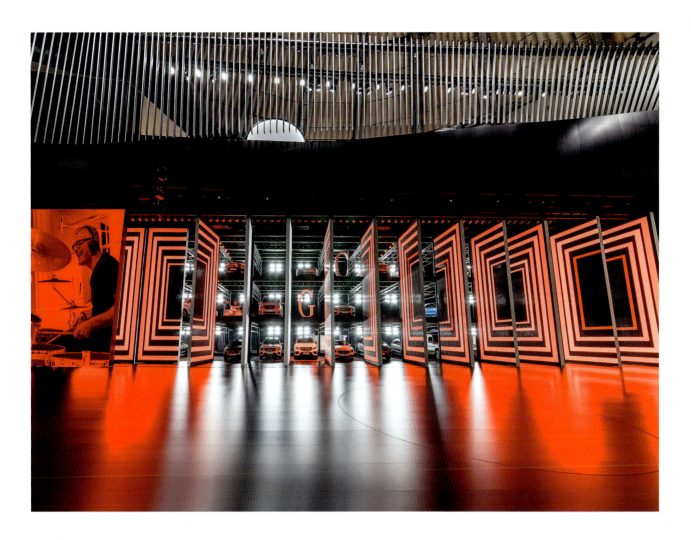

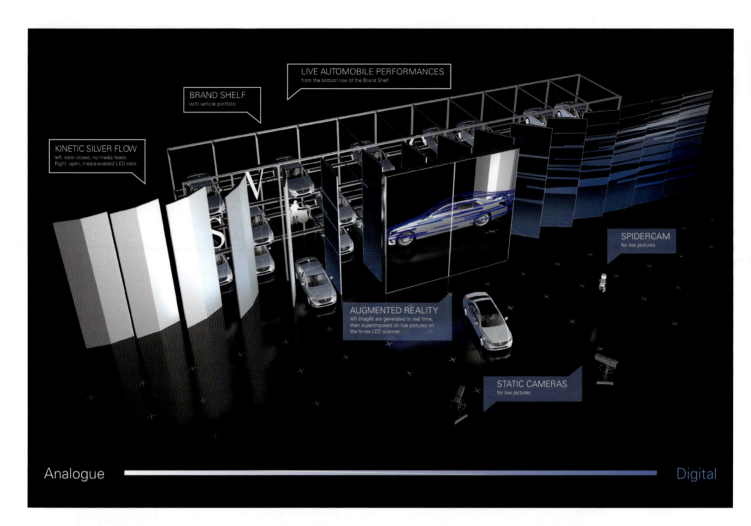

Mit der Leitidee „Mercedes Live!" wurden Fahrbewegungen sowie das Publikum wie bei Sportübertragungen live von einer Spider-Cam eingefangen, die Aufnahmen auf Medienflächen übertragen und diese mit Augmented-Reality-Ebenen überlagert.

With the central idea "Mercedes Live!", movements of the vehicles and of the public was recorded live by a spider cam. The recordings were broadcast on the media screens with layers of augmented reality added.

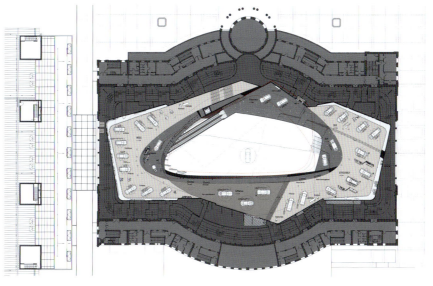

Size 9,000 m² | **Exhibitor** Daimler AG, Stuttgart | **Photos** Kristof Lemp, Darmstadt; Andreas Keller Fotografie, Altdorf | **Architecture** jangled nerves GmbH, Stuttgart | **Communication / Media Production** Atelier Markgraph GmbH, Frankfurt a. Main | **Lighting Design** TLD Planungsgruppe GmbH, Esslingen | **Construction** DISPLAY INTERNATIONAL Schwendinger GmbH & Co. KG, Würselen

KMS BLACKSPACE GmbH, Munich
Volkswagen AG, Wolfsburg
CES 2016, Las Vegas

NEU VERNETZT

540 Quadratmeter Standfläche bespielte die Münchner Agentur KMS BLACKSPACE für die Volkswagen AG auf der CES 2016 in Las Vegas. „Think New" lautete hier das Motto der auf Transparenz und Konnektivität fokussierten Inszenierung. Das neue Erscheinungsbild der Marke, das die Gestalter auf der weltweit größten Fachmesse für Unterhaltungselektronik präsentierten, zeigte ein Unternehmen, das sich selbst zwischen den Schlagworten Innovation, Nachhaltigkeit und Verantwortung verortet. Jene Themen wurden dementsprechend auch in der Standgestaltung aufgegriffen, wo sich kilometerlange, blaue Gurte kreuz und quer um die gesamte Präsentationsfläche spannten. So entstand eine transparente und ressourcenschonende Skulptur, anhand derer die Grenzen des VW-Bereichs gezogen wurden. Gleichzeitig wurde die Thematik der Vernetzung unausweichlich greifbar. Mittels Informationsstelen konnten die Besucher zudem Detailinformationen einholen, während Bildschirme über dem ausgestellten Showcar namens „Budd-e" dazu dienten, eine Reise von San Francisco zum Burning Man Festival mit dem elektrisch angetriebenen Fahrzeug zu visualisieren – Vernetzung und Nachhaltigkeit zogen sich demnach bis in die konkrete Narration durch.

NEWLY CONNECTED

At the CES 2016 in Las Vegas, the Munich-based agency KMS BLACKSPACE designed a 540 m² stand for Volkswagen AG. "Think New" was the slogan of the production with a focus on transparency and connectivity. The new look of the brand which the designers presented at the world's largest trade fair for entertainment electronics showed a company which places itself between the buzzwords innovation, sustainability and responsibility. These themes were picked up in the design of the booth, with kilometres of blue webbing criss-crossing the whole presentation area. The result was a transparent and resource-friendly sculpture, demarcating the borders of the VW area. At the same time, the theme connectivity was made tangible. Technical exhibits provided visitors with detailed information while screens in the background visualised a journey from San Francisco to the Burning Man Festival by an electrically driven model—networking and sustainability was the thread that ran through the narration.

Einen Blick in die Zukunft bot der Wolfsburger Automobilhersteller mit dem rein elektrisch angetriebenen „Budd-e", während der ebenfalls präsentierte e-Golf die unmittelbar bevorstehende Zukunft symbolisierte. Für die Vernetzung beider Modelle diente eine raumgreifende Inszenierung im Corporate Design der Marke.

With the "Budd-e", the car maker from Wolfsburg offered a glimpse of the future, while the e-Golf that was also on display was intended to symbolise the short-term future. The extensive presentation in the Corporate Design of the brand connected the two models.

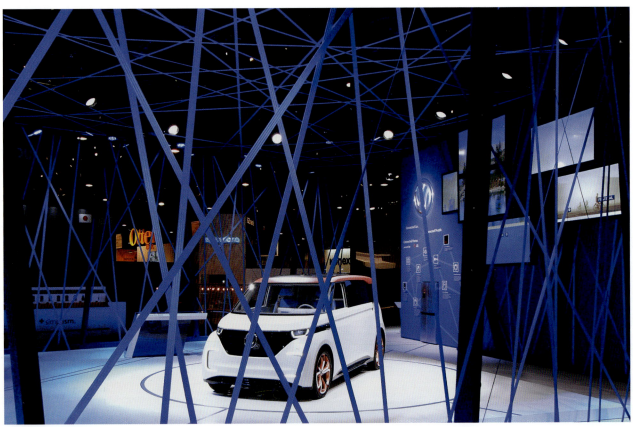

Die Gesamtlänge der Spanngurte entsprach der visualisierten Reiseroute von San Francisco zum Burning Man Festival in der Wüste Nevadas. Am Ende der Messe löste sich die Skulptur wieder in einzelne Gurte auf. Das von KMS BLACKSPACE entwickelte neue und transparente Erscheinungsbild kommuniziert dabei Volkswagens Markenwerte Innovation, Nachhaltigkeit und Verantwortung.

The total length of the tensioning straps was the distance between San Francisco and the Burning Man Festival in the Nevada desert. At the end of the fair, the sculpture was dismantled. The new and transparent appearance developed by KMS BLACKSPACE communicates Volkswagen's brand values—innovation, sustainability and responsibility.

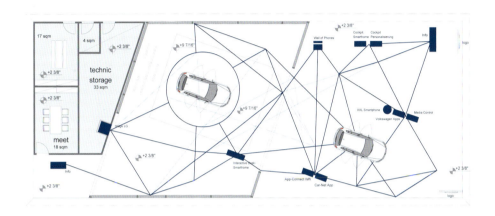

Size 540 m² | **Exhibitor** Volkswagen AG, Wolfsburg | **Photos** Lee Allen Photography, Birmingham | **Concept / Design / Graphics** KMS BLACKSPACE GmbH, Munich | **Archicecture / Lighting** rgb GmbH, Essen | **Construction** George P. Johnson Experiential Marketing, Torrance

Meiré und Meiré GmbH & Co. KG, Cologne
BMW AG, Munich
Internationale Automobil-Ausstellung (IAA) 2015, Frankfurt a. Main

URBANER LUXUS

Auf über 12.000 Quadratmetern auf zwei Ebenen präsentierte die BMW Group mit ihrem bisher größten Messestand auf der IAA 2015 die Produktpaletten von BMW, MINI und Rolls-Royce. Verbunden wurden die verschiedenen Markenbereiche mit einer etwa 400 Meter langen und bis zu 50 Meter breiten Fahrbahn. Die damit mögliche fahraktive Inszenierung dominierte den Auftritt architektonisch. Auf integrierten Bühnen wurden neue Technologie- und Produkthighlights der Marke BMW in abwechslungsreichen Shows präsentiert. Für den Auftritt von BMW interpretierten die Gestalter von Meiré und Meiré auf der Plaza der oberen Ebene in drei Showrooms die unterschiedlichen Aspekte der luxuriösen Welt des BMW 7ers: innovativ, ästhetisch, sportlich. Die „Seven Gallery" im oberen Geschoss zeigte, was moderner Luxus bedeutet: Ästhetik, Liebe zum Detail, handwerkliche Exzellenz sowie das Verschieben technologischer Grenzen in einer vernetzten Welt. Dargestellt wurde dies anhand von Fahrzeugdetails sowie mit Beispielen höchster Manufakturkunst aus anderen Bereichen. Im Erdgeschoss fanden die Besucher zudem die Themenbereiche BMW i und BMW M mit speziellen Lichtinszenierungen, das 50 Quadratmeter große Feldmassiv der Abteilung BMW X sowie die restliche BMW-Produktpalette. Für MINI entwarfen die verantwortlichen Gestalter von Meiré und Meiré den „Creative Hub". In jenem wurde sowohl das neue Corporate Design präsentiert als auch die Weltpremiere des neuen MINI Clubman gefeiert. Dabei stand die Kreativität in der Gestaltung der Inszenierung wie auch im abgebildeten Lebensstil der Zielgruppe im Mittelpunkt. Accessoires wurden daher genauso ausgestellt wie die Fahrzeuge und innovative neue Features.

Die beim BMW-Auftritt neben der Fahraktivität zentrale Highlightinszenierung in Form einer Rotunde bot wechselnde Perspektiven auf den neuen BMW 7er und geleitete den Besucher auf die großzügige Plaza im Obergeschoss.

As visitors passed along a highlight show housed in a rotunda, the heart of the BMW appearance besides the driving circuit, they were treated to changing perspectives of the new BMW 7 series, eventually arriving at a generous plaza on the upper floor.

URBAN LUXURY

On the 12,000 m² stand at the IAA 2015—its biggest booth yet—the BMW Group presented the product range of BMW, MINI and Rolls-Royce on two levels. The various brand areas were connected by a roughly 400 m long and 50 m wide circuit. The resulting active driving demonstrations architecturally dominated the presentation. On stages integrated, visitors could watch diverse shows to get to know new technology and product highlights. For the presentation of BMW, the designers from Meiré und Meiré interpreted the different aspects of the luxurious world of BMW 7 in three showrooms at the plaza on the upper floor: innovative, aesthetic, athletic. The "Seven Gallery" in the upper storey showed what contemporary luxury means: aesthetics, attention to detail, excellent craftsmanship as well as the way technological limits are being pushed back in a connected world. This was demonstrated both in vehicle details and in examples of manufacturing excellence from other areas. On the ground floor, visitors also found the themed areas BMW i and BMW M with special light shows, the 50 m² rock massif of the BMW X department as well as further BMW products. For MINI, the responsible designers from the Cologne agency Meiré und Meiré came up with the "Creative Hub". Here, both the new Corporate Design was presented as well as the world début of the new MINI Clubman. The focus of the design was on creativity and the lifestyle of the target group. Matching accessories were therefore presented alongside the vehicles and their innovative, new features.

Digitalisierung intelligent genutzt: Erstmals ermöglichte BMW den Besuchern, anhand einer App hinter die Kulissen zu blicken und vertiefende Inhalte zu den Innovationen zu entdecken. Neben einem Audioguide zur Ausstellung bot sie zudem Augmented Reality Features, die unter anderem den BMW 7er in neuen Dimensionen erlebbar machten.

Making intelligent use of digitalisation: for the first time, BMW offered an app that allowed visitors to take a look behind the scenes and to discover more in-depth information about the innovations. Besides an audio guide to the exhibition, the app also offered augmented reality features, which allowed the BMW 7 series to be experienced in new dimensions.

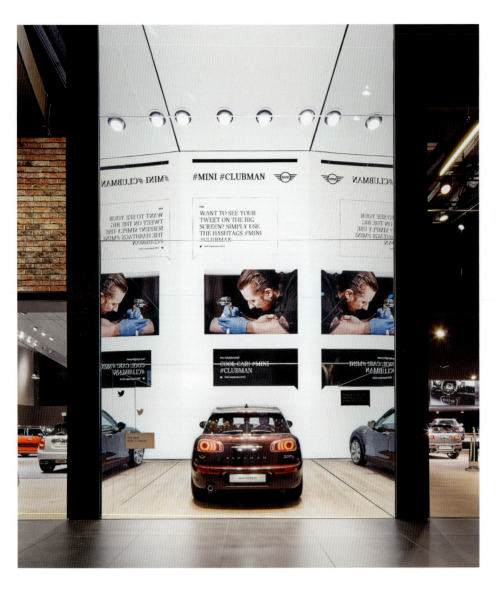

Meiré und Meiré präsentierte MINI zwischen tradierter Eleganz und Kreativität mit besonders urbaner Atmosphäre. Ein neun Meter hohes Schaufenster gab dabei Einblicke in die Welt des neuen MINI Clubman.

Meiré und Meiré presented MINI between traditional elegance and creativity, in particular in urban atmosphere. A nine-metre high shop window allowed insights into the world of the new MINI Clubman.

Size 11,960 m² | **Exhibitor** BMW AG, Munich | **Photos** diephotodesigner.de, Berlin; Achim Hatzius, Berlin | **Architecture / Design** Meiré und Meiré GmbH & Co. KG, Cologne | **Graphics** Djuma GmbH, Munich; catdesign GmbH & Co. KG, Kleve | **Lighting / Media** NIYU Media projects GmbH, Berlin; Production Resource Group AG, Hamburg | **Exhibition Planning** Blue Scope Communications Projektgesellschaft mbH, Berlin | **Construction** Winkels Ausstellungsbau GmbH, Kleve; Messeprojekt GmbH, Leipzig; metron eging GmbH, Eging a. See

Schmidhuber Brand Experience GmbH, Munich; Mutabor Design GmbH, Hamburg
AUDI AG, Ingolstadt
Internationale Automobil-Ausstellung (IAA) 2015, Frankfurt a. Main

KINETISCHER KOMPASS

Gestaltet von SCHMIDHUBER und Mutabor Design, präsentierte die AUDI AG unter dem Motto „the power of four" die vier Fokusthemen Audi ultra, Audi Technologies, Audi quattro und Audi Sport auf der IAA 2015 in Frankfurt. Noch vor der eigentlichen Produktpräsentation im Zentrum des 5.428 Quadratmeter großen Markengebäudes wurden die Besucher durch eine emotionale Ausstellung geleitet – den „Experience Walk". Den Auftakt dieser Inszenierung bildete die Fahrt mit einer Rolltreppe durch eine organisch vernetzte Leichtbauskulptur, die sich aus der Fassade des freistehenden Bauwerks entwickelte. Die Besucher erlebten damit die Themen Leichtbau, effiziente Motoren und alternative Kraftstoffe. Über ein virtuelles Fenster – ergänzt durch die Ebene der Augmented Reality – gab der folgende Ausstellungsbereich Audi Technologies einen spannenden Blick auf die Exponate im Inneren des Gebäudes frei. Ein Spiel mit Dimension und Perspektive erwartete die Besucher im Bereich Audi quattro: Temperaturen von -21 Grad Celsius schufen hier eine Welt aus Eis, in der Branding und Kunstwerk den quattro-Lifestyle illustrierten. Im Kontrast dazu stand der Weg durch das Thema Audi Sport: Intensive Rennsportakustik und dynamische LED-Installationen an Wänden und Decke lenkten den Blick auf die Rennsportikone Audi R18 in einer Steilkurve, die den nahtlosen Übergang in die eigentliche Fahrzeugausstellung bildete. Mit einem Ausblick auf die dynamisch angeordnete Audi-Flotte betraten die Messegäste schließlich das Herzstück des Auftritts, mit dem die eben erlebten Fokusthemen nun in einem Vierklang zusammengeführt wurden – wobei ein überdimensionaler Kompass im Zentrum auf das jeweilige Leitmotiv hinwies.

Noch vor der eigentlichen Produktpräsentation im Zentrum des Gebäudes wurden die Besucher unter dem Motto „the power of four" durch eine emotionale Inszenierung der vier Fokusthemen Audi ultra, Audi Technologies, Audi quattro und Audi Sport geführt.

KINETIC COMPASS

Designed by SCHMIDHUBER and Mutabor Design, AUDI AG's booth at the IAA 2015 in Frankfurt was themed "the power of four" and was dedicated to the four focus topics: Audi ultra, Audi Technologies, Audi quattro and Audi Sport. Before reaching the product presentation proper at the centre of the 5,428 m² brand building, the visitor was led on an emotional "Experience Walk" through the exhibition. This presentation started on an escalator passing through a lightweight sculpture with an organic network-like structure that evolved from the façade of the free-standing construction. In this way, visitors experienced the themes lightweight construction, efficient engines and alternative fuels first hand. Through a virtual window—supplemented by an augmented reality level—the next exhibition area "Audi Technologies" revealed an exciting view of the exhibits in the interior of the building. In the Audi quattro area, a play with dimension and perspective awaited visitors: temperatures of minus 21°C created a world carved out of ice in which the branding and artwork illustrated the quattro lifestyle. The path through the Audi Sport zone was in stark contrast to this: intensive racing sport acoustics and dynamic LED installations on the walls and ceiling directed attention to the iconic racing car Audi R18 in a banked curve that thus formed the seamless transition to the actual vehicle exhibition. With an outlook on the dynamically arranged Audi fleet, fairgoers finally reached the heart of the stand where the four focus themes experienced thus far came together under a huge, suspended compass which pointed to the respective leitmotif.

Even before they reached the actual product display at the centre of the building, visitors were guided under the slogan "the power of four" through an emotional presentation of the four focus themes: Audi ultra, Audi Technologies, Audi quattro and Audi Sport.

Im Audi quattro-Bereich überraschten die Gestalter mit einer -21 Grad Celsius kalten Eiswelt, während der Audi Sport-Abschnitt durch Rennsportklang sowie den Sportwagen R18 – positioniert auf einer Steilkurve – markiert wurde.

In the Audi quattro zone, the designers came up with a surprising ice world kept at minus 21°C, while the Audi Sport section was clearly dominated by the sound of motor sport and the sports car R18—positioned in a banked curve.

Im Zentrum des Messestands wies ein überdimensionaler Kompass auf die vier Leitthemen hin. Großformatige Medienflächen, auf denen reale Fahrzeuge als virtuell eingebettete, bewegliche Darsteller agierten, dominierten dabei den Raum.

At the centre of the trade fair stand, an outsized compass pointed to the four themed areas. Large-scale media screens on which real vehicles acted as virtually embedded, movable players dominated the space.

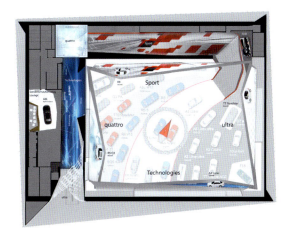

Size 5,428 m² | **Exhibitor** AUDI AG, Ingolstadt | **Photos** Andreas Keller Fotografie, Altdorf | **Architecture / Design** Schmidhuber Brand Experience GmbH, Munich; Mutabor Design GmbH, Hamburg | **Lighting** FOUR TO ONE LIGHTING DESIGN GmbH, Bornheim Media TFN GmbH & Co. KG, Hamburg | **Construction** NÜSSLI (Schweiz) AG, Hüttwilen

sons GmbH, Kempten
Kässbohrer Geländefahrzeug AG, Laupheim
INTERALPIN 2015, Innsbruck

GESPÜR FÜR SCHNEE

Auf der INTERALPIN 2015 in Innsbruck – Weltleitmesse für alpine Technologien – präsentierte die Kässbohrer Geländefahrzeug AG ihre Marke PistenBully in einem strahlend weißen Raum. Der etwa 1.250 Quadratmeter große Messestand, den die Agentur sons gestaltet hatte, wirkte wie eine Schneelandschaft, während geometrische Formen, die bewusst Erinnerungen an Snowparks evozierten, das aus jeder Perspektive unterschiedlich wirkende Standkonzept prägten. Auf schrägen Rampen inszenierte der schwäbische Hersteller neben dem neuen „PistenBully 100" auch den „400 ParkPro", der die Produktpalette um ein professionelles Werkzeug für die Präparation von Parks erweitert sowie gemeinsam mit den Experten von Schneestern entwickelt wurde, dem führenden europäischen Snowpark-Spezialisten. Jene waren mit einer Werkstatt ebenfalls auf dem Stand vertreten und erläuterten das Fahrzeug im Detail. So stellten die Kemptener Gestalter die Produkte in den Mittelpunkt des Geschehens, wodurch sonst schnell übersehbare Feinheiten wie Schaufelaufhängung oder Kettenspikes gut erkennbar wurden. Eine realitätsnahe Inszenierung ließ die Besucher zudem in eine alpine Welt eintauchen, in der die Pistenraupen als Helden des gesamten Auftritts in Erscheinung traten und auch beim Essen in der stilisierten Almhütte noch präsent waren. Historische Fotos, Zitate an die Rustikalität alpiner Umgebungen sowie klare Formen waren dabei die prägenden Elemente des schneeweißen Messestands.

„PistenBullys gehören in ihr natürliches Revier: an steile Hänge, in die Welt des Winters mit Eis, Kälte und Schnee – dazu die Behaglichkeit der Hütten. Diese Welt haben wir in die Sprache der Architektur übersetzt", erklärten die Gestalter ihr Konzept.

SENSE OF SNOW

At the INTERALPIN 2015 in Innsbruck—the world's leading fair for alpine technologies—Kässbohrer Geländefahrzeug AG presented their PistenBully marque in a bright, white space. The roughly 1,250 m² of the exhibition stand designed by the agency sons was like a snow landscape. Shaped by geometrical forms that deliberately evoked memories of snow parks, the stand appeared different from every perspective. On inclined ramps, the Swabian manufacturer presented not only the new "PistenBully 100" but also the "400 ParkPro", which complemented the product range with a professional tool for the preparation of snow parks developed in collaboration with the experts from Schneestern. Europe's leading snow park specialist was likewise represented on the stand with a workshop where the vehicle was explained in detail. In this way, the designers from Kempten put the products at the heart of the presentation, making fine details that might otherwise have been overlooked like the bucket suspension or the chain spikes easy to recognise. The realistic setting allowed visitors to immerse themselves in an alpine world in which the piste preparation vehicles appeared like the heroes of the whole exhibition and were still omnipresent even when eating in the stylised alpine hut. Historical photos, quotes referring to the rustic alpine environment and clear lines were formative elements of the snow-white booth.

"PistenBullys belong in their natural environment: steep slopes, a winter wonderland with ice, cold and snow— combined with the cosiness of the huts. This is the world we translated into architectural language", was how the designers explained their concept.

Es schien, als sei der zweigeschossige Messestand aus einem riesigen Schneeblock herausgefräst worden. Dabei wirkte alles stark reduziert und lebte von der Spannung zwischen Kalt und Warm.

The two-level trade fair stand appeared to have been carved out of one huge block of snow. The very reduced look lived from the interaction of warm and cold.

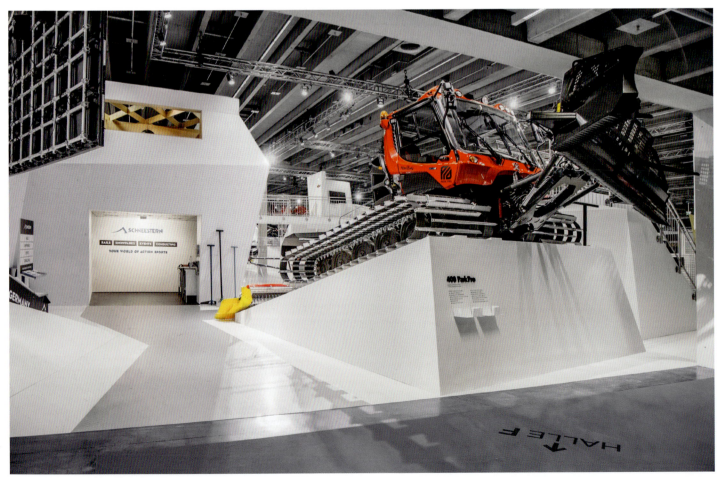

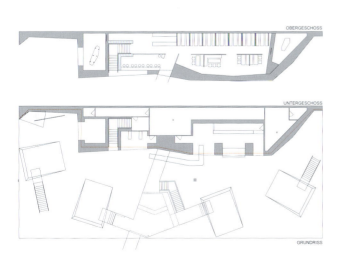

Size 1,245 m² | **Exhibitor** Kässbohrer Geländefahrzeug AG, Laupheim | **Photos** sons GmbH, Kempten; Martin Uhlmann; Kässbohrer Geländefahrzeug AG, Laupheim | **Architecture / Design** sons GmbH, Kempten | **Construction** System Standbau GmbH, Salzburg

INTERVIEW
MARKUS MÜLLER-KEMPF
(SONS GMBH)

Der Messeauftritt auf der Interalpin 2015 für die Marke PistenBully der Kässbohrer Geländefahrzeug AG entstand nach einem intensiven Strategieworkshop mit dem Unternehmen. Wie wichtig ist für Sie bei Ihrer Arbeit diese Nähe und starke Zusammenarbeit mit dem Kunden? Und welche Strategien wurden hier erarbeitet?

Bei der Betreuung der Marke ist viel Bauchgefühl wichtig, das einerseits durch die Projekte und andererseits durch die persönliche Nähe zum Unternehmen entsteht – insbesondere zu Vorstand, Marketing und Vertrieb. Gerade für eine Neuentwicklung in dieser Dimension ist eine solch enge Kommunikation der Beteiligten ganz zentral für den gemeinsamen Erfolg. Denn das macht eine authentische Markendarstellung möglich! Genau auf dieser Grundlage wurden im Strategieworkshop einige Schwerpunkte für den weiteren Markenauftritt gelegt: So sollte der Stand auf der Interalpin nicht nur Besuchermagnet, sondern gleichzeitig auch Treffpunkt für die gesamte Branche werden. Wichtig war es dabei für uns als Team, ein Erlebnis auf Basis der spezifischen Unternehmenspersönlichkeit zu schaffen und den PistenBully in seinen markenrelevanten Kontext zu stellen.

Wie spiegeln sich die Ergebnisse des Workshops in Ihrem architektonischen Entwurf wider?

Der Workshop fand im Snowpark „Motolino Fun Mountain" in Livigno statt. Hier konnten wir direkt im Einsatzgebiet des PistenBullys einen emotionalen Zugang zur Marke aufbauen und aufgrund der gemeinsam erarbeiteten Strategie bereits mit der Entwurfsplanung beginnen, die direkt in ein erstes Modell im Maßstab 1:87 übertragen wurde. Darauf aufbauend entstand im weiteren Verlauf ein Standkonzept, welches die vorherrschenden Produkteigenschaften – das steile Bergauffahren im Schnee – klar definierte. Die auf steilen Hängen einer abstrakten Winterlandschaft stehenden Fahrzeuge wurden zum Mittelpunkt der Inszenierung und erhielten durch die zurückhaltende Standarchitektur den nötigen Raum für den Dialog zwischen Kunden und Mitarbeitern. Dank der Möglichkeit, die tonnenschweren Produkte zu berühren, sie aus allen Blickwinkeln zu betrachten und damit hautnah zu erleben, konnten Markenwerte wie Emotionalität, Authentizität und Kundennähe, die sich im Verlauf der Zusammenarbeit herauskristallisiert hatten, weitergetragen werden.

Auch beim Aufbau war ein Hand-in-Hand-Arbeiten aller Beteiligten notwendig, um die tonnenschweren Fahrzeuge auf dem Stand zu präsentieren. Wie präzise musste die „Handarbeit" ausgeführt sein und welche besonderen Herausforderungen mussten bewältigt werden?

Der Aufwand war tatsächlich enorm und erforderte handwerkliches Geschick: Wir konnten ihn dank detaillierter Planung jedoch bereits im Vorfeld kalkulieren und austesten. Zunächst wurde dafür ein Rampenprototyp entwickelt, bei dem wir Aufbau, Transportbedingungen und vor allem die Statik untersuchen konnten. Schließlich sollten die abstrakten Schneeberge zwölf Tonnen schwere Fahrzeuge tragen. Da allein das Auflegen der Ketten von Hand für die PistenBullys pro Fahrzeug 18 Meter Länge und damit eine zweiwöchige, vorverlegte Aufbauphase benötigte, drehte sich die gesamte Logistik von Beginn an um die exakte, fast chirurgisch-präzise Fahrzeugpositionierung. Für den weiteren Ablauf bedeutet das beispielsweise aber auch, dass der Bodenbelag erst nach der Positionierung verlegt werden konnte. Der eigentliche Standbau wurde mit einem standardisierten Messebausystem umgesetzt und in der zweiten Ebene als kantige Bergoptik individualisiert. Dank des hohen Vor-Ort-Einsatzes aller Beteiligten und der engen Zusammenarbeit zwischen Kunde, Agentur und der für die handfeste Umsetzung verantwortlichen Messebaufirma System Standbau aus Salzburg war so eine Realisierung trotz hohem Kostendruck erst möglich.

⟶ **Markus Müller-Kempf** studierte Produktdesign und Innenarchitektur an der Staatlichen Akademie der Bildenden Künste, München. Nach verschiedenen Stationen im Design bei der BMW Group in München verantwortet er seit 2008 die Bereiche Corporate Architecture und entwickelt Marken im gesamten Corporate Identity bei sons.

> www.go-sons.de

The presentation at the Interalpin 2015 for the PistenBully brand of Kässbohrer Geländefahrzeug AG was the result of an intensive strategy workshop with the company. How important for your work is this proximity and close collaboration with the client? And what strategies have you developed to do so?

When looking after a brand, your gut feeling is very important. On the one hand, this develops through the projects themselves and on the other through close personal contact to the company—in particular to management, marketing and sales. Particularly when developing something new on this scale, close communication among all those involved is paramount for the shared success. Because that is what makes an authentic brand presentation possible! It was on precisely this basis that a number of focal points were decided on at the strategy workshop for the brand appearance in future: the booth at the Interalpin was not just to be a crowd puller, but at the same time meeting point for the entire sector. For us as a team, it was important to create an experience on the basis of the specific corporate personality and to position the PistenBully in terms of its relevance for the brand.

How are the results of the workshop reflected in your architectural design?

The workshop took place at the "Motolino Fun Mountain" snow park in Livigno. Being in the area in which the PistenBully is deployed enabled us to gain emotional access to the brand and to start with the development of the design on the basis of the strategy elaborated on together. This was transferred directly to a first model on a scale of 1:87 which in turn formed the basis for the resulting stand concept around the clearly defined main product feature, namely the ability to drive up steep inclines in the snow. Vehicles standing on steep slopes of an abstract winter landscape became the centre of the presentation and the reduced stand architecture provided the necessary space for dialogue between customers and staff. The possibility to touch the heavyweight products, to inspect them from all angles and thus to experience them at first hand transported brand values such as emotionality, authenticity and customer proximity which had emerged in the course of our work with the client.

The stand build also required everyone to work hand in hand in order to present the extremely heavy vehicles on the stand. How precise did the "hands-on work" have to be and what special challenges had to be managed?

It was indeed a hugely complex task which required a good deal of manual dexterity. Thanks to the detailed planning, we were however able to calculate and test everything out beforehand. First, a prototype ramp was developed which we used to test the structure, transport conditions and above all the statics. After all, the abstract snow mountain had to bear vehicles weighing twelve metric tonnes. As attaching the chains by hand for the PistenBullys took 18 metres in length per vehicle and thus required the build phase to be brought forward two weeks, the whole logistics right from the start were about the precise, almost surgically accurate positioning of the vehicles. However, this also meant, for instance, that the flooring could not be laid until after the positioning. The actual stand was built using a standardized stand construction system and individualised on the second level with an angular mountain look. The huge on-the-spot commitment of everyone concerned and the close collaboration between customer, agency and booth construction firm System Standbau from Salzburg were what made the realisation of the stand possible, despite the ever-present cost constraints.

→ **Markus Müller-Kempf** studied product design and interior architecture at the Academy of Fine Arts in Munich. After various design posts in the BMW Group in Munich, since 2008 he has been responsible for the areas Corporate Architecture and brand development as part of Corporate Identity at sons.

> www.go-sons.de

tisch13 GmbH, Munich
AUDI AG, Ingolstadt
CES 2016, Las Vegas

AUTOMOBILE AND TRANSPORTATION

GEORDNETES CHAOS

Zum sechsten Mal in Folge präsentierte sich die AUDI AG 2016 auf der CES in Las Vegas. Gestaltet von der Münchner Kreativschmiede tisch13 stand die Architektur des Auftritts dabei unter dem Motto „Audi Nexus" – ein Synonym für Vernetzung, Datenströme und künstliche Intelligenz, womit das Oberthema „Audi Intelligence" in Zusammenhang mit der digitalen Vernetzung sowie Innovationsideen zur Mobilität der Zukunft aufgegriffen wurde. Ein Netzwerk aus spiegelnden Aluminiumprofilen mit einer Gesamtlänge von vier Kilometern verlieh der Grundidee des Messestands dabei ihre Form. An den Knotenpunkten verbunden ergab sich ein dreidimensionales Raster, das als Präsentationsraum für Technikexponate sowie die Fahrzeuge diente. Die auf Hochglanz polierten Profile reflektierten den gesamten 500 Quadratmeter großen Messestand, der von drei Seiten für die Besucher begehbar war, während die Rückseite aus einer 60 Quadratmeter großen LED-Wand gebildet wurde, auf der sich das Netzwerk digital fortsetzte. So entstand nicht nur eine visuell beeindruckende Tiefenwirkung, den Gestaltern gelang zudem ein faszinierendes Spiel von Licht und Reflektionen.

ORGANISED CHAOS

AUDI AG presented itself at the 2016 CES in Las Vegas for the sixth time in a row. Designed by Munich's creative workshop tisch13, the booth architecture was inspired by the slogan "Audi Nexus", a synonym for networking, data flows and artificial intelligence, picking up the overarching theme "Audi Intelligence" in connection with digital networking and innovative ideas on mobility of the future. A network of reflective aluminium profiles with a total length of four kilometres gave the underlying idea of the stand a shape. Connected at the joints, there emerged a three-dimensional grid that served as presentation space for technical exhibits and vehicles. The highly polished profiles reflected the entire 500 m² of the stand. While the stand was accessible by visitors from three sides, the rear wall consisted of a 60 m² LED wall on which the network was continued in digital form. The result was not only a visually impressive sense of depth, the designers also achieved a fascinating interplay of light and reflections.

Der „Audi Nexus" zeigte eine hochreaktive Architektur, bei der das Eintauchen in die Struktur zentraler Bestandteil des Messeauftritts war und die Marke Audi mit all ihren thematischen Facetten im Raum erlebbar machte. Die Messegäste wurden damit zum aktiven Bestandteil der „Audi Intelligence".

The "Audi Nexus" showed a highly reactive architecture. Immersion in the structure was a central element of the booth, making the Audi brand and all its facets spatially tangible. Fairgoers thus became an active part of "Audi Intelligence".

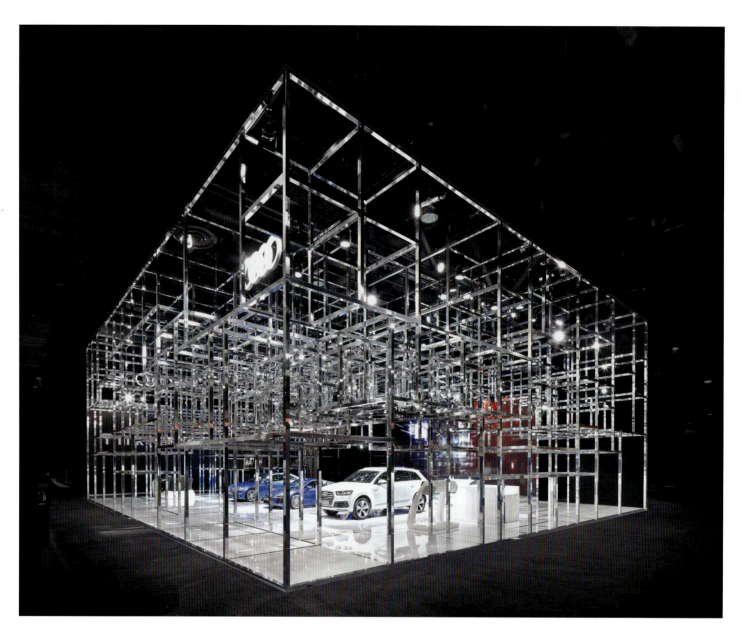

Das im ersten Moment verwirrend erscheinende Chaos des Messestands konnten die Besucher bei genauerer Betrachtung als klare, vernetzte Struktur begreifen, in der sich das Thema des Auftritts mehrfach wiederfinden ließ.

What at first glance appeared to be confusing chaos, could upon closer inspection be understood by the visitors as a clear, networked structure in which the themes of the exhibition were picked up again and again.

Size 500 m² | **Exhibitor** AUDI AG, Ingolstadt | **Photos** Andreas Keller Fotografie, Altdorf | **Architecture** tisch13 GmbH, Munich; Bathke Geisel Architekten, Munich | **Design / Graphics / Media** tisch13 GmbH, Munich | **Lighting** FOUR TO ONE LIGHTING DESIGN GMBH, Bornheim | **Construction** Expotechnik International Holding GmbH & Co. KG, Taunusstein

ELECTRONICS, TECHNOLOGY, AND SCIENCE

→ Elektronische Geräte sowie technologische Neuerungen sind aus unserem Alltag – egal in welcher Größe und Ausprägung – nicht mehr wegzudenken und bestimmen unsere Welt. Hersteller können sich demzufolge nicht mehr allein auf die Produktion, Weiterentwicklung und Verbesserung ihrer Fabrikate konzentrieren, sondern müssen auch über deren sinnvolle Einbindung in unser Leben nachdenken. Diesen Aspekt dann auch noch entsprechend zu präsentieren, bedeutet eine gewisse Herausforderung, die nicht nur in der Produktausstellung, sondern vor allem in der räumlichen Inszenierung als ganzheitliches Bild zum Ausdruck kommt.

→ It is hard to imagine our everyday lives without electronic devices and technical innovations—albeit in different ways and to differing degrees—and they certainly define the world we live in. Manufacturers can therefore no long focus solely on the production, further development and improvement of their products. They also have to think about how they can be incorporated into our lives in a useful way. Presenting this aspect is quite a challenge which finds its overall expression not only in the product display, but also and above all in the spatial presentation.

→ 142

→ 146

→ 130

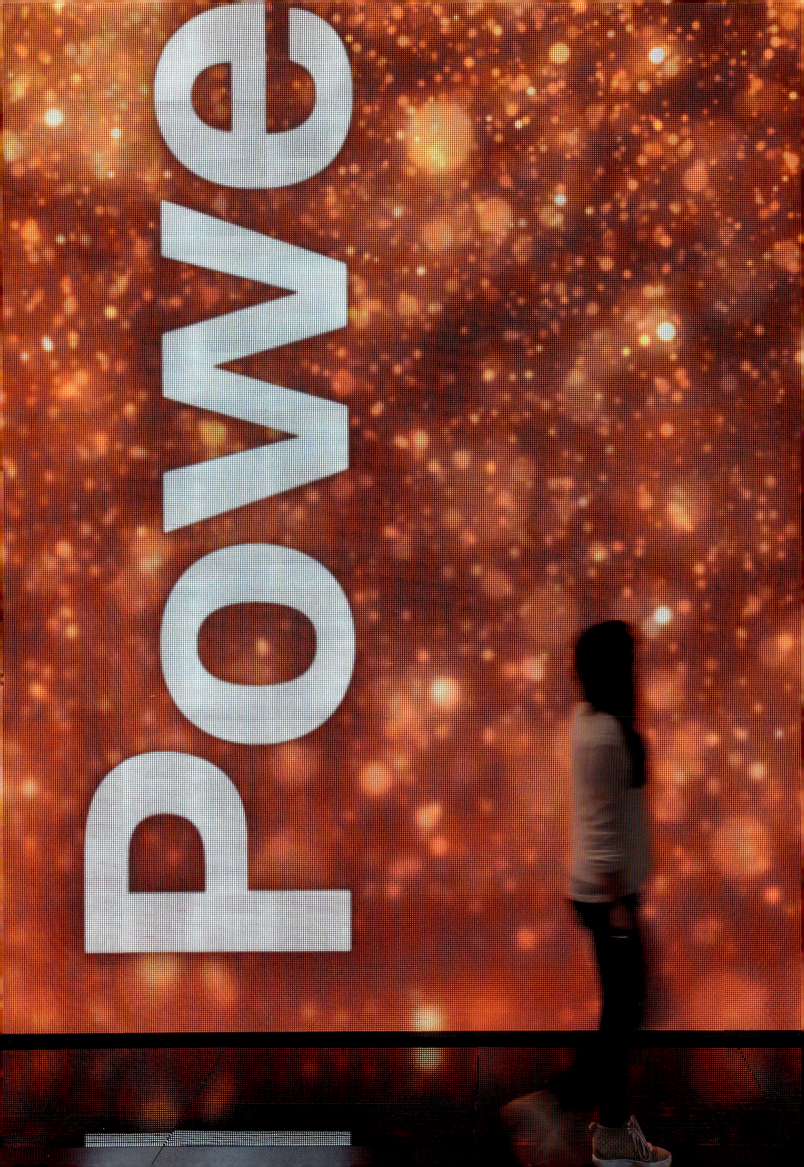

Atelier Markgraph GmbH, Frankfurt a. Main
Viessmann Werke GmbH & Co. KG, Allendorf (Eder)
ISH 2015, Frankfurt a. Main

LEUCHTTÜRME DES WANDELS

Für den Klimaschutz liegt das größte Potenzial im Bereich der Heiztechnik: Die Technologien und Produkte sind dafür auf dem Markt, dennoch herrscht hier ein „Modernisierungsstau" – bedingt durch die Komplexität des Themas sowie die Unsicherheit beim Endkunden. Um dies zu ändern, wurde bei der Gestaltung des Messeauftritts für die Viessmann Werke auf der ISH 2015 in Frankfurt dort angeknüpft, wo sich die breite Öffentlichkeit gut auskennt: in der Automobilität. Denn Hybridisierung, Elektrifizierung und Konnektivität sind hier wie dort die bestimmenden Themen. Konzipiert vom Frankfurter Atelier Markgraph boten dementsprechend drei „Leuchttürme des Energiewandels" Orientierungspunkte auf dem 2.260 Quadratmeter großen Messestand und lenkten mit ikonografischen Visualisierungen die Aufmerksamkeit der Besucher immer wieder auf die drei zentralen Themen. Dabei wurden physikalische Prinzipien durch eine generative, wissenschaftlich präzise und gleichzeitig reduzierte Darstellung verständlich gemacht. Tiefer in die Themen eintauchen konnten die Messegäste zudem in den Innenräumen der Türme und anhand von medial eingebundenen Produkten die neuesten Entwicklungen selbst testen.

LIGHTHOUSES OF CHANGE

The greatest potential for climate protection lies in the field of heating technology: Although the technologies and products are already on sale, there is a "renewal backlog" due to the subject's complexity and consumer uncertainty. To change this, the Viessmann booth design at ISH 2015 in Frankfurt took its cues from something the general public is more familiar with—automobility. The idea being that hybridisation, electrification and connectivity are the decisive topics in both fields. Developed by Frankfurt-based Atelier Markgraph, three "lighthouses of the new energy era" provided orientation points on the 2,260 m² booth which used iconic visualisations to draw the attention of the visitors again and again to the three central themes. Physical principles were made easily understandable in a generative, scientifically precise and at the same time low-key way. Fairgoers could literally deep dive into the topics inside the towers where they could use media-integrated products to test out the most recent developments for themselves.

Hybrid – Power – Connect: Auf dem Messestand der Viessmann Werke wurden der hocheffiziente Mix von fossilen und regenerativen Energieträgern in einem Gerät, ein smart vernetztes Energiemanagement sowie die Strom produzierende Heizung unter den Schlagwörtern Hybridisierung, Elektrifizierung und Konnektivität dem Publikum präsentiert.

Hybrid—Power—Connect: Those were the key words used to present to present the highly efficient mix of fossile and renewable energy sources in one, a smartly connected energy management and a heater producing electricity

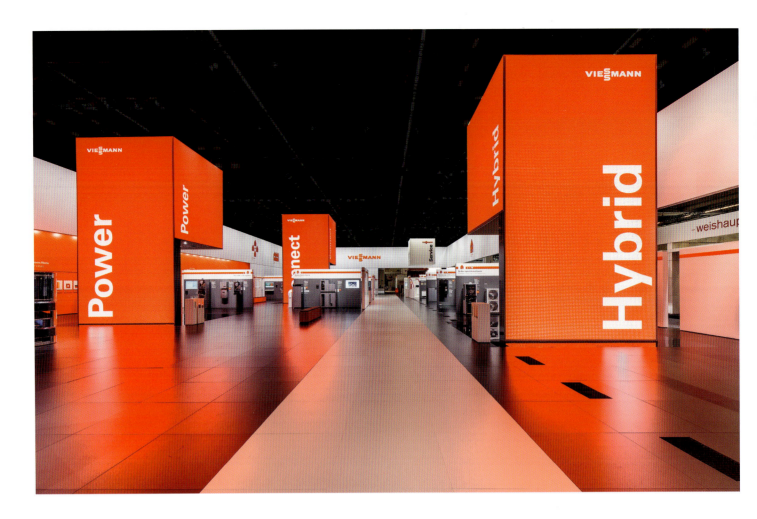

Drei „Leuchttürme des Energiewandels" markierten die zentralen Themen, boten Orientierung und gliederten einen Messestand voller aktueller und zukunftsfähiger Lösungen. Im Umfeld der Leuchttürme wurden thematisch zugeordnet die Produkte und Technologien gruppiert.

Three "lighthouses of the new energy era" marked out the central topics, offered orientation and divided up a trade fair stand that was full of current and future-proof solutions. The products and technologies were grouped thematically near the respective lighthouses.

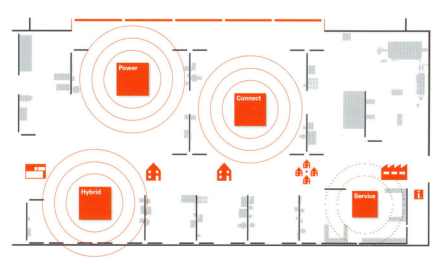

Size 2,260 m² | **Exhibitor** Viessmann Werke GmbH & Co. KG, Allendorf (Eder) | **Photos** Kristof Lemp, Darmstadt | **Architecture / Design** Atelier Markgraph GmbH, Frankfurt a. Main | **Graphics** Atelier Markgraph GmbH, Frankfurt a. Main; apfel, hübsch, Berlin; Leko Werbeservice, Weinstadt | **Lighting** Neumann&Müller GmbH & Co. KG, Esslingen | **Media** Production Resource Group AG, Oststeinbek; arora-electronic GmbH & Co. KG, Fuldabrück; NSYNK Gesellschaft für Kunst und Technik mbH, Berlin | **Musik** kling klang klong, Berlin | **Construction** mac messe- und ausstellungscenter Service GmbH, Langenlonsheim

D'art Design Gruppe GmbH, Neuss
Electrolux Hausgeräte GmbH, Nuremberg
IFA 2015, Berlin

SAUBER ZU TISCH

Für den langjährigen Kunden AEG / Electrolux Hausgeräte gestaltete die Neusser D'art Design Gruppe bereits zum achten Mal in Folge den Messeauftritt auf der IFA in Berlin. 2015 entwickelten die Designer die bereits 2014 präsentierte Architektur weiter und ergänzten diese mit einem sinnlichen Konzept. Die beiden Themenbereiche „Taste" und „Care" erhielten dabei eine individuelle Markengeschichte, welche die unterschiedlichen Produktkategorien inhaltlich vereinte. Moderierte Erlebnistouren ergänzten diese Präsentationen und führten die Besucher in die Welt des Geschmacks beziehungsweise der Wäschepflege ein. „Taking Taste Further" lautete beispielsweise das Motto der Geschmackswelt: Über fünf Erlebnisstationen konnten die Messegäste hier erfahren, wie der berühmte Caesar Salad durch die Optimierung aller Zubereitungsschritte und unter Einsatz der smarten AEG-Küchengeräte perfektioniert werden kann. Parallel zur Taste-Tour startete auch der Rundgang zum Thema Wäschepflege: Mit „From Just Cleaning to Caring" wurde thematisiert, wie der Lebenszyklus von Kleidungsstücken nachhaltig verlängert und Lieblingsstücke dauerhaft geschützt werden können. Neben den innovativen Produkten aus den beiden Bereichen stand auf dem 3.000 Quadratmeter großen Messestand zudem das Trendthema Connectivity im Fokus der Präsentation: Mit der App „My AEG" wurde den Besuchern noch mehr Vernetzung und Unterstützung im Alltag des Kochens und Waschens versprochen.

„Unser Konzept stellt die Kunden von AEG / Electrolux Hausgeräte klar in den Vordergrund: Erlebnistouren bringen den Besuchern die Produktqualitäten rund um die Hauptbereiche Kochen und Waschen von AEG multisensorisch näher", erklärten die Gestalter ihren Entwurf.

"Our concept puts the customers of AEG / Electrolux Hausgeräte at the centre of attention: discovery tours use multisensory means to convey to visitors the product qualities in AEG's main areas—cooking and laundry", is how the designers explained their design.

CLEAN TASTE

For their longstanding customer AEG / Electrolux Hausgeräte, Neuss-based D'art Design Gruppe designed the trade fair appearance at the IFA in Berlin for the eighth consecutive time. In 2015, the designers refined the architecture already presented in 2014, supplementing it with a sensuous concept. The two groups "Taste" and "Care" each received an individual brand story that combined the different product categories thematically. Facilitated tours of discovery complemented these presentations and gave visitors an introduction to the world of taste and laundry care. "Taking Taste Further", for instance, was the tagline of the taste world: at five stations, fairgoers could find out how the famous Caesar salad can be perfected by optimising all the preparation steps and using smart AEG kitchen appliances. In parallel to the Taste tour, their was a circuit tour of the topic laundry care: "From Just Cleaning to Caring" explained how life cycles of clothing can be prolonged and favourite garments protected for the long term. Alongside the innovative products from the two sections, the trend theme connectivity was the focus of the presentation of the 3,000 m² booth: the "My AEG" app promised to provide visitors with even more connectivity and support in their day-to-day cooking and washing.

„Taking Taste Further": Bei jeder Station der Geschmackstour wurde ein Zubereitungsschritt auf dem Weg zum perfekten Gericht thematisiert. Die dazugehörigen Rezeptkarten lagen zur Mitnahme aus, damit Besucher den Caesar Salad à la Sternekoch Christian Mittermeier auch zu Hause perfekt zubereiten können.

"Taking Taste Further": Each station of the Taste tour looked at one step in the preparation on the way to the perfect dish. Recipe cards were available as give-aways so that visitors would be able to make the Caesar Salad à la gourmet chef Christian Mittermeier perfectly at home.

Size 3,000 m² | **Exhibitor** Electrolux Hausgeräte GmbH, Nuremberg | **Photos** Lukas Palik Fotografie, Dusseldorf | **Architecture / Design** D'art Design Gruppe GmbH, Neuss | **Construction** HOLTMANN GmbH & Co. KG, Langenhagen

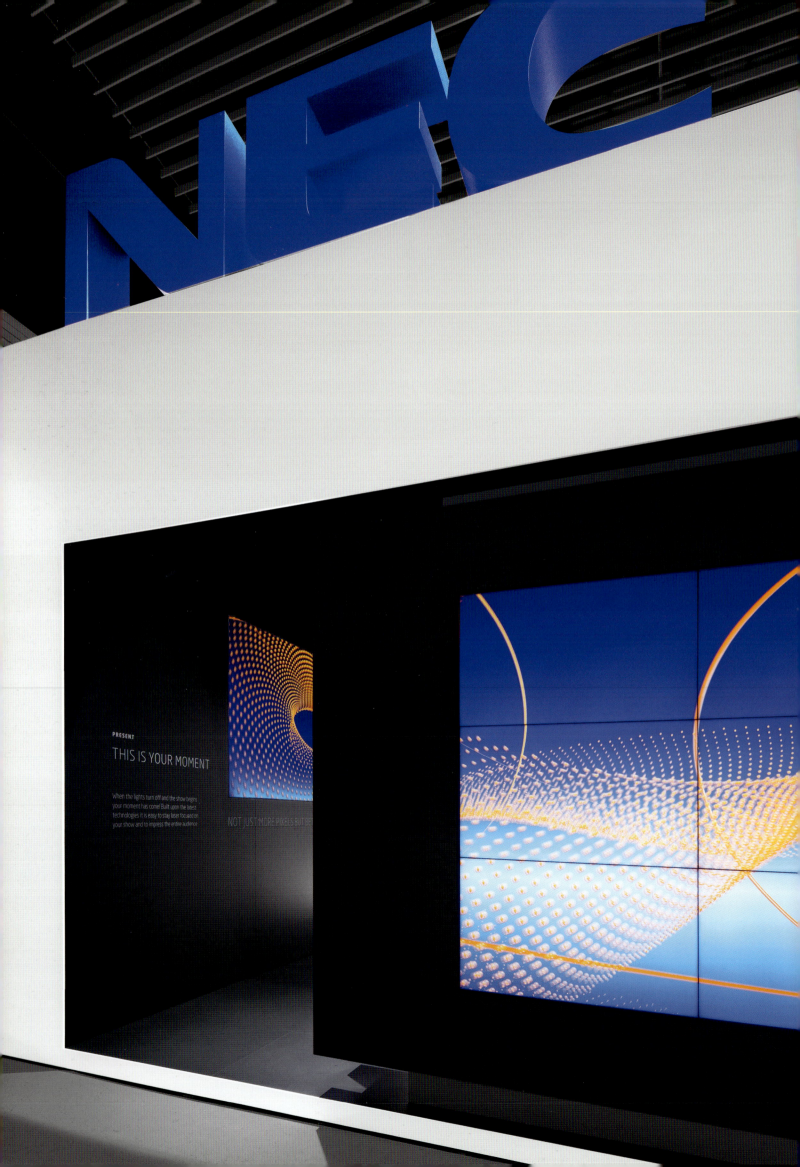

D'art Design Gruppe GmbH, Neuss
NEC Display Solutions Europe GmbH, Munich
ISE 2016, Amsterdam

DER TAKT DER BILDER

Im Fokus des Messeauftritts von NEC Display Solutions Europe auf der ISE 2016 in Amsterdam – Leitmesse für professionelle Audio-, Video- und elektronische Systeme – stand das Thema Interaktivität, um den positiven Einfluss der NEC Displaytechnologie auf Businessabläufe erfahrbar zu machen. Dementsprechend konnten die Besucher alle Produkte des Anbieters live und in direkter Anwendung erleben. Dabei eröffnete bereits die Fassade des 425 Quadratmeter großen Messestands den medialen Dialog: Hier integrierte Videowände setzten optische Akzente und visualisierten mit einer 3D-Animation das Motto „Orchestrating a brighter world". Den Gegenpart zu diesem weiß und hell gestalteten Auftakt bildete die Medieninszenierung im schwarz gehaltenen Show-Bereich mit integriertem Live-Studio. Der gesamte Schwarzraum wurde fließend über Laser-Projektionen mit animierten Bewegtbildern bespielt, um das Leitmotiv räumlich-medial zu inszenieren. Dabei war der von der D'art Design Gruppe gestaltete Messestand generell architektonisch und visuell dreigeteilt: Während die „Show Area" vorwiegend schwarz geprägt war, wurde der Kommunikationsbereich im Zentrum des Stands mit Holz verkleidet. Die Produkte selbst konnten die Messebesucher schließlich in der weißen „Test Area" – unterstützt von Vorführ- und Multitouch-Stationen – erleben.

Die D'art Design Gruppe entwickelte für NEC Display Solutions Europe ein interaktives Messedesign, das unter dem Motto „Y-our World is our Showroom" auf der ISE 2016 in Amsterdam dreidimensional erlebbar wurde.

D'art Design Gruppe developed an interactive trade fair design for NEC Display Solutions Europe that could be experienced in 3-D at the ISE 2016 in Amsterdam under the tagline "Your World is our Showroom".

THE RHYTHM OF THE IMAGES

The theme of the appearance of NEC Display Solutions Europe at the ISE 2016 in Amsterdam—leading trade fair for professional audio, video and electronic systems—was interactivity. The company wanted to demonstrate in a tangible way the positive influence of NEC display technology on business processes. Visitors were able to experience all the products live and in use. The façade of the 425 m² booth already opened the media dialogue: Integrated video walls provided optical highlights and visualised the slogan "Orchestrating a brighter world" in a 3D animation. The counterpart to this bright white prelude was the media production in the black show area with integrated live studio. The whole black room was brought to life by laser-projected animated moving images that afforded the leitmotif a spatial and media expression. The booth designed by D'art Design Gruppe was divided architecturally and visually into three: while the show area was mainly black, the communication zone at the centre of the stand was clad with wood. Finally, the products themselves could be experienced by the trade fair visitors in the white test area, supported by demonstrations and multitouch stations.

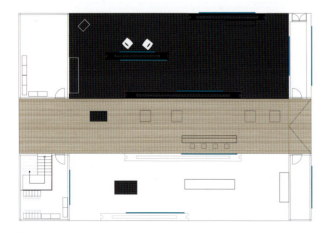

Auf sogenannten Blades – im Stand integrierte Medienwände – wurde mit der Animation „Curve" ein immersives Raumerlebnis aus Rhythmus, Melodie und Bewegtbild kreiert. Das dirigierende Key Visual fand sich dabei in allen Bereichen wieder und diente zur Illustration der fünf Kernthemen des Auftritts: Share, Present, Analyse, Review und Control.

On so-called blades—media walls integrated in the booth—an immersive spatial experience of rhythm, melody and moving images was created with the "Curve" animation. The key visual was to be found in all three areas and helped illustrate the five core themes of the presentation: Share, Present, Analyse, Review and Control.

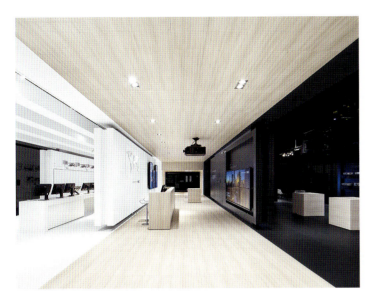

Size 425 m² | **Exhibitor** NEC Display Solutions Europe GmbH, Munich | **Photos** Lukas Palik Fotografie, Dusseldorf | **Architecture / Design** D'art Design Gruppe GmbH, Neuss | **Lighting / Technical** GAHRENS + BATTERMANN GmbH, Bergisch Gladbach | **Media** m box bewegtbild GmbH, Berlin | **Construction** Holtmann GmbH, Langenhagen

eins:33 GmbH, Munich
BEKO Deutschland GmbH, Neu-Isenburg
IFA 2015, Berlin

STADT-ERHOLUNGS-GEBIET

Mit dem Messestand für BEKO Deutschland auf der IFA 2015 in Berlin konnten die Münchner eins:33 eine Trilogie fortsetzen, die zur IFA 2013 begann. Während sich die Standgröße 2015 mit 1.700 Quadratmetern fast verdoppelte, blieb die Grundkonzeption aus architektonischen und städtebaulichen Elementen sowie der sozialen Interaktion dazwischen bestehen. So wurden 2015 wieder mit räumlich geschlossenen Einheiten offene, platzartige Flächen aufgespannt, die zum gemeinsamen Erkunden und Verweilen einladen sollten. Inspiriert von der Parklandschaft der New Yorker High Line wurden dabei Aspekte sozialen Engagements und Integration sowie aktiv genutzter landschaftlicher Flächen (Urban Gardening) hinzugenommen. Dementsprechend sollten Installationen aus Pflanzkästen und Setzlingen die Messegäste zum Mitmachen animieren und parkähnliche Bereiche mit echter Bepflanzung Zonen der Ruhe und Erholung inmitten des Messegeschehens bieten. Die Bedeutung von Grünflächen inmitten einer Megacity war somit stets spürbar und technische Installationen wechselten sich mit emotionalen persönlichen Momenten ab.

URBAN RECREATIONAL AREA

With the trade fair stand for BEKO Deutschland at the IFA 2015 in Berlin, Munich-based agency eins:33 continued a trilogy which began at the IFA 2013. While the size of the stand with 1,700 m² in 2015 almost doubled, the basic concept of architectural and urban planning elements as well as the social interaction between them remained. The 2015 booth once again contained both spatially closed units and open, square-like areas which were designed to encourage people to explore together and to stay a while. Inspired by the park landscape of the New York High Line, aspects of social commitment and integration as well as urban gardening were added. Installations consisting of planter boxes and seedlings were intended to encourage fairgoers to get involved and park-like areas with real plants offered zones for peace and regeneration in the midst of the hustle and bustle of the fair. The significance of green spaces within a megacity was thus always visible and technical installations alternated with personal emotional moments.

Soziale Interaktion und zwischenmenschliche Begegnungen im urbanen Umfeld wurden zur Inspirationsquelle und zum Leitkonzept, das sich aus architektonischen sowie städtebaulichen Themen und Elementen zusammensetzte.

Social interaction and human encounters in an urban environment became a source of inspiration and guiding concept which comprised themes and elements from architecture and urban planning.

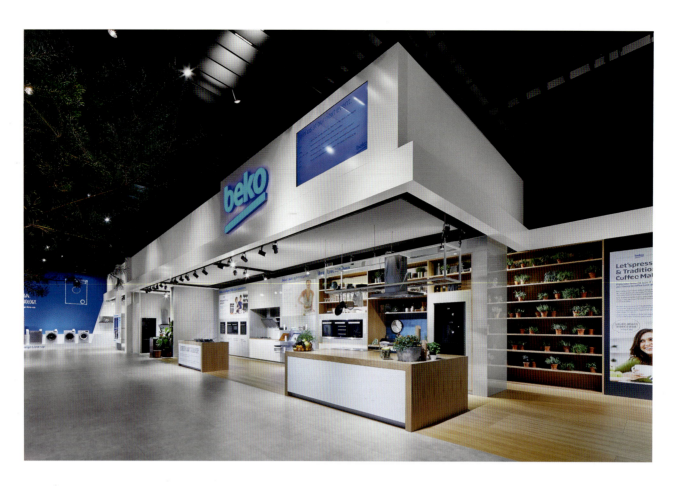

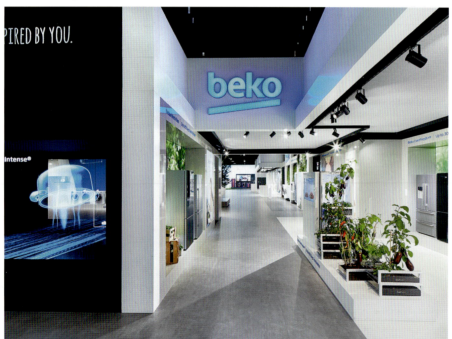

Der zentrale Platz, der zwischen den häuslichen Einheiten lag, wurde zum Ruhepol inmitten des Messetreibens: Unter lebenden Bäumen und einem künstlichen, wolkendurchzogenen blauen Himmel aus animierten LED-Paneelen fanden die Besucher einen Ort zum Entspannen.

The central square situated between the house-like units became a haven of peace away from the crowds: below living trees and an artificial, blue, cloud-dotted sky made of animated LED panels visitors found a place to relax.

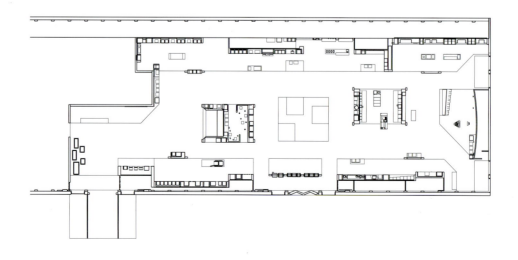

Size 1,730 m² | **Exhibitor** BEKO Deutschland GmbH, Neu-Isenburg | **Photos** Olaf Becker / BECKER LACOUR, Munich | **Architecture / Design** eins:33 GmbH, Munich | **Graphics** Jung von Matt AG, Hamburg | **Media** madhat GmbH, Offenbach a. Main | **Construction** Visage Messe- u. Ausstellungsbau GmbH, Cologne

333 years in the making

eins:33 GmbH, Munich
Gaggenau Hausgeräte GmbH, Munich
EuroCucina 2016, Milan

GESTERN, HEUTE, MORGEN

Auf der EuroCucina 2016 in Mailand feierte Gaggenau Hausgeräte ein ganz besonderes Jubiläum: Unter dem Motto „333 years in the making" nahm das Unternehmen, das sich von einer Nagelschmiede zum Küchengerätehersteller gewandelt hat, die Besucher mit auf eine Zeitreise durch die Firmenhistorie. Dabei bildete die Geschichte nicht nur den inhaltlichen Rahmen, sondern bespielte auch die Innenflächen der Fassade, die mit großformatigen Passepartoutausschnitten versehen war. Eine dieser trichterförmigen Öffnungen formte ein imposantes Entree, das die Besucher zum Ausgangspunkt ihres musealen Rundgangs leitete. Den Auftakt der 300 Quadratmeter großen Inszenierung von eins:33 bildete eine reale Schmiedewerkstatt, welche die Gründung im Jahr 1683 durch den Markgrafen Ludwig Wilhelm von Baden thematisierte. Hier fertigte ein Schmied am Amboss echte Eisennägel, auf deren Kopf die Jahreszahl der Gründung eingeprägt wurde. Mit dem Titel „Present is where past meets future" wurden die Besucher anschließend entlang einer Galerie, in der die Marke Gaggenau in einen zeitgeschichtlichen Kontext gesetzt wurde, zu einem der Höhepunkte des Rundgangs geführt: die Enthüllung des EB333 – eine Neuinterpretation des legendären 90 Zentimeter breiten Backofens. Im Zentrum des Messestands angekommen, fanden sich die Messegäste schließlich in einem strahlend weißen, rundum verglasten Raum, in dem Auszüge aus dem Produktportfolio museal präsentiert wurden und im Nebel scheinbar zu schweben schienen: der „Room of Perfection".

YESTERDAY, TODAY, TOMORROW

At the EuroCucina 2016 in Milan, Gaggenau Hausgeräte celebrated a very special anniversary: Under the tagline "333 years in the making", the company which evolved from a nail maker to kitchen appliance manufacturer took the visitors on a journey back through the history of the company. The history did not, however, only provide the content framework. It was also projected onto the inside surfaces of the façade which was furnished with large-scale passe-partout cut-outs. One of these funnel-shaped openings formed an impressive entrée that guided visitors to the starting point of their museum-like tour. The tour of the 300 m² presentation by eins:33 was kicked off by a real forge which referred to its formation in 1683 by Margrave Ludwig Wilhelm from the House of Baden. A smith working at the anvil was producing real iron nails on the head of which the year of foundation was stamped. Entitled "Present is where past meets future", the visitor was then led along a gallery in which the Gaggenau brand was placed in an historical context to one of the highlights of the tour: The unveiling of the EB333—a reinterpretation of the legendary 90 centimetre wide oven. Having reached the centre of the stand, fairgoers found themselves in a bright white, entirely glazed room, in which extracts from the product portfolio was presented like museum artefacts that appeared to be floating in a haze: the "Room of Perfection".

„Present is where past meets future" war das Motto der Inszenierung, die selbst keine räumliche Ausdehnung besaß, sondern die Besucher vielmehr über die Schwelle zwischen Vergangenheit und Zukunft beförderte.

"Present is where past meets future" was the slogan of the presentation which did not itself have any spatial expansion but rather transported visitors over the threshold between the past and the future.

Mit einem außergewöhnlichen Standkonzept zelebrierte Gaggenau Hausgeräte ihr Firmenjubiläum. Hierfür wurden die Besucher zu einer Zeitreise eingeladen, die im Gründungsjahr begann und die Evolution Gaggenaus inszenierte: von der Handwerkskunst der Nagelschmiede zur Perfektionstechnik für die private Küche.

Gaggenau Hausgeräte celebrated its anniversary with an unusual stand concept. Visitors were invited on a journey back in time to the foundation year and to trace its evolution over the centuries: from the craftmanship of nail making to perfect technology for the domestic kitchen.

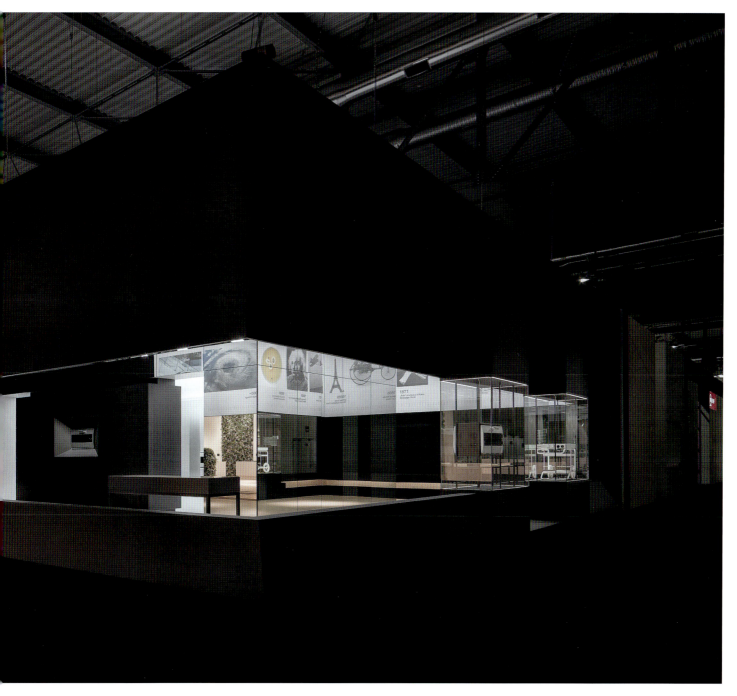

Herzstück des Messestands war der „Room of Perfection" – ein futuristisch anmutender, teilverspiegelter Glaskubus, der einen Ausblick in die Zukunft der Marke Gaggenau erahnen ließ. Dank einer hinterleuchteten, weißen Stoffdecke, die ein diffuses, museales Licht im Raum erzeugte, warfen die Besucher keine Schatten, die die Erhabenheit des Raums hätten beeinträchtigen können.

The heart of the booth was the "Room of Perfection"—a futuristic, partially mirrored glass cube which gave an outlook on the future of the Gaggenau brand. Thanks to a back-lit, white fabric ceiling which created a diffuse, museum-like light in the room, visitors did not create any shadows which could have adversely affected the sublimity of the room.

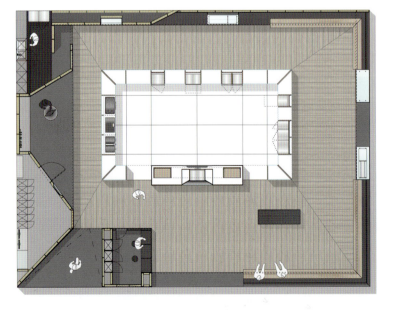

Size 300 m² | **Exhibitor** Gaggenau Hausgeräte GmbH, Munich | **Photos** Bodo Mertoglu, Murnau | **Architecture / Design / Graphics** eins:33 GmbH, Munich | **Lighting / Media** Neumann&Müller GmbH & Co. KG, Cologne; Statics H13 Ingenieure, Munich | **Construction** Raumtechnik Messebau & Event Services GmbH, Ostfildern

INTERVIEW
LINA MICUS (EINS:33)

In einer Zeit, in der mediale Exponate bei vielen Messeauftritten einen großen Raum einnehmen, bekam der Besucher beim Auftritt der Gaggenau Hausgeräte auf der EuroCucina 2016 als erstes Exponat einen Schmied bei der Ausübung seines Berufs zu sehen. Wird das reale (Er-)leben wieder wichtiger?

Manche Erlebnisse sind nicht durch eine virtuelle Inszenierung zu ersetzen! Und auch für Gaggenau ist es zunehmend wichtig, den Kontakt mit dem Kunden auf ein reales Erlebnis zu basieren: Die Marke soll sich für den Besucher anfassbar in einem Umfeld darstellen, das die Identität widerspiegelt – so auch auf der EuroCucina. Grundlage für die Inszenierung hier war die Gründung der Marke Gaggenau Ende des 17. Jahrhunderts als Nagelschmiede. Indem wir einen echten Schmied – umgeben von seinen Werkzeugen – auf dem Messestand beim Herstellen ebendieser Nägel zeigten, konnten wir die Thematik eindrucksvoll präsentieren. Zudem wurde die Inszenierung für die Besucher durch das Geräusch des Hämmerns besonders nahbar. Gerade solche realen Elemente werden in einer Zeit der Digitalisierung anders wahrgenommen: Sie treffen tiefer auf einer emotionalen Ebene und wirken beruhigend im Vergleich zur immer weiter beschleunigenden Umgebung.

Der futuristisch anmutende „Room of Perfection" bildet den Abschluss der Ausstellung. Wie schaffen Sie es, die präzise Handwerkskunst, die das Unternehmen ausmacht, hier ebenso zu präsentieren?

Die Präsentation der Handwerkskunst erfolgt in diesem Fall über die Geräte selbst. Denn trotz des Einsatzes moderner Techniken wie Laserschweißen oder den eines Reinraums beim Zusammenfügen der Einzelteile zum Premiumgerät setzt Gaggenau heute noch auf Handarbeit. Der Besucher kann dies dank eines Videos zur Verarbeitung zusätzlich nachempfinden. Auch unsere Materialwahl – Glas – als raumbildendes Element zeigt eine der wichtigsten Merkmale der Marke: Präzision. Die toleranzfreie Planung, welche Glas aufgrund seiner spezifischen Eigenschaften zulässt, findet sich daher ebenso bei den Bauteilen der hochklassigen Geräte wie bei der Gestaltung des „Room of Perfection".

Gaggenau feierte mit diesem Auftritt ein Jubiläum: 333 Jahre Firmengeschichte. Gab es für Sie als Gestalter besondere Herausforderungen für diese Inszenierungen?

Die Idee war es nicht nur, die Geschichte der Marke Gaggenau zu zeigen, sondern diese in den Kontext der Weltgeschichte zu setzen. Mittels einer Projektion am oberen Abschluss des Standes wurde der zeitgeschichtliche Rahmen dargestellt. Hier wurden die unterschiedlichen Ereignisse in die entsprechenden Jahrhunderte eingeteilt und – aufgrund ihrer Vielzahl – gegeneinander überblendet. So wurde den Besuchern auch visuell die Komplexität und Vielschichtigkeit der Geschichte verdeutlicht und anhand zunehmender Geschwindigkeit der Überblendungen auch der Aspekt der Beschleunigung der jüngeren Historie mit aufgenommen. Darunter eingeordnet findet sich die Markengeschichte, eingespannt zwischen Vergangenheit und Zukunft – eben vom Schmied bis zur Enthüllung der Neuauflage des legendären Backofens EB 333.

⟶ eins:33 wurde 1999 von Hendrik Müller gegründet, der das Büro seit 2007 gemeinsam mit seinem Partner Georg Thiersch leitet. Lina Micus ist seit 2008 ein fester Bestandteil des Teams. Das in München ansässige Büro arbeitet in den Bereichen Corporate Architecture, Markenkommunikation und Innenarchitektur.

> www.einszu33.com

In a time in which media exhibits take up a lot of space in many trade fair stands, the first exhibit that visitors to the appearance of Gaggenau Hausgeräte at the EuroCucina 2016 saw was a blacksmith doing his job. Is real life (experiences) becoming more important?

Some experiences can simply not be replaced by a virtual presentation. And for Gaggenau it is also becoming increasingly important to base customer contact on a real experience: The brand should present itself to visitors at first hand in surroundings which reflect the identity—and we did just that at the EuroCucina. The basis for the presentation was the foundation of the Gaggenau brand at the end of the 17th century as nail smith manufacturer. By putting a real blacksmith—surrounded by his tools—in the booth and getting him to make precisely these nails we were able to present the theme in an impressive way. What is more, the sound of the hammering made the presentation particularly accessible for visitors. In a time of digitalisation, such real elements are perceived very differently: They hit home on a deeper, emotional level and have a calming effect compared to the ever accelerating environment.

The futuristic "Room of Perfection" formed the finale of the exhibition. How did you manage to present the precise craftsmanship, which is what sets the company apart, here as well?

In this case, the presentation of craftsmanship is achieved via the appliances themselves. Despite the use of modern techniques such as laser welding or a clean room for the assembly of the parts into a premium appliance, Gaggenau still today relies on handwork. Thanks to a video, visitors get a good idea of the workmanship involved. The choice of material—glass—as space-shaping element, shows one of the brand's most important characteristics: precision. The no-tolerance planning which the special characteristics of glass allows is why it is to be found not only as components in the high-class appliances, but also in the design of the "Room of Perfection".

With this stand, Gaggenau was celebrating an anniversary: 333 years of corporate history. Did this pose you with special challenges as designer?

The idea was not just to narrate the history of the Gaggenau brand, but to put this in the context of world history. By means of a projection, the contemporary context was presented at the upper edge of the stand. The various events were divided into the centuries they concerned, cross-faded due to the large number. For the visitors, this visualised the complexity and multidimensional nature of history, including the aspect of acceleration in more recent history illustrated by the increasing speed of the cross-fading. Below that, is the brand history, tucked in between past and future—from blacksmith through to the unveiling of the new edition of the legendary EB 333 oven.

⟶ **eins:33** was founded by Hendrik Müller in 1999, who has led the office since 2007 together with his partner Georg Thiersch. Lina Micus has been part of the team since 2008. Located in Munich, the office works in the fields of corporate architecture, brand communication and interior architecture.

> www.einszu33.com

Heckhaus GmbH & Co. KG, Munich
NFON AG, Munich
CeBIT 2016, Hanover

RICHTIG VERBUNDEN!

Weithin sichtbar waren die vier Lettern des Cloud-Telefonanlagen-Anbieters NFON auf der CeBIT 2016 in Hannover. Die überdimensionalen Buchstaben dienten dabei nicht nur der Fernwirkung, sondern gleichzeitig als Sitzmodul für die Besucher des 105 Quadratmeter großen Messestands. Empfangen wurden jene von der sogenannten Cloud Lounge, die von einer minimalistischen, in hellem Holz gehaltenen Architektur geprägt und anhand deren Ästhetik die Konzentration auf das Wesentliche betont wurde. Der Einsatz von natürlichen Materialien wie Massivholz und Filz stand bewusst im Kontrast zu den hier ausgestellten, technischen Produkten. Aufgrund der durchdachten Struktur – entwickelt von der Münchner Agentur Heckhaus – war auf dem verhältnismäßig kleinen Stand dennoch genügend Raum für Besprechungsnischen, Arbeitsplätze zur Kundenberatung, ein absperrbares Lager sowie eine kleine Küche mit Bartresen. Als Blickfang dienten zudem blaue Haftnotizen, die an den immensen Lettern des Logos klebten und auf welche CI-konforme sowie unterhaltsame Weisheiten gedruckt waren –zum Beispiel „Long-term commitment is for marriages".

WELL CONNECTED!

The four letters of the cloud telephone system provider NFON were visible from a long way off at the CeBIT 2016 in Hanover. The huge letters not only attracted attention to the stand from a distance, they also served as seating for the visitors to the booth with a footprint of 105 m². They were received in the Cloud Lounge, that was shaped by a minimalist architecture constructed of light coloured wood and whose aesthetics emphasised the focus on the essential. The use of natural materials such as solid wood and felt was in deliberate contrast to the technical products on display here. Thanks to the well thought-through structure— developed by the Munich agency Heckhaus—the relatively small stand nevertheless offered enough space for consultation niches, workplaces for customer talks, a lockable store as well as a small kitchen with bar. The eye was drawn by blue post-it notes stuck to the vast letters of the logo and on which CI conform as well as entertaining messages were printed, for example "Long-term commitment is for marriages".

Trotz der minimalistischen Gestaltung präsentierte Heckhaus einen kontrastreichen Messestand mit klaren Formen und warmen Holzelementen, die mit dem hier ausgestellten Hardware-Sortiment kontrastierten.

Despite the minimalist design, Heckhaus presented a high-contrast booth with clear forms and warm wood elements which contrasted with the hardware range on display.

Zusammen mit dem überdimensionalen Logo erzeugten die blauen Haftnotizen eine hohe Aufmerksamkeit. Vielleicht lag es aber auch an den humorvollen Sprüchen, die darauf zu lesen waren ...

Together with the oversized logo, the blue post-its attracted a great deal of attention. But maybe that was also because of the witty sayings to be read there ...

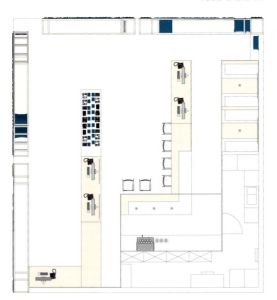

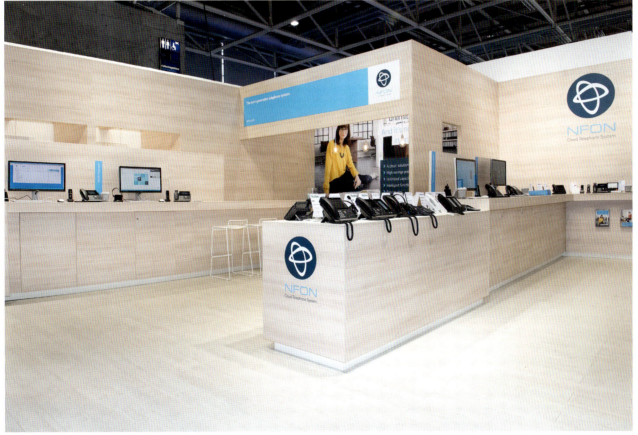

Size 105 m² | **Exhibitor** NFON AG, Munich | **Photos** Kai Löffelbein, Hanover | **Architecture / Design** Heckhaus GmbH & Co. KG, Munich | **Graphics** Zum goldenen Hirschen GmbH, Munich | **Lighting** UEBERKOPF GmbH, Hanover | **Media** NFON AG, Munich | **Construction** Messebau Franke GmbH, Bad Tölz

q~bus Mediatektur GmbH, Berlin
Deutsche Telekom AG, Bonn
CeBIT 2016, Hanover

FRÜHLINGS-BOTEN

Für den Messestand der Deutschen Telekom AG auf der CeBIT 2016 in Hannover entwickelten die Gestalter von q~bus Mediatektur einen Markenauftritt mit Frühlingscharakter. Im Fokus befand sich dabei eine frisch-offensive Aufbruchsstimmung im Sinne der Digitalisierung. Hierfür entstand im Zentrum des über 5.000 Quadratmeter großen Messestands das TRANSFORUM – ein Forum für Transformation. Jenes wurde von 18 beweglichen, magentafarbenen Blütenblättern überspannt, anhand derer der programmatische, frühlingshafte Aufbruch visualisiert werden sollte. Die Blätter waren Teil einer kinetischen Installation, mit der die Blüte zum Leben erweckt und damit unterschiedliche Raumsituationen generiert werden konnten. Rund um dieses Zentrum waren die Informationsbereiche angeordnet, in denen sich das florale Muster als Key Visual stets wiederfand: in Form von Schnittblumen, Leuchtobjekten, Projektionen sowie Pflanzenwänden. Zum Abschluss des Rundgangs wurden die Messegäste schließlich zu einer Fashion-Show geladen, auf der digitale Kleidung präsentiert wurde: Eingenähte Solarzellen, 3D-gedruckte Abendkleider und kinetische Anzüge verdeutlichten, was auf der ganzen Fläche ersichtlich wurde, nämlich die fortschreitende Digitalisierung unserer Lebenswelt.

Eine riesige Magenta-Blüte kündigte den digitalen Frühling an: Unter dem Motto „Digitalisierung. Einfach. Machen." präsentierte sich die Deutsche Telekom auf der CeBIT 2016 als innovativer und verlässlicher Partner für die Digitalisierung.

HERALDS OF SPRING

For the trade fair stand of Deutsche Telekom AG at the CeBIT 2016 in Hanover, the designers from q~bus Mediatektur came up with a brand appearance with a touch of spring, symbolising the fresh and vigorous pioneering spirit surrounding digitalisation. Appropriately, a forum for transformation—the TRANSFORUM—was therefore to be found at the heart of the 5,000 m² trade fair stand. The 18 moveable, magenta-coloured flower petals suspended above it were intended to visualize the programmatic, spring-like awakening. The petals were part of a kinetic installation which brought the flowers to life, thus generating different spatial situations. In the information zones arranged around this hub, the floral theme as key visual was omnipresent: in the form of cut flowers, light sculptures, projections as well as planted walls. At the end of the circuit tour, fairgoers were invited to a fashion show at which digital clothing was presented: wearable solar cells, evening dresses printed on 3D printers and kinetic suits illustrated just how digitalisation is advancing into every area of our lives, underlining the message that was to be found throughout the stand.

A huge magenta-coloured flower announced the digital spring: under the tagline "Digitalisation. Simply. Make it happen" Deutsche Telekom presented itself at the CeBIT 2016 as innovative and reliable partner for digitalisation.

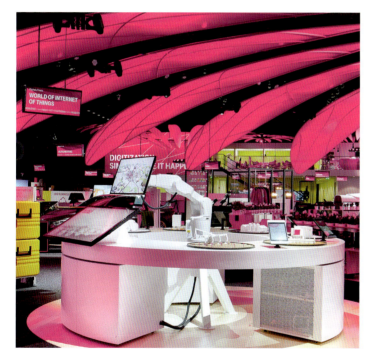

18 „Blütenblätter" mit einem Durchmesser von jeweils 35 Metern überspannten als kinetische Installation die zentrale Bühne – das TRANSFORUM – und repräsentierten die Digitalisierung als einen frühlingshaften, gedeihenden Prozess.

18 "flower petals", each 35 metres in diameter, spanned the central stage—the TRANSFORUM—as a kinetic installation, representing the digitalisation as spring-like, blossoming process.

Size 5,000 m² | **Exhibitor** Deutsche Telekom AG, Bonn | **Photos** Michael Setzpfandt, Berlin; Linus Lintner Fotografie, Berlin | **Architecture / Design** q~bus Mediatektur GmbH, Berlin

q~bus Mediatektur GmbH, Berlin
Deutsche Telekom AG, Bonn
IFA 2015, Berlin

MAGENTA-WELLE

Auf der IFA 2015 in Berlin erwartete die Besucher des Messestands der Deutschen Telekom AG ein 3.000 Quadratmeter großes Atelier – vollkommen in Magenta getaucht. Wie freistehend lehnten Printmotive von mehr als sieben Metern Höhe an den Hallenwänden, wobei auf Teilen der Bilder dynamische Projektionen zu sehen waren und Besucher mit ausgewählten Motiven interagieren konnten. Vor dieser Kulisse präsentierte das Bonner Unternehmen die Themen und Produkte der Magenta-Familie mit einem klaren Fokus auf den Alltag der Nutzer. Die Berliner Agentur q~bus Mediatektur entwickelte dafür eine Lichtchoreografie in Magenta, welche die Halle mehrmals pro Stunde in die Markenfarbe tauchte – unterstützt durch Video- und Gobo-Projektionen. Durch einen Parcours wurden die Besucher über den Stand geleitet und konnten somit verschiedene Erlebnisstationen durchlaufen: Ein Tandemspiel, digitales Seifenblasenpusten sowie verschiedene Aktionsfelder wurden durch eine dezentrale Bühne ergänzt, auf der eine Show unter dem Motto „Zuhause und Mobil werden eins: MagentaEins" zu sehen war. Die Gadgets, Wearables, smarte Fitness- und Sportgeräte, die hier präsentiert wurden, konnten anschließend im IFA-Sommergarten selbst ausprobiert werden.

MAGENTA WAVE

At the IFA 2015 in Berlin, visitors to the trade fair stand of Deutsche Telekom AG found a 3,000 m² studio—completely dipped in the colour magenta. Seemingly free-standing, printed motifs of more than seven metres in height leant against the walls of the hall; dynamic projections brought some of the images to life and visitors could interact with selected motifs. Against this backdrop, the company from Bonn presented the themes and products of the Magenta family with a clear focus on the everyday lives of the users. The Berlin-based agency q~bus Mediatektur developed a lighting choreography in magenta which plunged the hall in the brand colour several times an hour—supported by video and gobo projections. The visitors were guided round the stand on a circuit tour, passing a number of activity stations: a tandem game, digital bubble blowing and various action fields were supplemented by a central stage on which a show entitled "At home and on the move become one: MagentaEins". The gadgets, wearables, smart fitness and sport devices on display here could be tried out later in the IFA summer garden.

Nach fünf Messetagen konnte die Deutsche Telekom mehr als 150.000 Besucher auf dem 3.000 Quadratmeter großen Messestand verzeichnen, der 2015 erstmalig um einen „Digital Playground" im Außenbereich vor der Halle erweitert wurde.

After five trade fair days, Deutsche Telekom had recorded more than 150,000 visitors to the 3,000 m² stand. For the first time in 2015, the stand included a "digital playground" located in the grounds outside the hall.

Zu definierten Zeiten lief eine „Magenta-Welle" durch den gesamten Raum. Neben Video- kamen hierbei auch Gobo-Projektionen sowie Moving Lights zum Einsatz, um den Messestand komplett in die atmosphärische Markenfarbe zu tauchen.

At defined times, a magenta wave rolled through the entire space. Video and gobo projections were supplemented by moving lights, thus bathing the entire booth in the atmospheric brand colour.

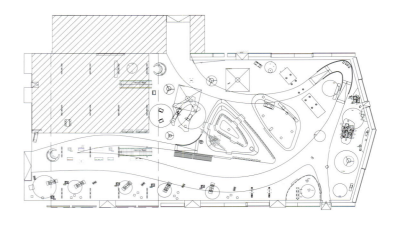

Size 3,000 m² | **Exhibitor** Deutsche Telekom AG, Bonn | **Photos** Michael Setzpfandt, Berlin; Linus Lintner Fotografie, Berlin | **Architecture / Design** q~bus Mediatektur GmbH, Berlin

raumkontakt GmbH, Karlsruhe
TechnologieRegion Karlsruhe GbR, Karlsruhe
EXPO REAL 2015, Munich

BEWEGUNG IM STAND

Auf der EXPO REAL 2015 in München konnten die Besucher einen informativen Einblick in die TechnologieRegion Karlsruhe erhalten. Inszeniert von der Karlsruher Agentur raumkontakt wurde hierfür die Dynamik des Standorts auf 110 Quadratmetern visuell greifbar gemacht: Großflächige, ondulierende Linienmuster fanden nicht nur auf großen, scheinbar über dem Stand schwebenden Kuben, sondern auch auf den Werbemitteln Verwendung, wodurch die Gestalter den gesamten Messestand visuell mit einer einheitlichen Dynamik füllten. Das filigrane, schwarze Muster auf weißem Grund versetzte dabei den gesamten Auftritt in Schwingung. So verschwanden Standkanten, räumliche Bezüge lösten sich auf und mit dem Raum wurde eine bewegte Leichtigkeit repräsentiert. Mit der reinweißen Möblierung wurde schließlich sowohl ein Gegenpol zum optisch irritierenden Muster als auch zu den hervorstechenden roten Kuben geschaffen, auf denen die typografischen Elemente untergebracht waren.

STAND IN MOTION

At the EXPO REAL 2015 in Munich, visitors were able to obtain informative insights into the city of Karlsruhe as technological centre. Developed by the Karlsruhe agency raumkontakt, the dynamic character of the location was given a tangible appearance on the 110 m² of the stand: Large-scale, undulating line patterns were used not only on the cubes that appeared to be floating above the stand, but also on the advertising materials, in this way filling the whole booth visually with a uniform dynamic. The delicate, black pattern on a white background made the whole stand vibrate. The edges of the stand disappeared, spatial references were dissolved and the space represented a lightness of movement. The pure white furnishings were juxtaposed with the optically jarring pattern and the prominent red cubes bearing the typographical elements.

Die scheinbar beiläufig wechselnden Perspektiven erweckten die Architektur förmlich zum Leben und inszenierten optische Irritationen bis ins kleinste Detail: Von der Möblierung bis in die Cocktailkarte konnten die Besucher so immer wieder neue Überraschungen entdecken.

The apparently incidentally changing perspectives literally brought the architecture to life, producing optical irritations, right down to the last detail: from the furnishings through to the cocktail menu, the stand held many surprises in store for its visitors.

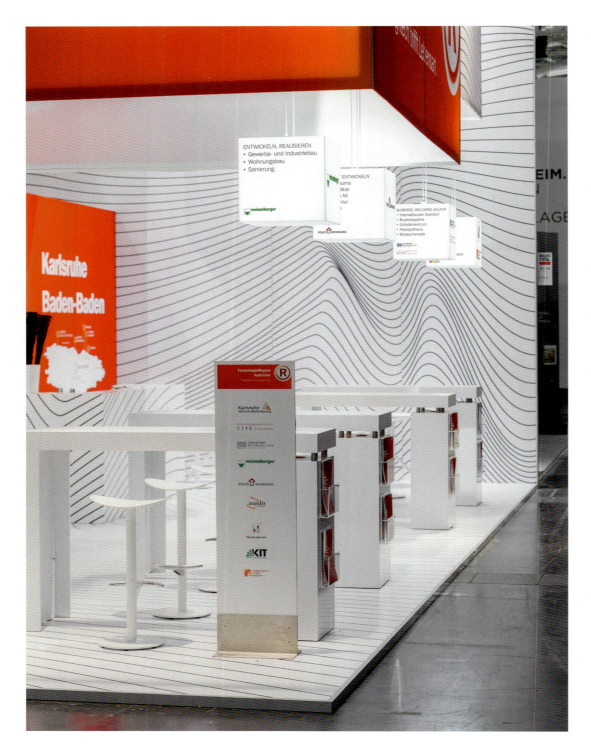

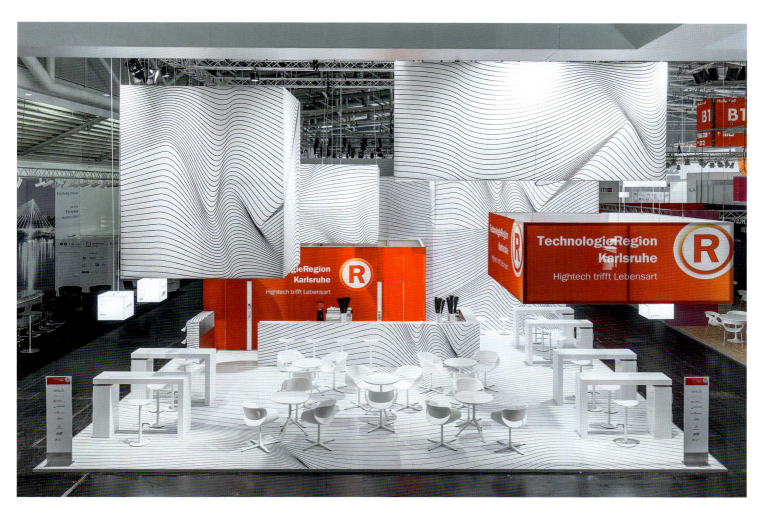

Mit intensivem Rot wurden visuelle Schwerpunkte gesetzt, die zudem einen starken Gegenpol zum ondulierenden Linienmuster des übrigen Messestands wie auch zum zurückhaltenden Weiß der Möblierung bildeten.

Visual focal points were created in vibrant red, which at the same time was in stark contrast to the undulating lines pattern of the rest of the booth and the restrained white furnishings.

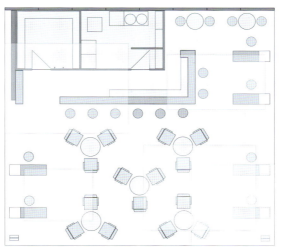

Size 110 m² | **Exhibitor** TechnologieRegion Karlsruhe GbR, Karlsruhe | **Photos** Jürgen Lenhardt / raumkontakt GmbH, Karlsruhe | **Architecture / Design / Graphics** raumkontakt GmbH, Karlsruhe | **Lighting** Megaforce Veranstaltungstechnik GmbH, Weingarten | **Construction** stinova Einrichtungs- und Verkaufs-Organisation GmbH, Achern

TRIAD Berlin Projektgesellschaft mbH, Berlin
Siemens AG, Munich
HANNOVER MESSE 2015, Hanover

AUF DIGITALER EBENE

Auf einer Fläche von 5.000 Quadratmetern inszenierte TRIAD Berlin den Messeauftritt der Siemens AG auf der HANNOVER MESSE 2015. Unter dem Motto „On the way to Industry 4.0" wurden die Themen Integration und Vernetzung in den Mittelpunkt gestellt und mittels einer futuristisch anmutenden Inszenierung die zukunftsweisenden Lösungen des Unternehmens im Bereich der Digitalisierung präsentiert. So wurden innerhalb des „Digitalization Forums", das alle Zielgruppen ansprach, die unsichtbaren Prozesse digitaler Produktionen mit multimedialen und interaktiven Elementen visualisiert: Während auf der linken Standhälfte Produkte ausgestellt waren, hatten Besucher auf der rechten die Möglichkeit, konkrete Anwendungsbereiche kennenzulernen. Im Zentrum befand sich hierbei eine überdimensionale Weltkugel mit Stadtlandschaften, deren einzelne Gebäude von den Messegästen an Terminals aktiviert werden konnten. Der Globus mit einem Durchmesser von 13,7 und einer Höhe von 5,6 Metern bildete zudem die Bühne für den Höhepunkt des Auftritts: eine von TRIAD Berlin konzeptionierte, stündliche Liveshow zwischen Moderator und „Digital Twin". In dieser entwickelte sich ein Dialog zwischen Mensch und digitalem Zwilling. Virtuelle und reale Produktionsprozesse wurden so verbunden und damit bewiesen, dass digitale und reale Welt ganz einfach miteinander verschmelzen können.

Im „Digitalization Forum" wurden die unsichtbaren Prozesse digitaler Produktionen erlebbar gemacht. Sein inszenatorisches Element war der „Digital Layer": In medialen, grafischen Visualisierungen überlagerte er das Realbild, um die Verschmelzung von realer und virtueller Welt bildlich zu übersetzen, wie hier am Beispiel der virtuellen Planung des Maserati Ghibli.

In the "Digitalization Forum", visitors could experience the invisible processes of digital productions. The dramatic element here was the "Digital Layer": In visualisations using media and graphics, it was superimposed over the real image to illustrate the merger of the real and virtual worlds, in this case for the virtual planning of the Maserati Ghibli.

ON A DIGITAL LEVEL

TRIAD Berlin had a space of 5,000 m² at their disposal for the design of the appearance of Siemens AG at the HANOVER FAIR 2015. Entitled "On the way to Industry 4.0", the themes integration and connectivity were the focal points and the forward-looking solutions of the company in the field of digitalisation were presented in a futuristic setting. Within the " Digitalization Forum", which addressed all target groups, the invisible digital processes were visualised with multimedia and interactive elements: While the left side of the stand was used to display products, on the right side visitors had the opportunity to experience actual fields of application. The centrepiece was an oversized globe covered with urban landscapes, the individual buildings of which could be activated by fairgoers at terminals. The globe, which was 13.7 m in diameter and 5.6 m in height, also provided a stage for the highlight of the stand: An hourly live show developed by TRIAD Berlin in which a dialogue developed between the human moderator and his "Digital Twin". Virtual and real production processes were connected, demonstrating how easily the digital and real world can merge with one another.

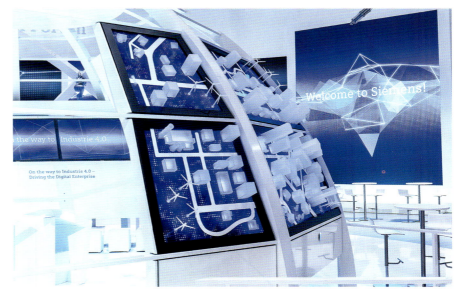

Im Zentrum des Forums befand sich eine überdimensionale Weltkugel. Hier konnten sich die Besucher interaktiv über die Lösungen des Ausstellers informieren. Zudem wurde das Thema „Digital Production" mit ausgewählten Exponaten erklärt.

The huge globe located at the centre of the forum offered visitors an interactive opportunity to find out more about the exhibitor's solutions. The topic "Digital Production" was also explained with carefully chosen exhibits.

Size 5,000 m² | **Exhibitor** Siemens AG, Munich | **Photos** Ulf Büschleb, Berlin | **Architecture / Design** TRIAD Berlin Projektgesellschaft mbH, Berlin

VAVE GmbH, Offenbach a. Main
Shanghai United Imaging Healthcare Co., Ltd., Shanghai
China International Medical Equipment Fair 2015, Shanghai

EINE RUNDE SACHE

Bereits zum zweiten Mal in Folge konnten die Offenbacher Designer von VAVE den Messestand für Shanghai United Imaging Healthcare Co. gestalten – Chinas größten Hersteller für bildgesteuerte, medizinische Produkte. Auf der China International Medical Equipment Fair 2015 in Shanghai setzten sie eine 900 Quadratmeter große Fläche in den Farben Blau und Weiß gekonnt in Szene. Die verschiedenen, hier gezeigten Instrumente standen dabei klar geordnet in einer futuristisch-sterilen Umgebung, wodurch der Eindruck zukunftsweisender Produkte verstärkt werden sollte. Gleichzeitig wurde dank der Weitläufigkeit des Messeabschnitts eine offene Atmosphäre geschaffen. In allen Bereichen wurde die schlichte Formgebung konsequent umgesetzt, wobei der Fokus klar auf der exakt komponierten, zum Teil indirekten Beleuchtung lag, mit der die Fabrikate von UIH betont und deren Form durch weitere große, runde Lichtelemente aufgegriffen wurde.

WELL-ROUNDED

This was the second time in a row that the Offenbach-based designers from VAVE had been entrusted with the design of the booth for Shanghai United Imaging Healthcare Co.—China's largest manufacturer of image-controlled, medical products. At the China International Medical Equipment Fair 2015 in Shanghai they presented the 900 m² space to great effect using a blue-and-white colour scheme. The various instruments shown here were clearly arranged in a futuristic-sterile environment, thus underlining the impression of future-oriented products. At the same time, the spaciousness of the trade fair section created an open atmosphere. The simple forms were found throughout the stand, with a clear focus on the precisely composed, sometimes indirect lighting which was used to emphasise the products of UIH, picking up their form in a series of large, circular light elements.

Auf der China International Medical Equipment Fair 2015 in Shanghai zeigte sich Shanghai United Imaging Healthcare Co. mittels einer klaren und schlichten Formensprache als zukunftsorientierter Hersteller medizinischen Equipments.

At the China International Medical Equipment Fair 2015 in Shanghai, Shanghai United Imaging Healthcare Co. used clear and simple shapes to present itself as a future-oriented manufacturer of medical equipment.

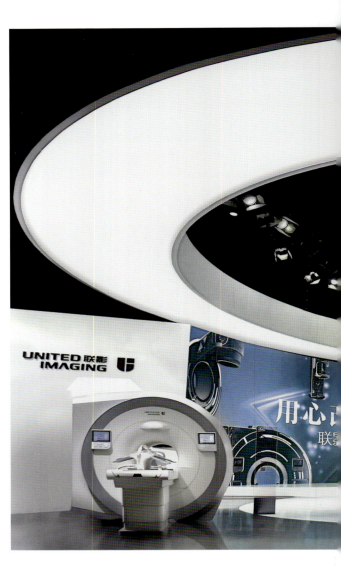

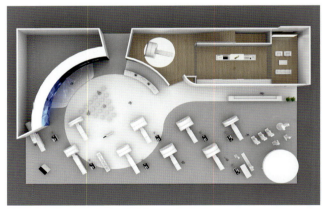

Im abgetrennten Café konnten sich Besucher schließlich vom Messetreiben erholen. Mit warmem Holzboden bot dieser Bereich eine kontrastvolle Möglichkeit, das Gesehene zu reflektieren.

Visitors could recover from the hustle and bustle of the fair in a separate café. The warm-coloured wooden floor was in stark contrast to the rest of the stand, offering an ideal setting in which to reflect on what they had seen.

Size 900 m² | **Exhibitor** Shanghai United Imaging Healthcare Co., Ltd., Shanghai | **Photos** Shanghai United Imaging Healthcare Co., Ltd., Shanghai | **Architecture / Design** VAVE GmbH, Offenbach a. Main | **Lighting / Construction** Ambrosius Exhibition Design and Building (Shanghai) Co., Ltd, Shanghai

WHITEvoid GmbH, Berlin
Vodafone GmbH, Dusseldorf
CeBIT 2016, Hanover

NETZ-BELEUCHTER

Unter dem Motto „Gigabit Network" präsentierten die Berliner Gestalter von WHITEvoid Vodafones Netzwerk als mehrgeschossige, komplexe Architektur, mittels derer die Dimensionen des Kommunikationskonzerns und des digitalen Raums greifbarer wurden. Als zentrales Element des 1.850 Quadratmeter großen Messestands wurden dafür Lichtröhren verwendet, deren einzelne Pixel individuell steuerbar waren. Für die Besucher der CeBIT 2016 in Hannover konnte so die Dynamik einer Kommunikation in einem Netzwerk visuell spannend verdeutlicht werden. Durch jene komplexe Lichtnetzwerk-Struktur wurden zudem die vier Themengebiete miteinander verbunden: Network, Unified Communications, Cloud and Hosting sowie Internet of Things. Dank verschiedener, begehbarer Ebenen konnte den Besuchern ein vielfältiger Blick auf die raumfüllende 360°-Lichtinstallation ermöglicht werden, womit ebenfalls deutlich wurde, dass das symbolische Netzwerk alles umspannt – genau wie das reale. Auf der obersten Etage befand sich schließlich eine Lounge und es wurde Raum für persönliche Gespräche geboten.

NETWORK ILLUMINATOR

Entitled "Gigabit Network", the Berlin-based designers from WHITEvoid presented Vodafone's network as a multi-storey, complex architecture with the help of which the dimensions of the communication group and the digital space were made more tangible. The central element of the 1,850 m² stand was made up of light tubes, each pixel of which could be individually controlled. For the visitors to the CeBIT 2016 in Hanover, this visualised the dynamics of communication in a network in an exciting way. The complex light network structure also served to combine the four themed areas with one another: Network, Unified Communications, Cloud and Hosting and the Internet of Things. Thanks to various, accessible levels, visitors were given many different views of the huge 360° light installation, showing that the symbolic network encompasses everything—just like the real one. The top level housed a lounge and offered space for individual consultations.

WHITEvoid arbeitete die Markenfarben von Vodafone deutlich heraus und zeigte anhand einer komplexen 360°-Lichtinstallation ein „Gigabit Network", das unser aller tägliches Leben fast schon lückenlos umspannt.

WHITEvoid worked with the brand colours of Vodafone and used a complex 360° light installation to visualise a "Gigabit Network" that encompasses almost every aspect of our everyday lives.

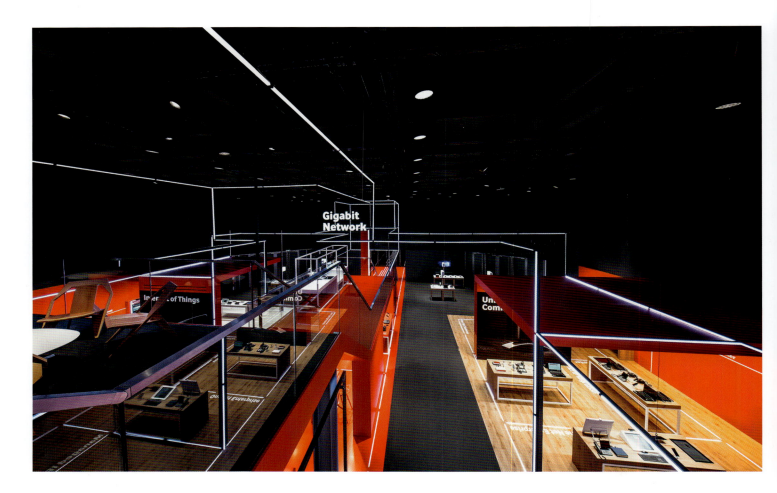

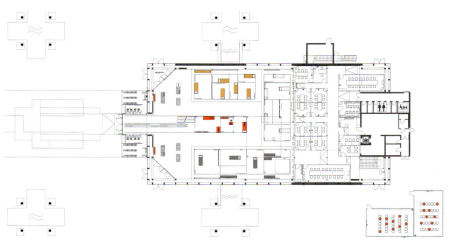

Alle Bereiche des Messestands waren durch die Lichtnetzwerk-Struktur miteinander verbunden. Die Besucher konnten jene dabei auf verschiedenen Plattformen aus den unterschiedlichsten Perspektiven betrachten, wenn sie sich entlang der Lichtstäbe bewegten.

All sections of the trade fair stand were connected with one another by the illuminated network structure. On various platforms visitors could observe it from all different perspectives as they moved along the light tubes.

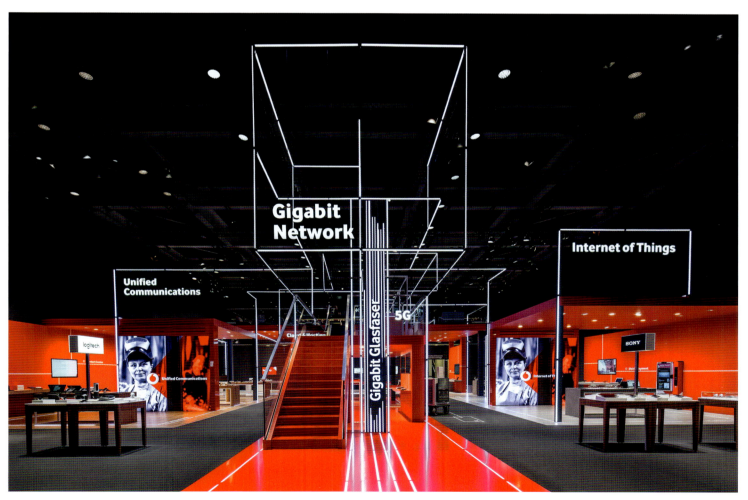

Size 1,850 m² | **Exhibitor** Vodafone GmbH, Dusseldorf | **Photos** RALPH LARMANN PERFORMANCE PHOTOGRAPHY, Hadamar | **Architecture / Design** WHITEvoid GmbH, Berlin | **Lighting** WHITEvoid GmbH, Berlin; Martin Kuhn Lichtdesign & Produktion, Berlin; music & light design GmbH, Leonberg | **Construction** Severich & Partner GmbH & Co. KG, Roetgen

IN- AND EXTERIOR

⟶ Die Gestaltung unserer Lebens- und Wohnräume gehört zum Ausdruck unserer eigenen Identität, die von vielfältigen Faktoren wie unserem Lebensgefühl, dem familiären und gesellschaftlichen Umfeld oder unseren Arbeits- und Lebensweisen geprägt ist. Und so wie wir uns mitsamt dieser Umstände kontinuierlich verändern, so verändern sich ebenfalls unsere Vorstellungen eines lebenswerten Umfelds, an das sich dementsprechend auch die Möbel, Einrichtungsgegenstände und Materialien immer wieder anpassen müssen. Umso wichtiger, dass die Inszenierungen von Produktlösungen für den Innen- und Außenraum dabei Welten eröffnen, die uns inspirieren und im besten Fall wiederum die Bühne für eine Präsentation unserer eigenen Persönlichkeit bieten.

⟶ The design of our living space and living rooms is an expression of our own identity which is in turn shaped by many different factors such as our attitude towards life, family or social environment or the way we work and live. And just as our circumstances are continuously changing, our ideas of what makes an environment worth living in are also changing so that furniture, furnishing and materials have to keep changing as well. It is therefore all the more important that presentations of product solutions for the interior and exterior open up worlds which inspire us and ideally offer a stage for the presentation of our own personality.

⟶ 170

⟶ 200

⟶ 188

Architekturbüro Wörner, Stuttgart
Willi SCHILLIG Polstermöbelwerke GmbH & Co. KG, Ebersdorf-Frohnlach
imm cologne 2016, Cologne

WOHLFÜHL-OASEN

„Ruhe, Stille, Sofa und eine Tasse Tee geht über alles", war sich schon der deutsche Schriftsteller und Journalist Theodor Fontane sicher. Und damit sollte er bis heute Recht behalten: Auf der imm cologne 2016 gestaltete das Architekturbüro Wörner aus Stuttgart den Messeauftritt der Willi SCHILLIG Polstermöbelwerke ganz im Sinne des Literaten. Insgesamt 19 individuell und separat präsentierte sowie gemütlich zusammengestellte Wohngruppen waren hier auf 1.000 Quadratmetern ausgestellt. Über jeder dieser Szenerien ordneten die Gestalter mehrere unterschiedlich große Aluminiumringe in Hellblau an. Die Ringe mit einem Durchmesser von 140 bis 240 Zentimetern waren mit sprinklerfähiger, weißer Gaze bespannt. Für jede der Exponatszenen entstanden so raumstrukturierende Wolkengebilde. Verstärkt wurde das Gefühl sich in abstrahierter Natur zu befinden durch die Fassade des Messestands, deren mehrdimensionale Aststruktur Einblicke in das Restaurant sowie Ausblicke auf die Ausstellung ermöglichte. Die Kreativen konzipierten somit einzelne Rückzugs- und Wohlfühloasen, in denen die Besucher – wie unter Wolken und Bäumen – Platz nehmen, verschnaufen und sich sogar dem Genuss einer Tasse Tee widmen konnten.

FEEL-GOOD OASISES

"Peace and quiet, a sofa and a cup of tea is all you need", the German writer and journalist Theodor Fontana was convinced of that. And this still holds true today: At the imm cologne 2016 the exhibition booth designed by Architekturbüro Wörner from Stuttgart for Willi SCHILLIG Polstermöbelwerke would have been to Fontana's taste. A total of 19 groups of furniture were displayed here on 1,000 m², some presented individually and separate, some comfortable and cosy. Above each of these scenarios, the designers arranged several light blue aluminium rings of different sizes. From 140 to 240 centimetres in diameter, the rings were covered in white gauze suitable for use with sprinklers. The resulting cloud formations structured the space for each of the arrangements of exhibits. The use of abstract references to nature that gave visitors a feeling of being outdoors was continued in the façade of the stand. The multidimensional branch structure allowed glimpses of the restaurant and views of the exhibition. The designers had thus created feel-good oases and retreats complete with clouds and trees in which visitors could take a seat, put their feet up and even enjoy a cup of tea.

Die bespannten und sich überlappenden Aluminiumringe waren bis auf 2,40 Meter abgehängt. Damit konnte eine unpersönliche Hallenstimmung vermieden und durch die fast normale Raumhöhe eine realistische Wohnwelt geschaffen werden.

The covered and overlapping aluminium rings were suspended down to a height of 2.40 metres. This avoided the impersonal hall atmosphere, and the almost normal room height created a realistic living space.

Begrenzend und gleichzeitig offen: Dank der Aststruktur waren schon durch die Fassade tiefe Ein- und Ausblicke möglich, wobei sich diese Gestaltung an den Wänden, die das Restaurant begrenzten, wiederfinden ließ – hier gestaffelt konstruiert und beidseitig in verschiedenen Farben von Hellgrün bis Dunkelblau lackiert.

Confining and yet at the same time open: Thanks to the branch structure that partitioned off the restaurant, the façade already allowed deep insights and outlooks. This design idea was continued on the walls, in this case in layers and lacquered on both sides in various shades from light green to dark blue.

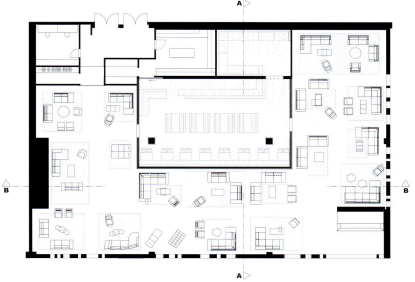

Size 1,000 m² | **Exhibitor** Willi SCHILLIG Polstermöbelwerke GmbH & Co. KG, Ebersdorf-Frohnlach | **Photos** KARL HUBER FOTODESIGN, Nagold | **Architecture / Design / Lighting** Architekturbüro Wörner, Stuttgart | **Construction** Visage Messe- u. Ausstellungsbau GmbH, Cologne

dan pearlman Markenarchitektur GmbH, Berlin
ROCA SANITARIO S. A., Barcelona
ISH 2015, Frankfurt a. Main

NEVER CHANGE A WINNING TEAM

… ist eigentlich eine alte Sportsweisheit und stammt vom englischen Fußballtrainer Alf Ramsey. Dennoch wird das Sprichwort seit seiner Entstehung immer wieder auf andere Bereiche übertragen. Das dachte sich wohl auch Roca, als das Unternehmen 2015 schon zum sechsten Mal in Folge dan pearlman Markenarchitektur mit der Entwicklung seines Messeauftritts auf der ISH in Frankfurt beauftragte: Mit über 500 Exponaten auf 680 Quadratmetern stellten die Gestalter hier die Produktvielfalt des spanischen Badezimmerausstatters unter Beweis. Thematisch sowie räumlich durch einen Gang in zwei unterschiedliche Bereiche gegliedert waren die beiden Produktpräsentationen „Bathroom Ambiences" und „Product Competence" hierbei um die zentral gelegene Plaza angeordnet: Auf der einen Seite befanden sich die einzelnen Kollektionen der Marke in Form von zwölf individuell ausgestatteten Badezimmersituationen. Direkt gegenüber wurde die technologische Kompetenz von Roca mit ausgestellten Armaturen, WC-Technologien und Materialinnovationen deutlich gemacht. Besondere Objekte wie beispielsweise Smart Toilets oder individuell anpassbare Badmöbel wurden zudem in begehbaren Räumen inszeniert.

NEVER CHANGE A WINNING TEAM

… is actually an old sports adage and stems from the English football coach Alf Ramsey. However, since it was coined the saying has been often been transferred to other areas. This is presumably what Roca was thinking when in 2015 the company commissioned dan pearlman Markenarchitektur to develop their trade fair stand at the ISH in Frankfurt for the sixth time in a row. With more than 500 exhibits on 680 m², the designers demonstrated the product variety of the Spanish bathroom outfitters. Divided both thematically and spatially by an aisle into two areas, the two product presentations "Bathroom Ambiences" and "Product Competence" were arranged around a central plaza: on one side, the individual collections of the brand were presented in the form of twelve individually equipped bathroom situations. Directly opposite, Roca's technological competence was illustrated with a display of fittings, WC technologies and innovative new materials. Special objects such as smart toilets or bathroom furniture that can be adapted to individual needs were presented separately in walk-in rooms.

Raffiniert: dan pearlman Markenarchitektur machte die Besucher mit Blickmöglichkeiten durch die halbtransparente Lamellenfassade neugierig und lockte sie so in das Zentrum des Messestands. Von hier aus konnten die Besucher die Produktbeispiele von Roca entdecken.

Artful: with possibilities to get glimpses of the inside through the semi-transparent slatted façade dan pearlman Markenarchitektur aroused the curiosity of visitors, thus enticing them into the centre of the booth. From here, the visitors could discover examples of Roca's products.

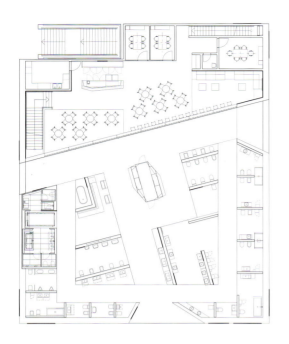

Besondere Aufmerksamkeit erntete eine Badezimmerwelt in edlen Gold- und Cremetönen: Die Premiumkollektion Armani Roca entstand aus einer seit 2010 bestehenden Kooperation und zeichnet sich durch hohe Qualität aus.

A bathroom world in fine shades of gold and cream received a lot of attention: The premium collection Armani Roca was the result of a collaboration initiated in 2010 that is characterised by its high quality.

Size 680 m² | **Exhibitor** ROCA SANITARIO S. A., Barcelona | **Photos** diephotodesigner.de, Berlin | **Architecture / Design / Graphics** dan pearlman Markenarchitektur GmbH, Berlin | **Lighting** weißpunkt und purpur, Berlin | **Construction** DISPLAY INTERNATIONAL Schwendinger GmbH & Co. KG, Würselen

Heine/Lenz/Zizka Projekte GmbH, Frankfurt a. Main
Alape GmbH, Goslar
ISH 2015, Frankfurt a. Main

PURISTISCH UND AUSSAGEKRÄFTIG

Als Premiumanbieter für individuelle Waschtischlösungen und Maßanfertigungen aus glasiertem Stahl durfte Alape auf der Weltleitmesse für Bad, Energie- und Klimatechnik – der ISH in Frankfurt – 2015 selbstverständlich nicht fehlen. Dementsprechend boten die Kreativen von Heine/Lenz/Zizka sowohl dem Badmöbelhersteller als auch dessen handwerklicher Präzisionskompetenz hier eine selbstbewusste Bühne. Auf 250 Quadratmetern kombinierten sie unterschiedlichste Materialien – Stahlemaille, Massivholz und Kupfer – vor einer elegant weißen Kulisse und übertrugen damit die besonderen Eigenschaften des Werkstoffs – Präzision, Leichtigkeit und filigrane Anmutung – in den Entwurf. Dabei waren die Präsentationsflächen für die zahlreichen ästhetischen Waschplatzlösungen in insgesamt acht musealen Produktinseln zu finden. Einige von ihnen wurden von der Decke abgehängt, waren nur mittels dünner Stahlrohre gehalten und schienen fast zu schweben. Andere, ebenfalls von Stahlrohren eingerahmt, wurden dagegen auf dem Boden verankert und mittels akzentuierender Lichtführung präsentiert. Zusätzlich und als besonderer Blickfang war im hinteren Zentrum des Stands eine ebenso eindrucksvolle wie spektakuläre Skulptur aus Stahlplatinen platziert.

Preisgekrönt: Der Messestand wurde vom Kommunikationsverband FAMAB für herausragende Markenerlebnisse in der Messekommunikation mit dem Gold Award in der Kategorie „Best Stand Design" aus der Hauptkategorie „Architecture" ausgezeichnet.

PURISTIC AND EXPRESSIVE

As premium supplier of individual wash basin solutions and bespoke glazed steel products, Alape was, of course, to be found at the world's leading fair for bathroom, energy and air-conditioning technology—the ISH in Frankfurt in 2015. The creative minds from Heine/Lenz/Zizka offered a suitably self-assured stage both for the manufacturer of bathroom furniture and its skilled craftsmanship. On a footprint of 250 m², they combined all different materials—enamelled steel, solid wood and copper—against an elegant white backdrop, thus incorporating the special characteristics of the material—precision, lightness and delicate appearance—in the design. The presentation areas for the numerous aesthetically pleasing wash basin solutions were to be found in a total of 8 museum-like product islands. Some of them were suspended from the ceiling, held merely by thin steel tubes and almost seemed to be floating. Others, likewise framed by steel tubes, were anchored to the floor and presented using special lighting effects. In addition, and as a special eyecatcher, a spectacular sculpture of steel slugs was placed to impress at the rear centre of the stand.

Prize-winning: The exhibition stand received the Gold Award in the category "Best Stand Design" in the main category "Architecture" from the FAMAB Association for Direct Business Communications for outstanding brand experiences in trade fair communication.

Mit der zentral platzierten Skulptur aus scheinbar zweckentfremdeten, weiß glasierten Stahlplatinen thematisierte der Aussteller seine Suche nach einer Einheit aus Form, Funktion und Material.

The centrally positioned sculpture of seemingly alienated white-glazed steel slugs picked up the theme of the exhibitor's search for a unity of form, function and material.

Size 250 m² | **Exhibitor** Alape GmbH, Goslar | **Photos** Achim Hatzius, Berlin | **Architecture / Design / Graphics** Heine/Lenz/Zizka Projekte GmbH, Frankfurt a. Main | **Construction** HOLTMANN GmbH & Co. KG, Langenhagen

Interior Architecture and Furniture Design-Programme / Oslo National Academy of the Arts, Oslo
Oslo National Academy of the Arts, Oslo
Stockholm Furniture & Light Fair 2016, Stockholm

GESELLSCHAFTS-KRITISCHES BÄLLEBAD

Norwegen gilt als das Land, in dem der weltpolitisch kontrovers diskutierte Rohstoff Öl wie aus Sturzbächen fließt, sodass die Haupteinnahmequelle der Nation scheinbar niemals zu versiegen droht. Doch selbst die skandinavische Halbinsel blieb vom Ölpreissturz nicht verschont und steht nun vor einer ernsthaften Problematik: Die Erträge, die das schwarze Gold abwirft, gehen bedrohlich zurück, weswegen zahlreiche Arbeitsplätze und Existenzen gefährdet sind. Norwegen muss sich und seine Wirtschaft also neu erfinden. Diese Thematik veranschaulichten Studierende des Master-Studiengangs „Interior Architecture and Furniture Design" der Oslo National Academy of the Arts mit einem Messestand auf der Stockholm Furniture & Light Fair 2016. Auf 24 Quadratmetern beleuchteten sie sowohl gesellschaftskritisch, als auch spielerisch die Zukunft der norwegischen Gesellschaft und Wirtschaft: Hinter einem großen Becken – voll mit schwarzen Kunststoffquadern – platzierten sie eine vertikale Holzwand mit etwa 800 herausnehmbaren Plättchen. Wurden diese entfernt, war die jeweils dahinter liegende Fläche sichtbar, entweder in Schwarz oder naturbelassen. Damit konnten die Besucher der Messe aktiv dazu beitragen, nach und nach Titel sowie Thema des Messestands zu enthüllen: „IS THIS IT?"

SOCIO-CRITICAL BALL POOL

Norway is the country where the commodity oil that is discussed so controversially in world politics appears to flow in such torrents that the nation's main source of income will seemingly never dry up. Yet even the Scandinavian peninsula has not been left unscathed by the plummeting price of oil and is now facing a serious problem: The revenue generated by the black gold is shrinking at an alarming rate and numerous jobs and livelihoods are at risk. Norway and its economy therefore need to reinvent themselves. Students studying for a masters in "Interior Architecture and Furniture Design" at the Oslo National Academy of the Arts illustrated this theme on a stand at the Stockholm Furniture & Light Fair 2016. They used the 24 m² of the stand to take a critical and yet playful look at the future of Norwegian society and economy: Behind a large pool full of black plastic cuboids, they placed a vertical wooden wall covered by around 800 removable platelets. When removed, the surface behind them was revealed, either black or natural wood colour. In this way, the visitors to the trade fair could make an active contribution as the title and theme of the booth was gradually exposed: "IS THIS IT?"

Von der willkommenen Entspannungsoase über ein spannendes Spieleparadies, bis hin zum nachhaltigen Denkanstoß: Mit dem rechteckigen Bällebad konnten sämtliche Bedürfnisse der Besucher abgedeckt und erfüllt werden.

From a welcome relaxation oasis and exciting play area right through to providing food for thought: the rectangular ball pool took into account and satisfied all the needs of the visitors.

Unter der Leitung der Professoren Toni Kauppila, Sigurd Strøm und Karin Knott wollten die Studierenden Nina Balliot, Christo-pher Hansen, Fatimah Mahdi, Hanna Nordh, Emma Staubo, Bruno Gabriel Suraski und Isak Wisløff mit der Inszenierung kritisch, ernst, aber auch ironisch verspielt aufzeigen, dass Norwegen wesentlich mehr zu bieten hat als nur den Rohstoff Öl.

Guided by the professors Toni Kauppila, Sigurd Strøm and Karin Knott, the students Nina Balliot, Christopher Hansen, Fatimah Mahdi, Hanna Nordh, Emma Staubo, Bruno Gabriel Suraski and Isak Wisløff wanted their production to show in serious yet tongue in cheek way that Norway has a lot more to offer than just the commodity oil.

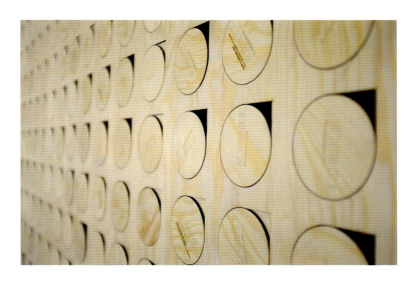
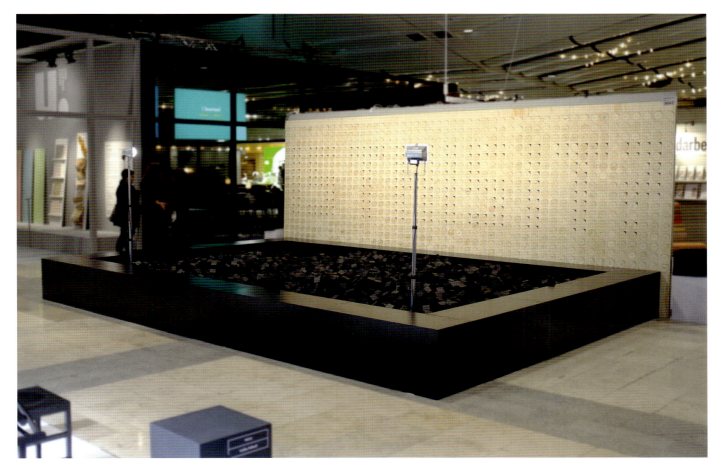

Size 24 m² | **Exhibitor** Oslo National Academy of the Arts, Oslo | **Photos** Toni Kauppila, Oslo; Bjørg Aabø, Oslo |
Architecture / Design Interior Architecture and Furniture Design-Programme / Oslo National Academy of the Arts, Oslo

INTERVIEW
TONI KAUPPILA
(OSLO NATIONAL
ACADEMY OF THE ARTS)

Bei den Masterstudiengängen im Bereich Design an der Oslo National Acedemy of the Arts – den Sie als Professor leiten – wird besonderer Wert auf „Socially Responsive Design" gelegt. Was können wir uns darunter vorstellen?

Da unser Studienprogramm sich mit der Gestaltung von Räumen, Objekten und Dingen befasst, verbringen wir viel Zeit mit der Untersuchung des ständigen Wandels innerhalb unserer Gesellschaften, um die Zusammenhänge zwischen Designeingriffen und den betreffenden Kulturen besser zu verstehen. Wir arbeiten mit einer Idee von doppelter Klientel, wo es um die jeweilige Aufgabe geht, aber auch um den Beitrag für eine Gesellschaft im Allgemeinen. Am faszinierendsten finden wir die sozialen Sachverhalte, bei denen Design innerhalb gesellschaftlicher Aktivitäten agiert. Wir leben in einer Zeit, in der wir mit der Komplexität kultureller Vielfalt konfrontiert werden. Um unser Wohlbefinden (was auch immer das künftig bedeuten mag) zu steigern, müssen wir die Zusammenarbeit zwischen dem einen und dem anderen und das Aufeinandertreffen sich überschneidender Absichten verbessern. Die meisten dieser Angelegenheiten sind sozialer Natur. In genau diesen Herausforderungen und Chancen sehen wir das Potenzial unseres Designs. Im Gegenzug regt es unsere Gewohnheit nach vielfältigen Ergebnissen zu suchen an; noch immer sind die Material-Workshops unser Ausgangspunkt, wir erleben aber mehr und mehr Projekte, die mittels einer Bandbreite von Medien ausgearbeitet werden müssen.

Auch bei Ihrem Auftritt auf der Stockholm Furniture and Light Fair präsentieren Sie Ihren Studiengang mit einer Installation

Auf dieser Messe haben wir verschiedene Ziele verfolgt. Zunächst einmal wollten wir uns zukünftigen Studenten als interessanter Studienort zeigen, gleichzeitig aber auch der Industrie als fortschrittlicher Forschungspartner. Um diesen Eigenschaften Ausdruck zu verleihen, war es unser Ziel, unseren ganzheitlichen wie auch analytischen Ansatz anhand dieser bewohnbaren Installation zu manifestieren. Und anstatt lediglich mit unserer Absicht zu provozieren, lockten wir die Besucher in das (soziale) Setting, ganz so als ob die Erfahrung unseres Messestands für sich selbst sprechen könnte. Unsere andere Absicht auf der Messe richtet sich kritisch an die Möbelindustrie und stellt die Frage, ob wir an alternativen „Produkten" arbeiten sollten, um es mit den bestehenden Typologien aufzunehmen, die häufig noch immer mehr oder weniger dasselbe in Grün sind. Dieser ontologische Anspruch ist nicht nur unsere akademische Pflicht, sondern vielmehr unsere Neugier auf die Gegebenheiten, die heute und in der Zukunft fernab der gängigen Ware zu haben sein könnten.

Das Motto Eures Entwurfs „IS THIS IT?" wird erst durch das Handanlegen der Besucher sichtbar. Lässt sich durch das spielerische Erleben ein solch ernstes Thema besonders gut darstellen?

Genau das, glaube ich, ist, was wir hoffen zu erreichen. Der Zeitaufwand, den ein normaler Messebesucher aufbringt, um die endlosen Stände zu durchkämmen, ist sehr gering. Es ist eine große Herausforderung, komplexe Forschungsergebnisse in so einem kurzen Moment zu vermitteln. Deswegen haben wir eine einfach zugängliche Installation als Chill-out-Pool gestaltet, die zum Erholen der Füße im Treiben der Ausstellungshalle einlädt. Ist der Besucher aber erst einmal drinnen, dann kann er über ein breites Lernangebot mehr darüber erfahren, was die jungen Designer, die bald ihren Hochschulabschluss machen, zu sagen haben. Auf den zweiten Blick dann stellt sich der eher naiv aussehende Spielplatz als ein Forum für einen professionellen Dialog heraus. Die andere Diskursebene kommt zum Vorschein, während der Besucher sich auf die kritische Meinung der Studenten sowohl zu Norwegens Ölindustrie als auch zu dem Status Quo der Möbelindustrie einlässt; parallel dazu herrscht aber der Optimismus, dass dem sozialen Potenzial unserer Gesellschaften, für das Gemeinwohl zu arbeiten, Priorität eingeräumt wird. Diese stetig kritische und reflektierte Praxis, die mit der Hilfe von Designerfindungen sorgfältig ausgearbeitet wurde, ist genau der Kern unseres akademischen Programms.

⟶ **Prof. Toni Kauppila** ist Leiter des Bereiches Innenarchitektur und Möbeldesign an der Oslo National Academy of the Arts in Norwegen. Sein Ansatz ist es, Forschung, Lehre und Praxis eng miteinander zu verknüpfen, hin zu einem nachhaltigen Laboratorium, um die architektonischen und gestalterischen Prozesse, die aus sozialen und unternehmerischen Ansätzen entstehen, zu entwickeln – auch in seinem forschungsbasierten Architectural Practice ND.

> www.khio.no | www.nd.fi

On the Master of Arts courses at the Oslo National Academy of Arts, design section—which you lead—they particularly value "Socially Responsive Design". What exactly does that mean?

As a study programme dealing with the design of spaces, objects and things, we spend a lot of time investigating the ever-changing affairs within our societies, to understand better the relationship between our design interventions and the cultures they relate to. We work with an idea of a double clientele, where there is the particular task at stake and then there is the contribution to the society at large. We find the social issues most intriguing, where the design is operating within the activities of the community. We live in an era in which we are confronted with the complexity of cultural diversity. For the sake of advancing our well-being (whatever that means in the future), we need to enhance the collaboration with one and the other and the encounter of overlapping agendas. Most of these matters are social by nature. It is in those challenges and opportunities that we see the potential of our design. In return, it stimulates our practice to seek for outputs that are more varied; the material workshops are still our home base, but more and more we see projects that need to be elaborated through a variety of media.

You took part in the Stockholm Furniture and Light. Your MA students developed an installation which picks up a socially relevant topic. What made you choose this topic?

Our objectives at this particular fair were manifold. First of all, we wanted to present ourselves as an interesting place to study for future students, but also to get the industry to see us as a progressive research partner. To express these qualities, our aim was to manifest our holistic and analytical approach within the field through this inhabitable installation. And rather than only provoking with our aim, we lured the audience generously into the (social) situation, as if the experience of our stand could stand for itself. The other embedded agenda critically confronts the furniture industry, and whether we should elaborate alternative 'products' to rival the existing typologies, that still are to a large extent more or less small variations of the same. This ontological interest is not only our academic obligation, but also more our curiosity about the contemporary and future conditions that may be beyond the current merchandise on offer.

The slogan of your design—"IS THIS IT"—can only be seen when the visitor touches it. Can such a serious topic be better displayed with the help of a playful experience?

That I believe is exactly what we were hoping to achieve. The amount of time spent by a normal fair visitor scanning through the never-ending stands is very little. To communicate complex research findings in such a fleeting moment is very challenging. That's why we designed an easily accessible installation as a chill-out pool to rest your feet while drifting through the exhibition halls. But once in it, there is an offering to learn more about what the young, soon-graduating designers have to say. The rather naïve looking playground reveals itself at second glance as a forum for a professional dialogue. The other level of discourse emerges as the visitors engage with the students' critical view both towards the Norwegians' oil-based economy and the furniture industry's status quo, but paralleling with the optimism for prioritising the social potential in our societies to work for the common good. This continuously critical and reflective practice elaborated through the design interventions is at the very core of our academic programme.

→ **Prof. Toni Kauppila** is the Head of the Interior Architecture and Furniture Design Oslo National Academy of the Arts, Norway. His approach is—also in his research-based Architectural Practice ND—to closely connect research, teaching, and practice into an ongoing laboratory for developing the social and entrepreneurial approaches emerging from the architectural and design processes.

> www.khio.no | www.nd.fi

raumkontor Innenarchitektur | Andrea Weitz und Jens Wendland GbR, Dusseldorf
Deutsches Tapeten-Institut GmbH, Dusseldorf
imm cologne 2016, Cologne

PANOPTIKUM DER EIGENHEITEN

Während der imm cologne 2016 war auf dem Messestand des Deutschen Tapeten-Instituts gebaute Poesie vorzufinden. Für den Auftritt hatten sich die Gestalter von raumkontor Innenarchitektur etwas ganz Besonderes überlegt: Sie bespielten die insgesamt 80 Quadratmeter auf drei unterschiedlichen Ebenen mit vier verschiedenen Raumszenarien. Als ein Spiegelbild unseres komplexen Lebens wurden diese Räume mittels einer enorm hohen Dichte an Elementen – wie beispielsweise Möbeln oder Gebrauchsgegenständen – in verschiedenfarbige, individuelle Welten verwandelt. In Rot, Grün, Blau und Gelb wurde den Besuchern vermittelt, dass räumliche Gestaltung immer auf persönlichen Eigenheiten sowie der Entfaltung der Individualität basieren muss. Die zahlreichen Überlagerungen ermöglichten dabei eine Vielfalt der Lesarten und wurden so zum Ausgangspunkt von Identifikation, Teilhabe und lustvollem Umgang mit der Welt. Raum wurde zum Ereignis. Letztlich lieferte der Aussteller gleichzeitig einen Vorschlag, wie der Endverbraucher eben solch persönliche Raumkreationen auch Zuhause ganz einfach generieren kann: Tapete macht aus Wänden ein Zuhause!

COMPOSITION OF SINGULARITIES

What was to be seen on the trade fair stand of the Deutsches Tapeten-Institut during the imm cologne 2016 can be described as built poetry. The designers from raumkontor Innenarchitektur had come up with something rather special for the stand: they created four different room scenarios on the total footprint of 80 m² spread over three different levels. As a mirror image of our complex lives, these rooms were transformed using an extremely high density of elements—such as furniture or articles of daily use—into different coloured, singular worlds. The message conveyed to visitors by the red, green, blue and yellow rooms was that spatial design must always be based on personal characteristics and will always be an expression of individuality. The numerous superimpositions and layering this involved could be interpreted in different ways and thus became the starting point for identifying and engaging with the world and having fun in the process. Finally, the exhibitor offered a suggestion how the end user can very simply create such rooms at home: Wallpaper turns walls into a home!

Während der Messe fand zum ohnehin schon spektakulären Auftritt zusätzlich eine mehrtägige Performance statt: Die Räume wurden mit prägnanten Typen belebt. So konnten die Besucher Hipster, Hund und Nerd dabei beobachten, wie sie in den Räumen miteinander und mit dem Set-Material interagierten.

During the trade fair, the spectacular booth was supported by a performance that lasted several days: The rooms were brought to life by concise characters. Visitors could watch how hipster, dog and nerd interacted with one another in the rooms and with the set materials.

Verschrobenes, Künstlerisches, Trash, Hochkultur des aktuellen Möbel- und Produktdesigns, Morphing und Montage – das Samplen als Konzeption des digitalen Denkens wurde auf dem Messestand als Lebenskonzept in die analoge Welt zurückgeführt.

Eccentric, artful, trashy, high culture of current furniture and product design, morphing and composition—sampling as a concept of the digital mindset was restored on the stand to the analogue world as a concept for life.

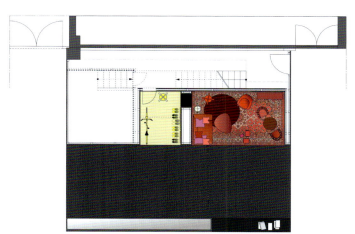

Express Yourself: Beim Betrachten der vier farbigen Raumszenarien, die den Besuchern wie Bühnenbilder präsentiert wurden, konnten sie sich schnell wiedererkennen und sich so mit der Marke identifizieren.

Express yourself: As visitors looked at the four brightly coloured room scenarios that were presented to them like stage sets they quickly recognized themselves, encouraging them to identify with the brand.

Size 80 m² | **Exhibitor** Deutsches Tapeten-Institut GmbH, Dusseldorf | **Photos** HANS JÜRGEN LANDES FOTOGRAFIE, Dortmund | **Architecture / Design** raumkontor Innenarchitektur | Andrea Weitz und Jens Wendland GbR, Dusseldorf | **Construction** schnaitt Internationale Messe- und Ladenbau GmbH, Bergheim

Schmidhuber Brand Experience GmbH, Munich
Franz Kaldewei GmbH & Co. KG, Ahlen
ISH 2015, Frankfurt a. Main

POLYGONALES ORCHIDEEN-WUNDER

Auf der ISH 2015 in Frankfurt sorgten der Produzent von emaillierten Badewannen und Duschflächen Franz Kaldewei und dessen langjähriger Gestaltungspartner SCHMIDHUBER einmal mehr für Aufsehen: Die Münchner Kreativen entwickelten für den mit 750 Quadratmetern größten Messeauftritt der Unternehmensgeschichte eine eindrucksvolle Standarchitektur. Ausgehend von der Strahlkraft der Marke war jene inspiriert von eintreffenden Lichtstrahlen, die den Markenraum in dreidimensionale Facetten brachen. Die Facettenkanten liefen dabei nicht parallel zueinander, sondern an verschiedenen Fluchtpunkten sowohl horizontal als auch vertikal zusammen. Die Fassaden, die sich dadurch nach innen neigten, schufen ein dynamisches Spiel aus Perspektive sowie Proportion und kreierten im Zentrum der Ausstellung einen eindrucksvollen Lichthof, das Atrium der Sinne. Hier schwebte eine Kugel aus weißen Orchideen über den Köpfen der Besucher und ein Meer aus 3.000 Blüten bildete die Bühne für die neuen Waschtische aus Stahlemaille. Hell, zart und mit einem dezenten Duft stellte diese Inszenierung damit einen sinnlichen Gegenpol zur Polygonalität des umgebenden Raums dar.

POLYGONAL ORCHID DELIGHT

At the ISH 2015 in Frankfurt, the producer of enamelled bathtubs and shower trays Franz Kaldewei and their long-standing design partner SCHMIDHUBER once again caused a stir: For the 750 m² stand, the largest in the history of the company, the creative heads from Munich developed an impressive booth architecture. With the "radiance" of the brand as the starting point, it was inspired by rays of light that hit the brand space, breaking it into three-dimensional facets. The edges of the facets did not run parallel to one another but merged at various vanishing points both horizontally and vertically. The façades which leant inward as a result created a dynamic play of perspective and proportion and at the centre of the exhibition produced an impressive courtyard, the atrium of the senses. A sphere of white orchids floated over the heads of the visitors and a sea of 3,000 flowers formed the stage for the new wash basins of enamelled steel. Bright, delicate and pleasantly scented, this presentation was a sensual contrast to the polygonally shaped space that surrounded it.

Spiel mit Perspektive und Proportion: Da die Kanten der einzelnen Raumfacetten nicht auf einen einzigen, sondern mehrere Fluchtpunkte zuliefen, ergaben sich perspektivisch ungewöhnliche Blickwinkel zwischen den Wegen des Messestands.

Play with perspective and proportion: As the edges of the individual facets of the room merged on several rather than a single vanishing point, this produced unusual perspectives between the paths through the booth.

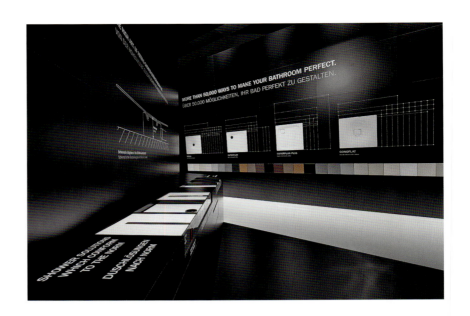

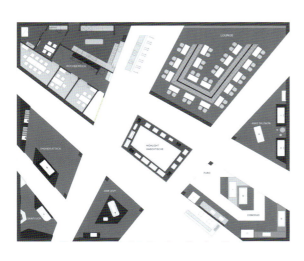

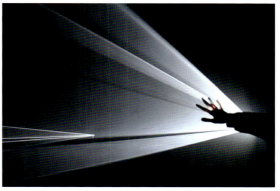

Die polygonale Architektur verkörperte die Eigenschaften der Marke: dezente Opulenz, nobler Purismus und zeitlose Eleganz. Die Produkte wurden mittels klarer Linien, dunkel glänzender Oberflächen und geometrischer Formen in Szene gesetzt.

The polygonal architecture embodied the characteristics of the brand: refined opulence, fine purism and timeless elegance. Clear lines, dark shiny surfaces and geometric forms were used to set off the products to great effect.

Size 750 m² | **Exhibitor** Franz Kaldewei GmbH & Co. KG, Ahlen | **Photos** Olaf Becker / BECKER LACOUR, Munich | **Architecture / Design** Schmidhuber Brand Experience GmbH, Munich | **Graphics** Kolle Rebbe GmbH, Hamburg | **Lighting** TLD Planungsgruppe GmbH, Taufkirchen | **Construction** Raumtechnik Messebau & Event Services GmbH, Ostfildern

spek DESIGN GbR, Stuttgart
Gerriets GmbH, Umkirch
Stage|Set|Scenery 2015, Berlin

BÜHNENREIF

Auf der Stage|Set|Scenery in Berlin, der Fach- und Kongressmesse für Veranstaltungstechnik, trifft einmal im Jahr die Branche aus den Bereichen Theater-, Bühnen- und Showausstattung aufeinander – eine Menge Inszenierungsexperten, aus deren Masse es herauszustechen gilt. Beispielhaft gelungen ist dies 2015 dem Umkircher Unternehmen Gerriets, für das die Stuttgarter Gestalter von spek DESIGN auf 220 Quadratmetern ein bühnenbildartiges Ausstellungskonzept entwickelten. Hierzu rahmten und strukturierten sie den Stand mit zahlreichen dunklen Papierboxen, die zu mehr oder weniger transparenten und geschlossenen Wänden zusammengefügt wurden, indem man sie unterschiedlich dicht aneinanderreihte und stapelte. Dadurch ergab sich eine räumliche sowie konzeptionelle Teilung des Messestands in zwei unterschiedlich aufgebaute Bereiche: Während in der Bewirtungszone Empfangstheke und Bar als zentrale Elemente wahrgenommen wurden, lag das Hauptaugenmerk in der Präsentationszone auf didaktischen Exponaten sowie Produktneuheiten.

STAGE WORTHY

At the Stage|Set|Scenery in Berlin, the specialist trade fair and convention for event technology, the world of theatre, stage and show equipment meets up once a year—a load of experts in creating spaces and all of them trying to stand out in the crowd. In 2015, Gerriets, a company from Umkirch, did just that in an exemplary fashion. With the help of the Stuttgart-based designers spek DESIGN they developed an exhibition concept on 220 m² along the lines of a stage set. To achieve this, they framed and structured the booth with numerous dark-coloured paper boxes which were combined to form more or less transparent and closed walls depending on how closely together the boxes were arranged in rows and piles. This divided the stand both spatially and in terms of concept into two differently constructed areas: While in the catering zone the reception counter and bar were perceived as the central elements, in the presentation zone the main focus was on educational exhibits as well as product innovations.

Akzente in Gerriets-Blau, kombiniert mit einem eindrucksvollen Himmel aus blauen Schirmleuchten, rundeten den Messeauftritt ab.

Dashes of Gerriets blue combined with an impressive ceiling of lights with blue lampshades rounded off the booth.

Von spek Design ebenfalls neu entwickelt ist „PaperBox" das erste System aus schwer entflammbarer Wellpappe mit B1-/M1-Zertifizierung und deshalb im öffentlichen Bereich einsetzbar. Durch das modulare Prinzip sowie die scharnierartige Verbindung konnten unterschiedliche Wandformationen aufgebaut werden, sei es versetzt und halbtransparent oder orthogonal und geschlossen.

Also newly developed by spek Design, "PaperBox" is the first system made of flame-resistant corrugated cardboard to receive B1/M1 certification and as such therefore suited for public spaces. Thanks to the modular principle and the hinge-like connections, it was possible to build various different wall formations, be it offset and semi-transparent or orthogonal and closed.

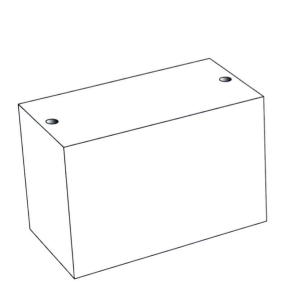

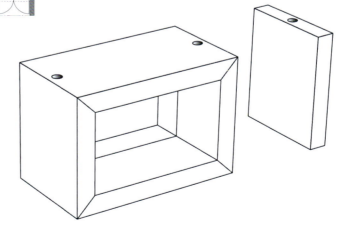

Size 220 m² | **Exhibitor** Gerriets GmbH, Umkirch | **Photos** spek DESIGN GbR, Stuttgart | **Architecture / Design** spek DESIGN GbR, Stuttgart | **Graphics / Media / Construction** Gerriets GmbH, Umkirch | **Lighting** music & light design GmbH, Leonberg

Stefan Zwicky Architekt, Zurich
NR Neue Räume AG, Zurich
neue räume 2015, Zurich

NEUE (AUSSTEL-LUNGS-)RÄUME

Was für den einen lediglich die Quadratmeteranzahl eines einzelnen Messestands sein kann, bietet für den Architekten und Designer Stefan Zwicky Raum für über 100 nationale sowie internationale Aussteller. Der ambitionierte Schweizer kuratierte 2015 bereits zum achten Mal die 8.000 Quadratmeter große und fünf Tage andauernde Wohn- und Möbelausstellung „neue räume" in einer alten Industriehalle des Quartiers Oerlikon im Norden Zürichs. Mit der mittlerweile größten Designplattform der Schweiz bot er damit insgesamt 110 Ausstellern aus den Bereichen Möbel, Leuchten, Küchen, Bäder, Textilien, Boden- und Wandbeläge eine Bühne für ihre Produkte und Neuheiten in einer einheitlichen Ausstellungsarchitektur. Mit 2.000 Laufmetern Bauabspanngewebe teilte er die komplette Halle in Bereiche für ebenso namhafte wie unbekannte Gestalter auf. So stellten sich beispielsweise auf der Sonderfläche „Young Labels" aufstrebende Jungdesigner dem Publikum vor, während nur einige Meter entfernt Urgesteine der Szene alte Klassiker und neue Kollektionen präsentierten. Dank der einheitlichen Ausstellungsarchitektur entstand für die Besucher also die Möglichkeit, die gezeigten Produkte unter den gleichen Bedingungen zu beurteilen.

NEW (EXHIBITI-ON) ROOMS

What for some is the number of square metres needed for a single trade fair stand, for architect and designer Stefan Zwicky offers space for more than 100 national and international exhibitors. In 2015, for the eighth time in succession the ambitious Swiss national curated the five-day lifestyle and furniture exhibition "neue räume" on the 8,000 m² of a factory hall in the Oerlikon quarter of north Zürich. With what is meanwhile Switzerland's biggest design platform, he offered a stage in a uniform exhibition architecture for the products and innovations of a total of 110 exhibitors from the fields of furniture, lighting, bathrooms, textiles, floor and wall coverings. Using 2,000 linear metres of building marker webbing, he divided up the entire hall into areas for both well-established and unknown designers. In the special section "Young Labels", for instance, budding young designers presented themselves to the general public, while just a few metres away veterans of the community presented timeless classics and new collections. Thanks to the uniform exhibition architecture, visitors had the opportunity to judge the products on display under the same conditions.

Wo wären wir nur ohne Papier? Auch die Gestalter des Schweizer Atelier Oï sind sich der Notwendigkeit des essenziellen Werkstoffs bewusst und zeigten eine Installation, mit der sie sich dem Wissen über Papier und dessen Verarbeitung widmeten.

Where would we be without paper? The designers of the Swiss Atelier Oï are aware of the necessity of the essential material and presented an installation dedicated to knowledge about paper and its processing.

Auch das formforum Schweiz war in der Ausstellung zugegen. Der Verein fördert seine Mitglieder im Bereich der zeitgenössischen und experimentellen Gestaltung in vielerlei Hinsicht. Auf der Messe verschaffte er ihnen zusätzlich eine Möglichkeit zur öffentlichen Präsenz.

The formforum Schweiz was also represented at the exhibition. The Swiss association promotes and supports its members in the field of contemporary and experimental design in many ways. At the trade fair, the association gave them an opportunity to reach a wider audience.

Durch die Kampagne „neue räume in the city" waren die Designobjekte nicht nur in der Messehalle zu finden. In den Schaufenstern, Innenräumen und Innenhöfen von 35 ausgewählten branchenfremden Geschäften und Gastronomiebetrieben waren zusätzlich Möbel, Leuchten und Textilien beteiligter Hersteller ausgestellt.

Thanks to the campaign "neue räume in the city", the design objects were not only to be found in the exhibition hall. The manufacturers participating in the campaign exhibited additional items of furniture, lamps and textiles in the shop windows, rooms and courtyards of 35 selected shops and restaurants.

Size 8,000 m² | **Exhibitor** NR Neue Räume AG, Zurich | **Photos** Constantin Meyer Photographie, Cologne | **Architecture / Design** Stefan Zwicky Architekt, Zurich | **Public Relations** Public Relation Communication / Claudia Neumann, Cologne | **Graphics** wapico AG, Berne | **Construction** Strickler Reklamen AG, Zurich

Studio Aisslinger, Berlin
DEDON GmbH, Lüneburg
Salone del Mobile 2016, Milan

WELCOME TO THE JUNGLE …

… ist nicht nur der Titel des weltberühmten Kassenschlagers der Hardrock-Band Guns N' Roses, sondern war mit Sicherheit auch der erste Gedanke der Besucher des Messeauftritts von DEDON auf dem Salone del Mobile 2016 in Mailand. Das Berliner Studio Aisslinger schwang hierbei die kreative Feder und verwandelte die 1.800 Quadratmeter große Fläche in eine wahrhaft grüne Dschungelszene. Auf dem tropisch gestalteten Stand konnten die Messegäste dabei die Produktpalette des exklusiven Herstellers handgeflochtener Outdoor-Möbel begutachten und ausprobieren: Teilweise unter sogenannten „Jungalows" waren acht Sitzgruppen lässig angeordnet. Mit diesen unaufdringlichen, doch mit grünen Gewächsen umschlungenen Konstruktionen konnte eine Verknüpfung zwischen der Lebendigkeit des Dschungels sowie der Ruhe eines Bungalows geschaffen werden. Durch diverse Kletter- sowie Hängepflanzen, reflektierende Spiegelflächen und mit Blättercollagen bespielte Rückwände sorgten die Gestalter zudem dafür, dass sich die Besucher von der Dschungelszenerie verschlungen und als Teil der Installation fühlten.

WELCOME TO THE JUNGLE …

… is not only the title of the world-famous hit of the hard rock band Guns N' Roses, but without a doubt also the first thought that came to the mind of visitors to the DEDON exhibition booth at the Salone del Mobile 2016 in Milan. The designers from Berlin-based Studio Aisslinger were the creative minds behind the stand, transforming the 1,800 m² area into a truly green jungle scene. What the fairgoers got to inspect and try out on the tropically designed stand was the product range of the exclusive manufacturer of hand-woven outdoor furniture casually grouped in eight seating arrangements, in some cases under so-called "Jungalows". These unobtrusive constructions covered in greenery established a link between the vibrancy of the jungle and the peace and quiet of a bungalow. Through the use of climbing and hanging plants, reflective mirrors and rear walls decorated with leaf collages, the designers also made sure that visitors felt engulfed by the jungle scenery and as part of the installation.

Der Gedanke an primitive Natur wurde mit dem Projekt neu interpretiert: Das Bureau Mirko Borsche aus München war für die frischen und modernen Blättercollagen an den Rückwänden des Messestands verantwortlich.

The project reinterpreted the idea of primitive nature: Bureau Mirko Borsche from Munich was responsible for the fresh and modern leaf collages on the rear walls of the booth.

Mit dem Messeauftritt gelang den Gestaltern des Studio Aisslinger eine liebevolle und detailreiche Erlebnisarchitektur. Während die Blätter in einer scheinbar echten, leichten Brise raschelten, bekamen die Besucher durch Lichtinstallationen ein Gefühl von realer Natur.

The designers from Studio Aisslinger came up with a lovingly designed themed architecture for the stand that was full of details. While the leaves rustled in what appeared to be a real gentle breeze, the sense of real nature was reinforced by light installations.

Size 1,800 m² | **Exhibitor** DEDON GmbH, Lüneburg | **Photos** DEDON GmbH, Lüneburg | **Architecture / Design** Tina Bunyaprasit und Werner Aisslinger / Studio Aisslinger, Berlin | **Graphics** Bureau Mirko Borsche, Munich | **Construction** viva Messe- und Ausstellungsbau GmbH, Hanover

Studio Aisslinger, Berlin
Kvadrat A/S, Ebeltoft
imm cologne 2016, Cologne

TEXTILE ARCHITEKTUR

Im Rahmen der imm cologne verwandelt sich einmal im Jahr die ganze Domstadt in ein Paradies für Designliebhaber – wobei die innovativsten Neuheiten der Möbelbranche nicht nur auf dem Messegelände zu finden sind: Mit den Kölner Passagen öffnen jedes Jahr pünktlich zur Messe zahlreiche Galerien, Hallen und weitere Veranstaltungsorte für eine Woche ihre Pforten. Einige Aussteller präsentieren sich beispielsweise in der Design Post Köln – einem Showroom in Köln-Deutz. 2016 waren in der ehemaligen Post-Bahnhofshalle insgesamt 35 Unternehmen vertreten – darunter auch der dänische Textilhersteller Kvadrat. Ziel ihres Auftritts war es, das eigene, umfassende Sortiment architektonisch zu inszenieren. Für dieses anspruchsvolle Ziel engagierten sie das Berliner Studio Aisslinger. Zum zentralen Element der 100 Quadratmeter großen Ausstellung wurde das „kvadrat cabin house" – eine farbenfrohe, kleine Hütte, die komplett aus Stoff zu bestehen schien. Sowohl innerhalb als auch außerhalb des kleinen Hauses fanden sich sämtliche Produktvariationen des Unternehmens auf geschickt-kreative Art und Weise überall im Raum verteilt sowie in sämtliche Möbel und Gegenstände integriert.

TEXTILE ARCHITECTURE

During the imm cologne, the cathedral city is transformed once a year into a paradise for design fans. And the most innovative novelties of the furniture industry are not just found in the exhibition grounds: In the "Cologne Passages" numerous galleries, halls and other event locations open their doors every year at exactly the same time as the trade fair for one week. A number of exhibitors, for instance, presented themselves at the Cologne Design Post—a showroom in Cologne-Deutz. In 2016, a total of 35 companies were represented in the former mail hall of the train station, including the Danish textile manufacturer Kvadrat. The goal of their stand was to present their own, extensive product range in an architectural setting. They commissioned Berlin-based Studio Aisslinger with this challenging task. The central element of the 100 m² exhibition was the "kvadrat cabin house"— a brightly coloured, little hut which seemed to be made entirely of fabric. Both inside and outside the little house, all the company's product variants were spread skilfully and creatively throughout the space and integrated into the furniture and other items on the stand.

Über zwei Stufen konnten die Besucher in die Hütte gelangen. Hier waren neben Tischen und Sitzgelegenheiten auch Wände und Boden, sogar die Dachuntersicht mit Stoffen von Kvadrat bespannt. Nicht einmal das Fahrrad, das neben der Hütte parkte, blieb von der Stoffoffensive verschont.

Visitors took two steps up to reach the hut. Not only the tables and seating, but also the walls and floor were clad in Kvadrat fabrics, as was the inside of the roof. Not even the bicycle propped up against the hut was left untouched by the fabric attack.

Textilerlebnis: Einige Stoffmuster hingen wie Baldachine an der Decke und als Quadrate an den Wänden. Andere waren über Stützböcke gehängt und auf Tischen drapiert, wiederum andere lagen auf dem Boden wie Teppiche oder Fliesen.

Textile experience: Some fabric samples were suspended like a canopy from the ceiling or attached as squares to the walls. Others were draped over trestles and tables, or placed on the floor like carpets or tiles.

Size 100 m² | **Exhibitor** Kvadrat A/S, Ebeltoft | **Photos** patricia parinejad photography, Berlin | **Architecture / Design** Tina Bunyaprasit und Werner Aisslinger / Studio Aisslinger, Berlin | **Construction** Günter Sand Bühnen- & Dekorationsbau, Berlin; Syncro ApS, Knebel; Kvadrat A/S, Ebeltoft

TRIAD Berlin Projektgesellschaft mbH, Berlin
hülsta-werke Hüls GmbH & Co. KG, Stadtlohn
imm cologne 2016, Cologne

FADENSPIEL

Nachdem die hülsta-werke Hüls schon 2015 auf der internationalen Einrichtungsmesse imm cologne ihr glänzendes 75. Jubiläum feiern konnten, übertraf sich der Möbelhersteller 2016 erneut selbst. Für die Gestaltung des Messeauftritts wurde die Kommunikations- und Kreativagentur TRIAD Berlin verpflichtet, die die Besucher mit ihrer Inszenierung buchstäblich einwickelte. Fast acht Kilometer Seil wurden dabei in Form einer kinetisch transparenten Skulptur vertikal über den 950 Quadratmeter großen Stand gespannt. So ergaben sich immer wieder neue Blickwinkel, Raumeindrücke und nicht zuletzt eine abstrakte Wohnwelt, in der die Besucher zahlreiche Räume mit Produktbeispielen begehen konnten. Durch die Seile, die zwar in bestimmte Richtungen gespannt, mit dem Luftzug aber dennoch ständig in Bewegung waren, wurde dem Messeauftritt zudem eine dynamische Leichtigkeit verliehen, womit sich das Unternehmen erneut zu seiner flexiblen Philosophie bekannte.

CAT'S CRADLE

Having celebrated their glittering 75th anniversary at the 2015 international furniture and interior design show imm cologne, at the 2016 fair the furniture manufacturer hülsta-werke Hüls once again outdid themselves. The communications and creative agency TRIAD Berlin was entrusted with the design of the exhibition booth and what they came up with was literally a wrap. Almost eight kilometres of rope were extended vertically across the 950 m² of the stand to form a kinetically transparent sculpture. The result were ever changing perspectives, spatial impressions and not least an abstract living world in which visitors could explore numerous rooms containing product examples. Although the ropes were tensioned in certain directions, they were constantly moving in the airflow, giving the stand a dynamic lightness that underlined the company's flexible philosophy.

Mit dem dynamischen Messestand symbolisierten die hülsta-werke Hüls ihre Fähigkeit, sich dem stets wandelnden Markt immer wieder neu anzupassen und damit jederzeit in Bewegung bleiben zu können.

The dynamic trade fair stand of hülsta-werke symbolised their ability to adapt to the constantly changing market and to stay in motion.

Eine kinetische und transparente Seilskulptur sorgte für viel Aufmerksamkeit. Die vertikal gesponnenen und auf kleinen Schienen gelagerten Seile schwangen lässig hin und her, kreierten eine abstrakte Wohnwelt und unterteilten den Stand in einzelne Bereiche.

A kinetic and transparent rope sculpture attracted a great deal of attention. The vertically spun ropes that were mounted in small tracks swung casually backwards and forwards, creating an abstract living world and dividing the stand into various sections.

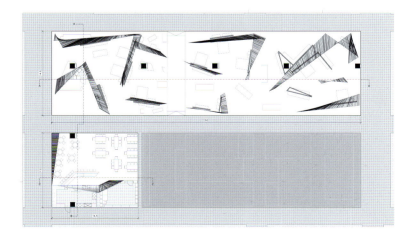

Size 950 m² | **Exhibitor** hülsta-werke Hüls GmbH & Co. KG, Stadtlohn | **Photos** Ulf Büschleb, Berlin | **Architecture / Design** TRIAD Berlin Projektgesellschaft mbH, Berlin

Ueberholz GmbH, Wuppertal
Fachverband Tischler Nordrhein-Westfalen, Dortmund
imm cologne 2016, Cologne

SINN-STIFTEND

Um unsere Umwelt physiologisch wahrzunehmen, stehen uns fünf Sinneseindrücke zur Verfügung. Jene Fähigkeiten griff die Wuppertaler Agentur Ueberholz bei der Gestaltung des Messeauftritts für den Fachverband Tischler Nordrhein-Westfalen auf der imm cologne 2016 auf und band vier dieser Sinne – Sehen, Tasten, Hören und Riechen – in das 40 Quadratmeter große Standerlebnis ein. So konnten die Besucher beispielsweise aus induktiven Lautsprechern in der Rückwand holzthematischen Geräuschen – wie von Kreissägen oder Klanghölzern – lauschen, während eine per iPad individuell steuerbare Duftmaschine mit verschiedenen Holzdüften – Birke, Fichte, Tanne, Eiche oder Ahorn – den Stand an entsprechenden Stellen beduftete. Zusätzlich unterstützten zahlreiche haptische sowie visuelle Exponate die Sinneserfahrungen. Jedoch gelang es den Gestaltern, die Besucher nicht nur mit sinnlichen Erfahrungen zu begeistern, sondern auch mit der Standarchitektur selbst: Vergrößert und auf Grobspanplatten lasierend gedruckt wurde das Foto einer Kopfholzscheibe begehbar. Dabei waren entlang der Jahresringe Stufen angeordnet, die als Sitzflächen dienten und Raum für persönliche Gespräche über handwerkliche Perfektion schufen.

MAKING SENSE OF WOOD

We have five senses at our disposal to physiologically perceive our environment. In their design of the trade fair appearance of Fachverband Tischler Nordrhein-Westfalen at the imm cologne 2016, Agentur Ueberholz from Wuppertal took up these abilities and incorporated four of the senses—sight, touch, hearing and smell—into the on 40 m² stand experience. Visitors could, for example, listen to wood-related sounds—such as circular saws or claves—played through inductive loudspeakers integrated in the rear wall, while a scent machine that could be individually controlled by an iPad with the fragrances of various types of wood—birch, fir, pine, oak or maple—perfumed certain parts of the stand. The experiences for the senses were supported by various tactile and visual exhibits. However, the designers did not only succeed in thrilling the visitors with sensual experiences. The architecture of the stand itself was also impressive: The photo of a head wood cross-section, enlarged and translucently printed on oriented strand boards, covered the floor. Steps arranged along the growth rings served as seating and created space for personal talks about perfect craftsmanship.

Während der Messe waren auf dem Stand kontinuierlich Schreiner anwesend, die mit den Besuchern interagierten, für Gespräche offen waren und damit neben ihrer Handwerks- und Beratungs- auch ihre Gestaltungskompetenzen unter Beweis stellen konnten. Ganz nach dem Standmotto: „Wir gestalten. Persönlich."

During the fair, the stand was constantly manned by carpenters who interacted with the visitors, were open for discussion and were able to demonstrate not only their craft and consulting competence, but also their design skills. True to the slogan of the stand: "We design. Personally."

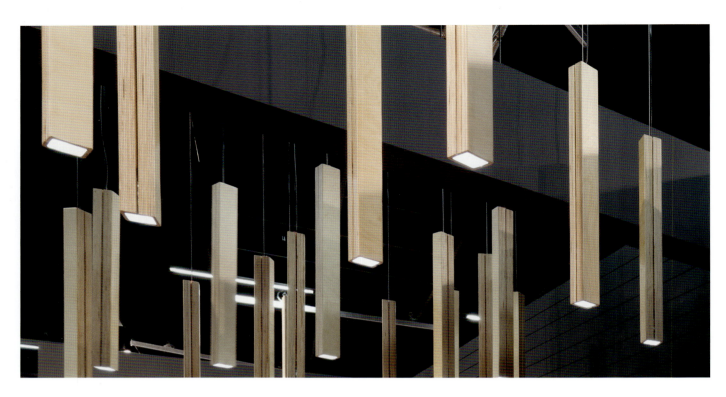

Abgependelte Klanghölzer mit integrierten Leuchten sorgten für zusätzliche Lichtquellen und verdeutlichten die Vielseitigkeit des Materials Holz. Mit dem Gesellenstück eines Geigenkastens wurde zudem die hohe Verarbeitungsqualität demonstriert.

Suspended claves with integrated luminaires provided an additional source of light and showed just how versatile wood is. A violin case produced as a test piece at the end of a carpentry apprenticeship also demonstrated the high standard of workmanship.

Size 40 m² | **Exhibitor** Fachverband Tischler Nordrhein-Westfalen, Dortmund | **Photos** Frank Dora / photoprop, Wuppertal | **Design / Graphics / Lighting / Media / Construction** Ueberholz GmbH, Wuppertal

INTERVIEW
ANDRÉ FÜSSER
(UEBERHOLZ GMBH)

Der Auftritt des Fachverbands Tischler Nordrhein Westfalen auf der imm Cologne 2016 stand ganz unter dem Motto „Wir gestalten. Persönlich.". Was bedeutet für Sie „persönlich"?

„Wir gestalten. Persönlich." ist ein Slogan des Fachverbands für alle Auftritte in der Öffentlichkeit und damit auch Grundlage unseres Entwurfskonzepts für die imm Cologne. Die Botschaft, die dahintersteckt, ist folgende: Tischler gestalten durch ihre handwerkliche Arbeit. Persönlich wird es durch die Beratung des Kunden und dessen Vorgaben, auch für den Raum. Damit möchte der Verband eine klare Abgrenzung zum Möbelhandel herstellen – schließlich fertigt der Tischler auf Maß! Für mich bedeutet „persönlich", einen Kontakt zu einem Kunden aufzubauen und alle Belange und Befindlichkeiten desjenigen zu verstehen und darauf einzugehen, statt Allgemeinplätze zu vertreten oder eine standardisierte Gestaltung zu verkaufen. „Persönlich" bedeutet im positiven Sinne „individuell" und „nicht egozentrisch". Wir Gestalter haben einen Dienst zu erbringen, der dem Kunden behilflich ist!

Holz und seine handwerkliche Bearbeitung spielen – selbstverständlich – die entscheidende Rolle bei der Standgestaltung. Dennoch wurden bei den Exponaten technische Lösungen integriert. Was wollten Sie damit erreichen?

Die Exponate mit technischen Lösungen zeigen, dass der Tischler mit vielfältigen, verschiedenen Aufgabenstellungen zu tun hat. So kann ein beim Tischler beauftragter Lautsprecher ebenso eine Holzbox wie auch eine individuelle Lösung mit unsichtbaren, induktiven Klangkörpern sein. Auch beim Einsatz von Licht in einem handwerklich hergestellten Produkt muss der Tischler Wissen um die dazugehörige Technik haben, damit er diese gekonnt und entsprechend der Kundenwünsche einsetzen kann. Auf dem Stand konnte die Berufsgruppe so eindrucksvoll und persönlich unter Beweis stellen, welche Kompetenzen sie in der gesamten Raum- und Objektplanung hat.

Welchen Unterschied macht es, einen Berufsverband oder ein Unternehmen zu inszenieren?

Zunächst ist ein Berufsverband gleich jedem Industriekunden, denn er muss die Marke ebenso wie ein Hersteller nach außen darstellen – auch wenn diese Marke „der Tischler" ist. In diesem Fall muss jedoch nicht nur ein Berufszweig oder eine Person, sondern eben auch die Kultur des Handwerks vermittelt werden. Das wiederum bedeutet, dass es sich um eine allgemeinere Darstellung als bei einem speziellen Produkt handelt und ich dafür eine Form entwickeln muss, die von möglichst vielen Interessenten verstanden wird. Um das zu erreichen, habe ich bei diesem Stand über die Sinneswahrnehmung argumentiert. Grundsätzlich bin ich jedoch der Ansicht, dass es wünschenswert wäre, diese Haltung auch bei Inszenierungen spezifischer Produkte anzuwenden, denn in Zukunft wird der Schwerpunkt auf der Vermittlung einer beziehungsweise unserer Kultur liegen und nicht nur auf Preis und Leistungsmerkmalen. Und dafür ist ein Kunde wie dieser Berufsverband ein sehr gutes Trainingsfeld!

⟶ **André Füsser**, Jahrgang 1961, studierte nach seiner Ausbildung zum Druckvorlagenhersteller Kommunikationsdesign an der Bergischen Universität Wuppertal bei Bazon Brock und Wolfgang Körber. Seit 1990 ist Füsser bei der Ueberholz GmbH für Entwurf und Projektleitung zuständig.

> www.ueberholz.de

The appearance of the Fachverband Tischler Nordrhein Westfalen at the imm Cologne 2016 was shaped by the slogan "We design. Personally.". What does "personally" mean for you?

"We design. Personally." is the slogan of the trade association for all public appearances and thus also the basis of our design concept for the imm Cologne. The message behind the slogan is as follows: carpenters design through their craft. Through the consultation with the customer and their requirements, it becomes personal, also in spatial terms. The associton wants to set itself apart from the furniture trade—after all the carpenter makes to measure! For me, "personally" means establishing contact to a customer and understanding all their concerns and attitudes and to respond to these, instead of representing platitudes or selling standardised design. "Personal" means "individual" in a positive sense and not "egocentric". We designers have to provide a service which helps the client!

Wood and handcrafted products made of wood—of course—play a key role in the design of the stand. And yet technical solutions were integrated into the exhibits. What was the idea behind this?

The exhibits with technical solutions show that carpenters have to handle many different tasks. If a carpenter is commissioned to build a loudspeaker it might involve making a wooden box or an individual solution with invisible, inductive resonating body. When using light in a hand-crafted product, the carpenter must also know about the related technology so that he can employ this skilfully and in line with the wishes of the customer. On the stand, the profession had the opportunity to prove in an impressive and personal way just what competencies they have in spatial and project planning.

What difference does it make if you are presenting a professional association or a company?

Initially, the professional association is just like any industrial customer as it has to present a brand just like a manufacturer—even if the brand is "the carpenter". However, in this case not only the profession or a person is being presented, but also the whole craft culture. This, in turn, means that the presentation is more general than for a specific product and I have to develop a form of expression that is understood by as many potential customers as possible. In this stand, I used sensory perception to get the message across. Generally speaking, however, I am of the opinion that it would be desirable to also apply this approach to presentation of specific products because in future the focus will be on conveying a specific culture or our culture, and not on price and product features. And a customer like this professional association is good practice!

⟶ **André Füsser**, born 1961, followed his apprenticeship in prepress production with a degree in communication design at the University of Wuppertal under Bazon Brock and Wolfgang Körber. Since 1990 Füsser has been responsible at Ueberholz GmbH for design and project management.

> www.ueberholz.de

LIFESTYLE

⟶ Die Frage, wie wir sein und zu wem wir gehören möchten, stellen wir uns vermutlich unser halbes Leben lang. Bei der Beantwortung präsentieren wir der Außenwelt vor allem unseren Lebensstil, der von der Wahl unserer Kleidung, Verhaltensweisen oder Freizeitbeschäftigungen stark gekennzeichnet ist. Unternehmen – von Modeproduzenten über Fahrradhersteller bis hin zu digitalen Musikdienstleistern – machen uns auf Messen die hierfür notwendigen Produkte und Dienstleistungen besonders schmackhaft und ermöglichen uns so, jenen Lebensstil zu zeigen, den wir bereit sind zu offenbaren. Selbstverständlich demonstrieren sie mit einer gekonnten Inszenierung zudem ihren eigenen Zeitgeist ...

⟶ We will presumably end up asking who we are and where we belong half our lives. We answer these questions above all in the way we present our lifestyle to the rest of the world and this is characterised by the clothes we choose, the way we behave and what we do in our free time. At trade fairs, companies—from fashion producers to bicycle manufacturers through to music service providers—want to make the products and services we need to do so particularly attractive, thus allowing us to demonstrate the lifestyle that we are prepared to reveal. And of course, with a skilful presentation they are also showing their own zeitgeist ...

⟶ 236

→ 220

→ 228

→ 212

,simple GmbH, Cologne
Curaden AG, Kriens
Internationale Dental-Schau (IDS) 2015, Cologne

FARBHYGIENE

Auf der Internationalen Dental-Schau (IDS) 2015 in Köln inszenierte die Kölner Agentur ,simple die Schweizer Traditionsmarke CURAPROX der Curaden AG mit einem farbigen Messestand, der sich deutlich von den anderen hygienisch-weißen Ständen abhob. Auf zwei Standflächen, die durch einen Gang getrennt wurden, präsentierten die Experten für Mundgesundheit neben Leistungen und Fabrikaten aus den Bereichen Zahnpflege und Prophylaxe einerseits den internationalen Markt und andererseits den Vertriebsbereich Deutschland, Österreich und Schweiz. Bei der Gestaltung setzte ,simple auf die Kraft der Farben, die ikonischen Zahnbürsten mit ihren expressiven Farbkombinationen sowie klaren Formen bildeten den Nukleus des Standkonzepts. Große Leuchtwände mit Produkt- und Kampagnenfotos, grafische Muster, starke Farben sowie das Herstellerlogo bildeten zudem den architektonischen Rahmen des 80 Quadratmeter großen Messestands. Farbige Bodenbeläge zonierten die Fläche nach Produktgruppen und Themen, während aufblasbare Schaumwolken den Auftritt von weitem markierten. An insgesamt fünf Showcases – zierliche Kommoden mit Waschbecken und Spiegel – konnten die Besucher schließlich Mundspülungen, elektrische Zahnbürsten sowie die schwarze Zahnpasta von Swiss Smile testen.

COLOURFUL HYGIENE

At the International Dental Show (IDS) 2015 in Cologne, the Cologne-based agency ,simple presented the time-honoured Swiss brand CURAPROX of Curaden AG with a colourful trade fair stand that was in stark contrast to all the other clinically white booths. The stand was divided into two parts, separated by an aisle. Besides showing services and products from the fields of dental care and prophylaxis, the experts for dental hygiene presented the international market on the one hand, and the sales territory Germany, Austria and Switzerland on the other. In their design, ,simple employed the power of colours; the iconic toothbrushes with their expressive combinations of colours and clear shapes formed the nucleus of the booth concept. Large illuminated walls displaying product and campaign photos, graphic patterns, vibrant colours and the manufacturer's logo also provided the architectural framework of the 80 m² trade fair stand. Coloured flooring zoned the space into product groups and themes while inflatable foam clouds made the stand easy to spot from a distance. At a total of five showcases—delicate dressing tables with wash basin and mirror—visitors could try out mouth rinses, electric toothbrushes and the black toothpaste by Swiss Smile.

Mit Bezug auf die Bürsten des Herstellers wurde der zweigeteilte Messestand von CURAPROX besonders farbig und verspielt gestaltet, wodurch sich der gesamte Auftritt deutlich von den umliegenden Ständen abheben konnte.

Making a reference to the manufacturer's brushes, CURAPROX's two-part stand was particularly colourful and playful, thus setting the whole presentation clearly apart from the surrounding booths.

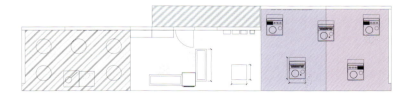
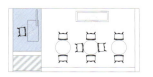

An einem Glücksrad konnten die Besucher die gesamte Produktpalette der Zahnzwischenraumbürsten begutachten, während die Farbkollektion der klassischen CURAPROX-Zahnbürste mit ausziehbaren Paletten aus Stegdoppelplatten gezeigt wurde.

Visitors could spin a wheel of fortune to examine the entire range of interdental brushes, while the colour collection of the classic CURAPROX toothbrushes was displayed in pull-out pallets made of double-walled sheets.

Size 80 m² | **Exhibitor** Curaden AG, Kriens | **Photos** Annika Feuss / Feuss Fotografie, Cologne | **Architecture / Design** ‚simple GmbH, Cologne | **Graphics** ‚simple GmbH, Cologne; Max Wettach GmbH, Kriens

ARNO Design GmbH, Munich
Messe München GmbH, Munich
INHORGENTA MUNICH 2016, Munich

ELEGANZ UND EXOTIK

Für die INHORGENTA MUNICH 2016 gestaltete ARNO Design gleich zwei Hallen und inszenierten auf rund 2.000 Quadratmetern den Glamour des roten Teppichs sowie die Eleganz Brasiliens der 1960er-Jahre. Bei der Neugestaltung der Halle A1 wurde bildlich der rote Teppich ausgerollt, damit sich jeder von seiner besten Seite zeigen konnte. Blumenbestückte Sitzmöglichkeiten in der Gangmitte sollten dabei die Messegäste sowohl zum Verweilen als auch zum Begutachten der hier inszenierten Sonderplatzierungen einladen. Einen exotischen Gegensatz bot dabei die Halle B1, die mit ihrer organischen Formensprache an Brasiliens beeindruckende Architektur und Kunst der 1960er- und 1970er-Jahre erinnern sollte. Mit Liebe zum Detail ermöglichten es die Gestalter damit, erneut die Größe und Zeitlosigkeit dieser Epoche – geprägt durch Bossa Nova, Gold, Edelsteine sowie exotische Gärten – zu genießen. Weiche Formen, die aus den berühmten Pflastersteinen der Copacabana entlehnt sind, harmonisierten mit der warmen Farbgebung, wobei mit der Gestaltung von Schaukästen und Bodenbelägen in Gold- und Bronzetönen zusätzliche Akzente geschaffen werden konnten.

Inspiriert von Oscar Niemeyer, Alexander Calder und Roberto Burle Marx verschmolzen in der Halle B1 aktuelle Farbtrends mit Gold- und Bronzetönen sowie der Schönheit der Natur zu einem charmanten Gesamtkonzept, das eine Reminiszenz an Brasiliens Kunst und Architektur der 1960er- und 1970er-Jahre darstellen sollte.

ELEGANCE AND EXOTICISM

For the INHORGENTA MUNICH 2016, ARNO Design designed two whole halls covering 2,000 m², recreating the glamour of the red carpet in one and the elegance of 1960s Brazil in the other. When redesigning Hall A1, the red carpet was metaphorically rolled out, this meant that everyone could show themselves at their best. Seating decorated with flowers in the middle of the aisle was intended to encourage them to rest a while and invite them to take a look at the special placements displayed here. In exotic contrast to this, the organic design idiom of Hall B1 was intended to remind fairgoers of Brazil's impressive architecture and art of the 1960s and 1970s. With their attention to detail, the designers allowed visitors to once again enjoy the greatness and timelessness of the era that had been shaped by the Bossa Nova, gold, precious stones and exotic gardens. Gentle forms borrowed from the Copacabana's famous cobblestones harmonised with the soft colour scheme. Display cabinets and flooring in shades of gold and bronze created additional design accents.

Inspired by Oscar Niemeyer, Alexander Calder and Roberto Burle Marx, current colour trends blended in Hall B1 with shades of gold and bronze as well as the beauty of nature to create a charming overall concept reminiscent of Brazil's art and architecture of the 1960s and 1970s.

Warm und erhaben wurden die Besucher in der Halle A1 empfangen – Bodenbelag, Sitzflächen und Deckenleuchten gestaltete ARNO Design hier als klare Referenz an den roten Teppich, woraufhin die hier ausgestellten Schmuckstücke noch mehr zum Strahlen gebracht wurden.

Visitors to Hall A1 received a warm and noble reception—flooring, seating areas and ceiling lights were designed by ARNO Design with a clear reference to the red carpet, making the pieces of jewellery on display here shine even more brightly.

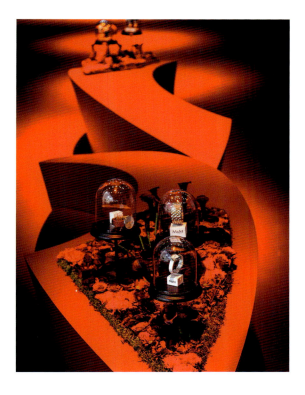

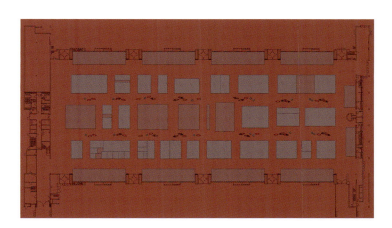

Size 2,000 m² | **Exhibitor** Messe München GmbH, Munich | **Photos** Ben Grna / ARNO Design GmbH, Munich | **Architecture / Design / Graphics / Construction** ARNO Design GmbH, Munich | **Lighting** Neumann&Müller GmbH & Co. KG, Munich

atelier 522 GmbH, Markdorf
Atomic Austria GmbH, Altenmarkt i. Pongau
ISPO MUNICH 2016, Munich

AB AUF DIE PISTE

Schlicht und geschmeidig zeigte sich der Skisportartikel-Hersteller Atomic Austria auf der ISPO MUNICH 2016. Bereits zum fünften Mal in Folge vom Markdorfer atelier 522 gestaltet entstand auf etwa 450 Quadratmetern eine große Bilderwelt in Verbindung mit verschiedenen Produktgruppen, die gut sortiert an den Wänden präsentiert wurden – und damit in ihrer Klarheit der Formensprache des Stands folgten. Die gesamte Inszenierung fiel dabei unter das Motto „#WEARESKIING" – eine groß angelegte Social-Media-Strategie, bei der nicht nur das Unternehmen selbst Bilder teilt, sondern auch Athleten und Hobbysportler einen großen Teil der weltweiten Impressionen beisteuern. Um dieser riesigen Bilderflut Herr zu werden, wurde der Auftritt durch eine großflächig angelegte Petersburger Hängung gegliedert – wobei digitale Elemente eine Einheit mit analogen Strukturen bildeten. In die Bildhängung integrierte Flat-Screen-Monitore boten neben dem Zugriff auf den digitalen Katalog unter anderem auch die Ski-Liveübertragung des Hahnenkamm-Rennens. So wurde die Community – vom Athleten über den Händler bis hin zum Fan – mit dem Hashtag #WEARESKIING gut aufgefangen und repräsentiert. Das technische Können des Herstellers wurde zudem durch eine schlichte, aber sichtbar technische Bauweise widergespiegelt, auf deren rechtwinkliger Grundstruktur klar abgegrenzte Produktbereiche entstanden. Gleichzeitig wurden auf einzelnen Wänden Zusammenstellungen von „Perfect Set-ups" gezeigt – stimmige Outfits für wintersportbegeisterte Besucher.

Mit dem Messedesign sollte die Social-Media-Kampagne „#WEARESKIING" integriert werden – eine Strategie, die auf geschickte Weise Aufmerksamkeit für die Marke erzeugt und eine gelungene Grundlage zum weiteren Generieren von Earned-, Paid- und Owned-Media-Inhalten bietet.

The trade fair stand was designed to integrate the "#WEARESKIING" social media campaign—a strategy which cleverly draws attention to the brand, providing a successful basis for the further generation of earned, paid and owned media content.

TAKE TO THE SKI LOPES

At the ISPO MUNICH 2016, the manufacturer of skiing equipment Atomic Austria was given a simple and smooth appearance. Designed for the fifth time in a row by Markdorf's atelier 522, this time they came up with a large world of images on around 450 m² combined with various product groups, the latter well arranged on the walls in line with the clear-cut design idiom of the stand. The whole production was under the slogan "#WEARESKIING"—a large-scale social media strategy in which not only the company shares images but also athletes and enthusiasts who contribute most of the impressions from around the world. To manage this enormous flood of photos, the presentation was grouped by means of a large-scale Petersburg hanging scheme in which digital elements were combined with analogue structures. Flat-screen monitors integrated in the picture hanging allowed access to the digital catalogue but also, among other things, to the live broadcast of the Hahnenkamm slalom race. In this way, the community—from athletes to dealers and fans—were captured by the hashtag #WEARESKIING and well represented. In addition, the technical competence of the manufacturer was reflected in a simple, but visibly technical construction, whose right-angled structure gave rise to clearly demarcated product areas. At the same time, some walls showed combinations of perfect set-ups for winter sport enthusiasts visiting the fair.

Durch die großangelegte Petersburger Hängung wurde die umfangreiche Bilderwelt des Messestands strukturiert, wobei das intensive Rot dem winterlichen Stand eine optisch warme Komponente gab.

The vast array of images to be seen in the booth was structured by means of a large-scale Petersburg hanging; visually, the vibrant shade of red lent the wintry stand warmth.

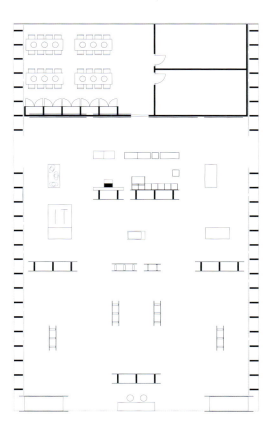

Size 445,5 m² | **Exhibitor** Atomic Austria GmbH, Altenmarkt i. Pongau | **Photos** Benedikt Decker / atelier 522 GmbH, Markdorf | **Architecture / Design** atelier 522 GmbH, Markdorf | **Graphics** Atomic Austria GmbH, Altenmarkt i. Pongau | **Construction** RUN Retail United AG, Hünenberg

b&z | Benz & Ziegler GbR, Munich
Spotify GmbH, Berlin
dmexco 2015, Cologne

LADUNGS-
IMPULS

Anlässlich der dmexco 2015 in Köln – weltweite Leitmesse und Konferenz für die digitale Wirtschaft – folgte der von Benz & Ziegler entworfene Messestand für Spotify in seiner visuellen Wirkung ganz klar der Corporate Identity des Musik-Streaming-Anbieters: Das Übereinanderschichten von Grundformen wie Dreiecken, Vierecken und Kreisen in Kombination mit einem Duoton-Farbkonzept wurde konsequent aufgegriffen und in die Architektur übersetzt. Dabei fand sich der „Burst" als expressives grafisches Element der Printkampagnen in der Standgestaltung wieder und sollte als etwas Energiegeladenes, Ungestümes beziehungsweise Aufstrebendes im Raum spürbar sein. Diese explosive Herangehensweise war bereits mit der Platzierung des 104 Quadratmeter großen Kopfstands erkennbar, der nicht einfach gerade auf das rechteckige Grundstück gesetzt wurde, sondern eine schräge Anordnung erfuhr und damit auf die Besucherströme reagierte. Neben den klaren geometrischen Formen, war vor allem die markante Farbgebung prägendes Element, denn der Farbdualismus wurde konsequent durchgespielt: aggressiv-frisch versus ruhig-entspannt. So entstanden nicht nur spannende grafische Effekte, sondern zugleich eine sinnvolle Zonierung: Weiß und Grau dienten als Basistöne, Grün und Schwarz für die Raumatmosphäre und gebaute CI, mit Flächen aus unbehandeltem Holz kam eine weiche Komponente als Akzent hinzu.

Die Formensprache der Architektur war eine räumliche Fortführung des „Burst" – ein grafisches Gestaltungselement, das Spotify in seinen Printkampagnen beziehungsweise als zentrales Element der CI verwendet. Jenes wurde nicht einfach in den Raum appliziert, sondern in der dritten Dimension weiterentwickelt und erlebbar gemacht.

The design idiom of the architecture was a spatial continuation of the "Burst"—a graphic design element that Spotify uses in its print campaigns and as a central element of its CI. And yet, it was not simply applied in the space, but represented in the third dimension and given a tangible form.

CHARGED
IMPULSES

On the occasion of the dmexco 2015 in Cologne—the world's leading trade fair and convention for the digital economy—the visual effect of the booth designed by Benz & Ziegler for Spotify very clearly mirrored the corporate identity of the music streaming provider: the layering of basic shapes like triangles, squares and circles combined with a two-tone colour scheme was systematically applied throughout and translated in the architecture. The "Burst", the expressive graphical element of the print campaign, was incorporated into the booth design and could be sensed in the space as something energy-charged, impetuous or emerging. This explosive approach was already evident from the way the 104-m² peninsula stand was positioned; it was not just simply placed on the rectangular plot but arranged at an angle in response to the flow of visitors. Besides the clear geometric shapes, the most dominant element was the striking colours. The two-tone colour scheme was rigorously applied: aggressive and fresh versus calm and relaxed. This not only produced exciting graphic effects, but at the same time provided helpful zones: white and grey were the base colours, green and black were used for the spatial atmosphere and built CI, with areas of untreated wood adding a softer touch.

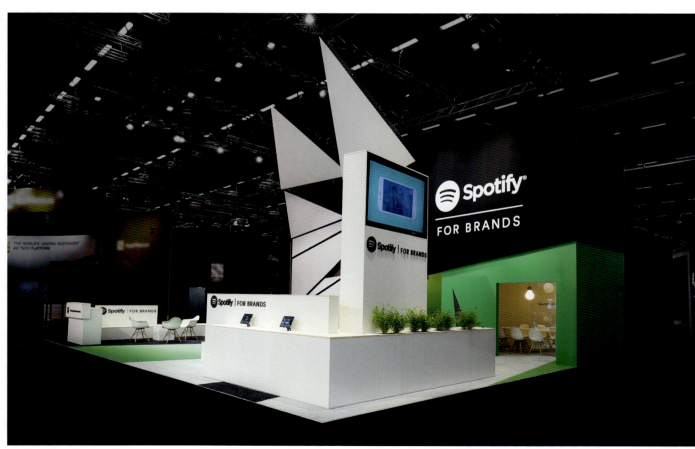

Zwischen der großen Medienfläche und den Sitzbereichen diente die gestalterische Verbindung dazu, die Blicke der Besucher auf die visuellen Informationen zu lenken ohne sie mit einer Vielzahl medialer Bespielungen zu überfordern, während mittels natürlicher Elemente die allgegenwärtige Nutzung von Musik-Streaming deutlich gemacht werden sollte.

The design created a connection between the large media wall and the seating areas which drew the attention of the visitors to the visual information without overwhelming them with a multitude of media projections. The use of natural elements was intended to make it clear just how omnipresent the use of music streaming has become.

Size 104 m² | **Exhibitor** Spotify GmbH, Berlin | **Photos** Thomas Stefan, Hamburg | **Architecture / Design** b&z | Benz & Ziegler GbR, Munich | **Construction** ATE Albersmeyer Touristik & Events e.K., Riedmoos; ESTETICO, s.r.o., Brünn

DFROST GmbH & Co. KG, Stuttgart
neubau eyewear / Silhouette International Schmied AG, Linz
opti 2016, Munich

MODERNE TRADITION

neubau eyewear, das Sublabel der Linzer Silhouette International Schmied AG, wurde auf der opti 2016 in München in einem mattschwarzen Kubus präsentiert, der aufgrund seiner Verschlossenheit die Neugier der Besucher wecken sollte. Die Gestaltung des 204 Quadratmeter großen Messestands übernahm die Stuttgarter Agentur DFROST, welche die Hommage des Herstellers an die sogenannte Millennials-Generation auf die Standfläche übertrug. Im Entree des Monoliths konnten Messegäste anhand von Collagen und Erklärungen mehr über die Traditionsmarke und deren Herkunft erfahren. Anschließend wurden sie durch einen zweiten Eingang zur eigentlichen Präsentation geführt, deren Tonalität im Kontrast zum Äußeren eher licht und hell gehalten war. Dieser Ausstellungsraum war ebenfalls zweigeteilt konzipiert und die beiden Bereiche durch eine Treppe gleichermaßen räumlich getrennt als auch verbunden: Im ersten Abschnitt, der an eine Galerie erinnerte, konnten die Besucher die Modelle in Ruhe begutachten und anprobieren, während sie im zweiten Teil bei gemütlichem Kaffeehausambiente Raum für Gespräche fanden. Genau wie die Fassade bestach auch die Innenraumgestaltung durch schlichte, rohe Materialien und individuelle Designelemente. Akzente wurden zudem durch grafische Statements gesetzt, wie zum Beispiel: „Miles away from Sacher cake."

MODERN TRADITION

neubau eyewear, the sublabel of the Linz-based Linzer Silhouette International Schmied AG, was presented at the opti 2016 in Munich in a matt-black cube, the closed sides of which were intended to arouse the curiosity of the visitors. The design of the 204 m² stand that stemmed from the Stuttgart agency DFROST transferred the homage paid by the manufacturer to the so-called millennial generation to the exhibition booth. At the entrance to the monolith, fairgoers could find out more about the long-established brand and its origins presented in the form of collages and explanations. They were then guided through a second entrance to the actual presentation whose tonality was bright and airy compared to the outside. This exhibition space was also made up of two areas, spatially divided and at the same time connected by a flight of stairs: in the first section, which was reminiscent of a gallery, visitors could examine and try on the models in peace and quiet, while in the second part there was space for discussion in a cosy, café-like atmosphere. Like the façade, the interior design impressed with its simple raw materials and individual design elements with graphic statements such as "Miles away from Sacher cake" added for effect.

Mit der Fassade des Messestands wurde kaum Einsicht ins Innere gewährt und so Neugier und Begehrlichkeit geweckt. Nur der schwebend wirkende Eingang sowie ein Ausschnitt in Form des Logos gaben Einblicke frei.

The façade of the booth allowed little insight into the interior, thus arousing curiosity and desire. Only the apparently floating entrance and a cut-out in the form of the logo allowed glimpses of the inside.

Auf der Münchner Messe entstand ein Ausstellungsraum mit Kaffeehauscharakter, der sich gleichzeitig innovativ und neu präsentierte – auch im Visual Merchandising.

At the Munich trade fair centre, an exhibition space was created which while exuding the flair of a Viennese café at the same time appeared innovative and modern—including the visual merchandising.

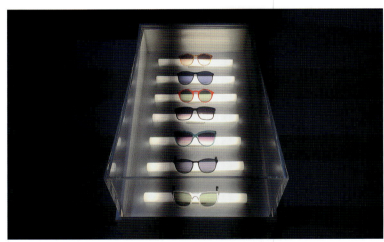

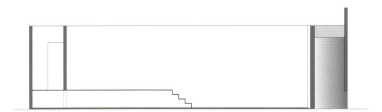

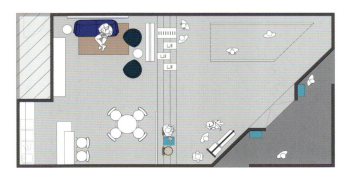

Size 204 m² | **Exhibitor** neubau eyewear / Silhouette International Schmied AG, Linz | **Photos** Duncan Longden Smith, Stuttgart | **Architecture / Design / Graphics** DFROST GmbH & Co. KG, Stuttgart | **Lighting / Construction** Raumtechnik Messebau & Event Services GmbH, Ostfildern

m|b|co Messe Bauer & Companions GmbH, Munich
K2 Sports Europe GmbH, Penzberg
ISPO MUNICH 2016, Munich

MESSEGAUDI

Der Messestand von K2 Sports Europe auf der ISPO MUNICH 2016 erinnerte nicht ohne Grund an eine Almhütte: Der Hersteller präsentierte als größte Neuerung seiner Skisparte den Skistiefel BFC (Build for Comfort), der es Trägern ermöglicht, ihre Skier wegzustellen und die Boots zur Après-Ski-Party einfach anzulassen. Diese neue Komfortdimension wollte m|b|co Messe Bauer & Companions anhand einer möglichst authentischen Skihüttenatmosphäre visualisieren – ohne dafür eine Massivholzbehausung bauen zu müssen. Stattdessen wurden bedruckte Oberflächen durch natürliche Materialien wie Echtholz oder Stein ergänzt und somit ein wirkungsvolles, plastisches Erscheinungsbild generiert. Drei Wände bildeten in dieser Form die schützende Rahmung für die traditionelle Almhüttenoptik des 374 Quadratmeter großen Messestands, auf dem die Produkte stilecht präsentiert wurden. Die skizzierten Kaminöffnungen wurden dabei genutzt, um Snowboards hängend zu inszenieren, während der Hersteller an der mit Stein verkleideten Bar inmitten der Schneesportfabrikate zu Getränken lud.

APRÉS-SKI FUN AT THE FAIR

It was no coincidence that the exhibition booth of K2 Sports Europe at the ISPO MUNICH 2016 reminded visitors of an alpine hut: The biggest innovation from their ski segment presented by the manufacturer was the BFC (Build for Comfort) ski boot, which allows the user to unfasten their skis and to simply leave the boots on for the après-ski party. m|b|co Messe Bauer & Companions wanted to visualise this new dimension of comfort by creating the atmosphere of an alpine hut as authentically as possible—but without having to build a solid wood hut. Instead, printed surfaces were supplemented with natural materials like real wood or stone, thus generating an effective and vivid appearance. Three walls of this kind formed the protective frame for the traditional alpine hut look of the 374 m² trade fair stand on which the products were presented in an authentic setting. The outlines of chimney openings were used to hang up the snowboards while the manufacturer offered drinks at the stone-clad bar amidst the snow sport products.

Hinter überzeugend bedruckten Wänden mit integrierten Holzelementen verbarg m|b|co Messe Bauer & Companions einen Messestand mit authentischem Almhüttenflair als symbolische Grundlage der innovativen Produkte des Sportartikelherstellers K2 Sports Europe.

Behind convincingly printed walls with integrated wooden elements, m|b|co Messe Bauer & Companions concealed a booth with the authentic flair of an alpine hut as the symbolic basis of the innovative products of the sports equipment manufacturer K2 Sports Europe.

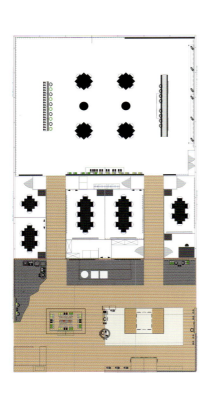

Kaminfeuer, Ledersofas und Geweihe an den teilweise bedruckten Holzwänden boten eine exzellente Grundlage für die Präsentation der neuen, für das Après-Ski geeigneten Skistiefel.

Open fire, leather sofas and antlers on the wooden and partly printed walls offered an excellent basis for the presentation of the new ski boots that are also suitable for the après ski party.

Size 374 m² | **Exhibitor** K2 Sports Europe GmbH, Penzberg | **Photos** Fotostudio Peter Schaffrath, Dusseldorf | **Architecture / Design / Lighting / Construction** m|b|co Messe Bauer & Companions GmbH, Munich | **Graphics** K2 Sports Europe GmbH, Penzberg | **Media** Imagic Productions GmbH, Taufkirchen / Vils

m|b|co Messe Bauer & Companions GmbH, Munich
Marker Völkl (International) GmbH, Baar
ISPO MUNICH 2016, Munich

GUT SORTIERT

Auf der schlichten Fassade des 656 Quadratmeter großen Messestands prangten lediglich die Logos der drei Hersteller Marker, Völkl und Dalbello, die sich auf der ISPO MUNICH 2016 gemeinsam mit der Botschaft präsentierten: „Noch bessere Technologien versprechen noch intensivere Erlebnisse". Frei nach diesem Motto konzentrierten sich die Münchner m|b|co Messe Bauer & Companions auf die Inszenierung eines funktionalen Auftritts in neutralen Farbtönen. Durch die Verwendung einer filigranen Architektur mit reduziertem Materialeinsatz wurde zudem ein einladendes und gleichzeitig technisch-präzises Ambiente geschaffen, mit dem die Aufmerksamkeit der Besucher geweckt werden sollte. Der zurückhaltende Auftritt bot den drei Herstellern viel Raum zur fokussierten Präsentation ihrer Innovationen, die so in ihrer gesamten Gestaltung und Farbgebung von den Messegästen intensiv und detailreich wahrgenommen werden konnten. Dank des klaren technischen Fokus konnten der Messestand zudem gut strukturiert sowie präzise Präsentationswände entwickelt werden. Lediglich einzelne Farbflächen nutzten die Münchner Kreativen, um Kontraste zu schaffen und die Kolorierung der gezeigten Produkte zu unterstreichen.

WELL STRUCTURED

The plain façade of the 656 m² trade fair stand only bore the logos of the three manufacturers Marker, Völkl and Dalbello, who shared a stand at the ISPO MUNICH 2016 with the common message: "Even better technologies promise even more intense experiences." Loosely interpreting this slogan, Munich-based m|b|co Messe Bauer & Companions chose to produce a functional stand in neutral colours. With delicate architecture and reduced use of materials, they created an inviting and at the same time technically precise ambiance that was designed to grab the attention of the visitors. The reserved booth offered the three manufacturers a lot of room for the focussed presentation of their innovations which fairgoers visiting the stand experienced intensively and rich in detail against the backdrop of the overall design and colour scheme. Thanks to the clear technical focus, the trade fair stand could be well structured and precise presentation walls be developed. The Munich designers worked solely with coloured surfaces to create contrasts and to underline the colouring of the products on display.

Bei dem Messestand für die drei Hersteller Marker, Völkl und Dalbello wurde der Fokus auf eine rein technische Gestaltung gelegt, um die innovativen Funktionen der Produkte in den Vordergrund zu stellen.

For the shared booth of the three manufacturers Marker, Völkl and Dalbello, the focus was placed on the pure technical design in order to showcase the innovative functions of the products.

m|b|co Messe Bauer & Companions gestalteten eine fast kühle, technisch-präzise und dabei innovativ-attraktive Atmosphäre, die durch farblich neutrale Flächen gekennzeichnet war.

m|b|co Messe Bauer & Companions designed an almost cool, technically precise and yet innovatively attractive atmosphere shaped by neutral coloured spaces.

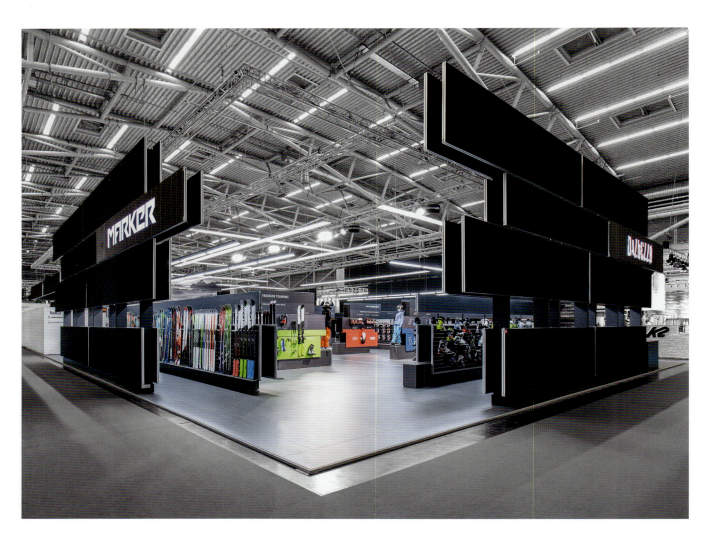

Size 656 m² | **Exhibitor** Marker Völkl (International) GmbH, Baar | **Photos** Fotostudio Peter Schaffrath, Dusseldorf | **Architecture / Design / Lighting / Construction** m|b|co Messe Bauer & Companions GmbH, Munich | **Graphics** Yearning Communications GmbH & Co. KG, Berg | **Media** Imagic Productions GmbH, Taufkirchen / Vils

Ozon. Büro für integrale Kommunikation., Munich
SRAM Europe Sales & Services BV, Nijkerk
EUROBIKE 2015, Friedrichshafen

KRAFTPAKET

Dynamisch wirkte die Architektur des Messestands von SRAM Europe Sales & Services – ein amerikanischer Fahrradkomponenten-Hersteller, dessen Auftritt auf der Friedrichshafener EUROBIKE 2015 Ozon. Büro für integrale Kommunikation. gestaltete. Um den Anspruch der Marke als „Forcemanager" zu festigen, entwickelten die Münchner Kreativen eine Architektur, die auch Ausdruck der Landschaften ist, in denen die Produkte von SRAM leben: MTB – Road – Urban. In den textilen Wand- und Deckenelementen, die in unterschiedlichen Winkeln zueinander abgehängt waren, fand sich dabei genügend Raum für Medienprojektionen, mit denen auf dem 390 Quadratmeter großen Messestand atmosphärische Welten inszeniert und die Produkte in konkreten Fahrsituationen dargestellt wurden. Diese fein abgestimmte Komposition aus Form, Farbe, großflächigen Projektionen, wechselnden Lichtstimmungen und der exklusiven Produktpräsentation vereinte die vielen verschiedenen Komponenten zu einem authentischen und unvergesslichen Markenerlebnis.

POWERHOUSE

The architecture of the trade fair stand of SRAM Europe Sales & Services—a US American manufacturer of bicycle components—whose appearance at the EUROBIKE 2015 in Friedrichshafen was designed by Ozon. Büro für integrale Kommunikation, conveyed a sense of dynamic movement. To reinforce the brand claim as "Force manager" the Munich-based designers developed an architecture, which also expressed the landscapes, in which SRAM's products are alive: MTB—Road—Urban. The textile wall and ceiling elements which were suspended at various angles to one another offered enough space for the media projections which were used to create atmospheric worlds on the 390 m² exhibition stand and to present the products in specific biking situations. This finely attuned composition of shape, colour, large-scale projections, changing light moods and the exclusive product presentation combined the many different components to form an authentic and unforgettable brand experience.

Weithin sichtbar war der rote Messestand des Fahrradkomponenten-Herstellers SRAM Europe Sales & Services, der sich sowohl durch seine expressiven Formen als auch durch die dreigeteilte Farbigkeit mit typografischen Elementen auszeichnete.

Easily visible from a distance, the red trade fair stand of bicycle component manufacturer SRAM Europe Sales & Services was characterised by expressive forms and also by the three-way colour scheme with typographical elements.

Die speziell für die Großprojektion entwickelten Filmsequenzen haben den Auftritt nicht nur emotional und inhaltlich aufgeladen, sondern auch einen direkten Kontext zwischen Produkten, Lebenswelten und Markenversprechen hergestellt.

The various film sequences, which were developed for the large projection, not only charged the stand both emotionally and in terms of content, but also created a direct association between products, living environments and brand promises.

Size 390 m² | **Exhibitor** SRAM Europe Sales & Services BV, Nijkerk | **Photos** Ozon. Büro für integrale Kommunikation., Munich | **Architecture / Design / Graphics / Media** Ozon. Büro für integrale Kommunikation., Munich | **Lighting** Ozon. Büro für integrale Kommunikation., Munich; MDS PAtec Veranstaltungstechnik GmbH, Munich | **Construction** artefakt Offenbach, Offenbach a. Main | **Textile Architecture** PARZINGER – TEXTILES BAUEN GmbH, Höslwang

Schmidhuber Brand Experience GmbH, Munich; Milla & Partner GmbH, Stuttgart
Bundesministerium für Wirtschaft und Energie, Berlin
Expo Milano 2015, Milan

WACHSEN UND GEDEIHEN

Unter dem Motto „Fields of Ideas" inszenierte SCHMIDHUBER gemeinsam mit Milla & Partner den Deutschen Pavillon auf der Expo Milano 2015. Die Gestaltung der 2.930 Quadratmeter großen Fläche will Antworten auf die zukünftigen, großen Herausforderungen der Welternährung geben – das übergreifende Leitmotiv der Expo. Dementsprechend griffen SCHMIDHUBER mit der Architektur die deutsche Feld- und Flurlandschaft in stilisierter Form auf und es entstand ein Gebäude als sanft ansteigende Landschaftsebene mit einer Themenausstellung im Inneren. Auf der frei begehbaren Ebene erinnerten Holzflächen aus verschiedenfarbigen heimischen Hölzern an die für Deutschland typische, parzellierte Landschaftsstruktur. Zentrales Gestaltungselement des Pavillons waren zudem stilisierte Pflanzen, die als „Ideen-Keimlinge" aus der Ausstellung an die Oberfläche wuchsen und ein großes Blätterdach entfalteten – als Verbindung zwischen Innen und Außen, Ausstellung und Architektur. Die Präsentation im Inneren, für die Milla & Partner verantwortlich zeichnete, erkundeten die Besucher entlang eines Wegs, der thematisch durch das „Erdreich" als wesentliche Quelle unserer Ernährung hoch in die urbane Welt führte. Im Mittelpunkt standen eine starke Umweltpolitik, innovative Unternehmen und Forschungsprojekte wie auch eine engagierte Zivilgesellschaft. Die Besucher entdeckten die Lebensmittelvielfalt aus Deutschland und deren Herstellung, lernten aber auch die Kehrseiten des Konsums kennen. Dabei wurden sie in die Ausstellung eingebunden: Mit dem „SeedBoard" – einem mobilen Interaktionsfeld aus Pappe – konnten Exponate gesteuert und je nach Interesse vertiefende Medieninhalte abgerufen werden.

Der Deutsche Pavillon diente zur Repräsentation einer klaren Haltung zum Expo-Thema „Feeding the Planet, Energy for Life", wobei Aspekte wie der wertschätzende Umgang mit der Natur ebenso greifbar wurden wie ein authentisches und einladendes Bild von Deutschland.

GROWING AND FLOURISHING

Under the tagline "Fields of Ideas", SCHMIDHUBER in collaboration with Milla & Partner designed the German Pavilion at the Expo Milano 2015. The design of the 2,930 m² space was shaped by the themes environmental policy, research and nutrition of the future—the overarching leitmotif of the Expo. Accordingly, SCHMIDHUBER picked up Germany's open field structure in the architecture in a stylised form. The result was a building with a gently sloping landscape level and a themed exhibition on the inside. On the freely accessible level, wooden surfaces of different coloured native woods were reminiscent of the landscape structure made up of parcels of land so typical for Germany. Another central design element of the pavilion were stylised plants which grew as "idea seedlings" out of the exhibition to the surface and spread into a huge roof of leaves—as the link between the interior and exterior, between exhibition and architecture. The interior exhibition, for which Milla & Partner was responsible, guided visitors along a path leading thematically through the "soil" as the main source of our nutrition upwards into the urban world. Central themes included a strong environmental policy, innovative companies and research projects as well as an engaged society. Visitors discovered the wide variety of foodstuffs in Germany and their production, learned about the downside of consumption. They were also actively involved in the exhibition: with the "SeedBoard"—a mobile interaction field made of a cardboard—exhibits could be controlled and, depending on the interests of the visitors, more in-depth media content could be retrieved.

The German Pavilion took a clear stance on the topic "Feeding the Planet, Energy for Life", making aspects such as respectful treatment of nature more easily accessible and painting an authentic and inviting image of Germany.

Das Konzept für den Deutschen Pavillon „Fields of Ideas" zeichnete sich durch eine besondere Verzahnung von räumlicher und inhaltlicher Präsentation aus: Wie Keimlinge entfalteten sich Ideen aus dem Inneren und wuchsen als ein großes Blätterdach an die Oberfläche.

The concept for the German Pavilion "Fields of Ideas" was characterised by a special interlinking of spatial and content presentation: like seedlings, ideas developed from the interior and grew up to the surface where they formed a large roof of leaves.

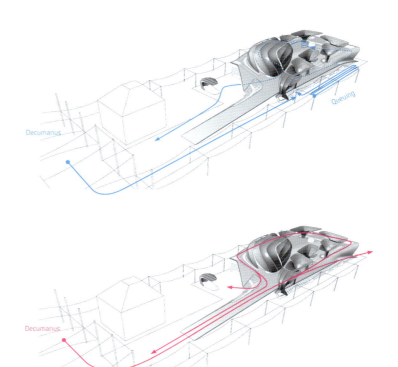

Das „SeedBoard" selbst enthielt keinerlei Elektronik oder Technologie, konnte aber zur Steuerung verschiedenster interaktiver Medienprojektionen genutzt werden. So erhielt jeder Besucher sein eigenes „Feld der Ideen".

The "SeedBoard" itself did not contain electronics or technology of any kind, but could nevertheless be used to control all different kinds of interactive media projections. In this way, every visitor obtained his own "Field of Ideas".

Size 2,930 m² | **Exhibitor** Bundesministerium für Wirtschaft und Energie (BMWi), Berlin | **Photos** Andreas Keller Fotografie, Altdorf | | **Management Company** Messe Frankfurt GmbH, Frankfurt a. Main **Architecture / Design** Schmidhuber Brand Experience GmbH, Munich; Milla & Partner GmbH, Stuttgart | **Construction** Nüssli (Deutschland) GmbH, Roth

LIGHTING

⟶ Licht ist – kurz gefasst – der für das Auge sichtbare Teil der elektromagnetischen Strahlung und damit eines der wichtigsten physikalischen Phänomene unserer Welt. Die wissenschaftliche Erklärung kann jedoch kaum die emotionale Wirkung von Licht und Schatten auf uns beschreiben: Es erzeugt Stimmungen und Atmosphären, verleiht Orientierung und dient als architektonisches Werkzeug. Kein Wunder also, dass Leuchtenhersteller auf ihren Messeständen ihre vielfältigen Kompetenzen – von der Gestaltung der Leuchten bis hin zu technologischen Höchstleistungen – mit allen ihnen zur Verfügung stehenden Komponenten ins rechte Licht rücken können.

⟶ Light is—in a nutshell—the visible portion of the electromagnetic spectrum and thus one of the world's most important physical phenomenon. The scientific explanation cannot, however, describe the emotional effect that light and shadow have on us: It creates moods and atmospheres, provides orientation and serves as a architectural tool. It is hardly surprising, therefore, that in their trade fair stands manufacturers of lights want to shed the best possible light on their multifaceted competences—from the design of lamps through to outstanding technological achievements—using all the components at their disposal.

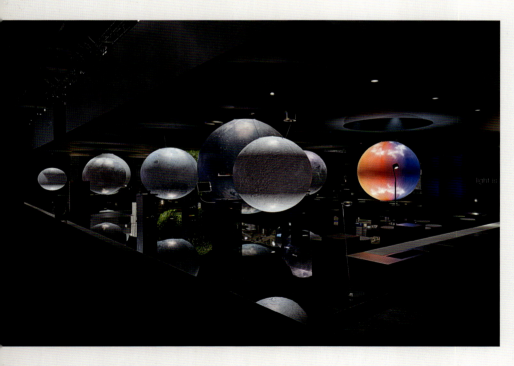

→ 282

→ 258

→ 228

Atelier Bernd Steinhuber, Vienna
Wever & Ducré bvba, Roeselare
Light + Building 2016, Frankfurt a. Main

(IM-)PROVI-SORIUM

„Wenn ein Produkt wirklich gut ist, braucht es keinen Schnickschnack – erst recht nicht, um es zu präsentieren." Dies war zumindest die Meinung des Wiener Architekten und Designers Bernd Steinhuber als er den 280 Quadratmeter großen Auftritt für Wever & Ducré auf der Light + Building 2016 in Frankfurt plante. Und das Ergebnis kann sich durchaus sehen lassen. Ergeben hat sich ein Messestand, der kreativ, unkonventionell und ein bisschen verrückt ist – genau wie Wever & Ducré. Spontan zusammengestellt aus einem Baugerüst und zwei Wänden, jeder Menge Kisten und ein paar bequemen Polstern ließen sich die Produkte des belgischen Herstellers von Leuchten harmonisch in die auffallende Raumgestaltung integrieren – sowohl die technischen Leuchten, die in Betonoptikboxen ausgestellt waren, als auch die Pendelleuchtenserien, die frei in den Gerüsten hingen. Weiterer Blickfang war zudem ein 72 Quadratmeter großes Kunstwerk, das der Street-Art-Künstler Knarf während der Messezeit live hinter der Bar entstehen ließ.

Dank der warmen Lichtfarbe am Stand, der langen Bar und den Lederkissen im Lounge-Bereich wirkte der Messestand sehr einladend. Abends ließen viele Besucher den Tag bis Messeschluss bei dem einen oder anderen belgischen Bier und Lounge-Musik gemütlich ausklingen.

IMPROVISED

"A really good product does not need any bells and whistles—particularly not to present it." This at least was the opinion of Viennese architect and designer Bernd Steinhuber when he was planning the 280 m² stand for Wever & Ducré at the Light + Building 2016 in Frankfurt. And the result was pretty impressive. The booth that he created is creative, unconventional and a bit crazy—just like Wever & Ducré. Spontaneously put together from scaffolding, a pile of boxes and a few comfy cushions, the products of the Belgian lighting manufacturer were integrated harmoniously into the remarkable spatial design—both the technical luminaires, which were exhibited in concrete optics boxes, as well as the hanging lamp series, which were freely suspended in the scaffolding. Another eye-catcher was a 72 m² work of art which the street artist Knarf created behind the bar during the fair.

Thanks to the warm colour of the stand lighting, the long bar and the leather cushions in the lounge area the booth was very welcoming. At the end of the trade fair day, many visitors whiled the evening away until closing hours over a beer or two and some lounge music.

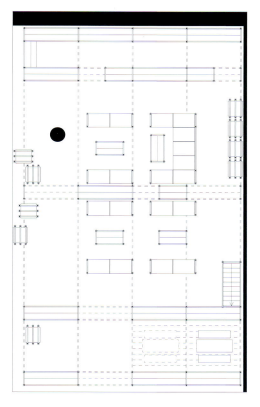

Hinter der Bar entwickelte der Street-Art-Künstler Knarf über die Messezeit ein Kunstwerk, wodurch er sowohl die künstlerische Komponente der Ausstellungsstücke betonte, als auch die urbane Stimmung auf dem Stand unterstrich.

Behind the bar, street artist Knarf was creating a work of art for the duration of the trade fair. This emphasised the artistic aspect of the exhibits and also the urban vibe of the stand.

Size 280 m² | **Exhibitor** Wever & Ducré bvba, Roeselare | **Photos** Paul Ott, Graz | **Architecture / Design** Atelier Bernd Steinhuber, Vienna | **Graphics / Lighting** Wever & Ducré bvba, Roeselare | **Construction** X-TEC GmbH, St. Margarethen a. d. Raab

INTERVIEW BERND STEINHUBER (ATELIER BERND STEINHUBER)

Ihre Inszenierung für Wever & Ducré auf der Light + Building 2016 bestach durch außergewöhnliche, improvisiert wirkende Akzente – wie die Konstruktion aus Baugerüsten und Kisten – und stand damit im Gegensatz zu vielen umliegenden "cleanen" Standarchitekturen. Sehen Sie darin eine Entwicklung hin zum Handgemachten, zum Unfertigen?

Tatsächlich sehe ich zukünftig eine Entwicklung in diese Richtung und es gibt viele Marken, die sich „atypisch" zeigen könnten, jedoch fehlt noch – sowohl von Unternehmern als auch von Gestaltern – der Mut zu diesem Schritt. Allerdings bin ich sicher, dass dieser mit jedem gelungenen Beispiel größer wird! Zudem sehe ich auch die Notwendigkeit zu einer solchen Inszenierung, um sich als Marke in der Bilderflut an Ähnlichem nicht zu verlieren. Dabei ist „unfertig und handgemacht" aber nur eine Strategie von vielen – wenn auch eine sehr wirkungsvolle und noch dazu kostenschonende!

Bei dieser Präsentation stellt sich unweigerlich die Frage, ob auch der Aufbau Handarbeit war?

Handarbeit war für uns ein zentrales Thema! Da ausgewählte Objektleuchten von Wever & Ducré in Handarbeit gefertigt werden, haben wir nach einem Stilmittel gesucht, mit dem wir den Bogen zum Produkt spannen können. Gleichzeitig wollten wir einen gestalterischen Gegenpol, der diametral in eine andere Richtung zeigt: Wir wollten etwas Industrielles, Vorgefertigtes, Systematisches. In Summe sollte daraus etwas entstehen, das selbstverständlich, situativ, faszinierend und gleichzeitig unterhaltend für die Besucher ist. Genau diese Selbstverständlichkeit konnten wir durch das Baugerüst erreichen. Zum einen wurde es seinem eigentlichen Zweck entsprechend verwendet – nämlich hoch oben liegende Wandflächen zu erreichen – zum anderen wurde es zum Regal für die Leuchten, und ganz neue, räumliche Nutzungsmöglichkeiten konnten so entstehen.

Zum Beispiel der bauliche Rahmen für ein Kunstwerk: Der österreichische Street-Art-Künstler Knarf trug über die gesamte Laufzeit der Messe ein zwölf auf sechs Meter großes Bild auf eine Wand innerhalb der Gerüststruktur auf – selbstverständlich in Handarbeit. Dabei war die einzige Vorgabe des Auftraggebers, den Claim „from belgium with love" einzubeziehen. Marken können sich selbst als kreativ beschreiben oder kreative Dinge tun, wobei sie zu tun weit mehr Sinn ergibt …

Durch das Kunstwerk, das während der Messe fertiggestellt wurde, veränderte sich auch der Stand kontinuierlich. Wie kam es zu dieser dynamischen Inszenierung und wie hat sie sich entwickelt? Was waren die Herausforderungen?

Die größte Herausforderung war, überhaupt einen Street-Art-Künstler zu finden, der mit dem Pinsel malt. Denn vom Sprayen war das Messebüro – wen wundert's – nicht so begeistert. Nein, ganz im Ernst: Die eigentliche Herausforderung war, die gesamte Geschichte um diesen Auftritt zu erzählen: Knarf hatte im Auftrag von Wever & Ducré anlässlich der Art Basel in Miami einen ersten Teaser für die Marke geschaffen, indem er ein ganz ähnliches Werk in den öffentlichen Raum gebracht hat. Fotos dieser künstlerischen Intervention wurden dann auch noch als aktuelles Katalogcover des Unternehmens genutzt. So wurde daraus eine Erzählung in Bildern und Medien – und zwar vor, während und nach der Messe. Dies entspricht eben genau unseren Vorstellungen, denn wir verstehen Messestände als ein Kommunikationswerkzeug, das nicht nur als „schönes Foto" verwendbar sein soll. Sofern die Strategie stimmt, entstehen gerade durch die sozialen Netzwerke großartige Möglichkeiten, die Menschen an der richtigen Stelle abzuholen – und das weit über die wenigen Messetage hinaus. Diese Vorgehensweise haben wir zwar nicht erfunden, aber wir nutzen sie!

⟶ **Bernd Steinhuber**, Jahrgang 1972, studierte zunächst Architektur an der TU Graz, bevor er gemeinsam mit Martin Lesjak, Andreas Reiter und Peter Schwaiger 1999 das Architekturbüro INNOCAD in Graz gründete. Seit 2009 existiert nun sein eigenes Atelier, wo er sich gleichwohl mit Produkten, Grafik und (Innen-) Architektur auseinandersetzt.

> www.berndsteinhuber.com

Your stand for Wever & Ducré's appearance at the Light + Building 2016 impressed with its extraordinary, seemingly improvised touches—such as the construction of scaffolding and boxes—and was thus in stark contrast to many of the "clean" stand architectures surrounding it. Do you see a trend towards the self-made and unpolished?

I do indeed see a development in this direction in future and there are many brands which could show themselves in an "atypical" way, but at the moment both the companies themselves and the designers don't quite have the courage to take this step. However, I am sure that with every successful example it will grow. Moreover, I also see a need for such presentations so that brands don't lose themselves in the flood of similar images. Having said that, "unpolished and self-made" is just one of many strategies—albeit a very effective and, what is more, a cost-saving one!

This presentation raises the question whether the build was also done "by hand"?

Handiwork was a central them for us. As selected architectural lamps by Wever & Ducré are made by hand, we were looking for a stylistic device with which we could establish a link to the product. At the same time, we wanted a design counterpoint which pointed diametrically in another direction: We wanted something industrial, prefabricated, systematic. The result in sum should be self-evident, situational, fascinating and at the same time entertaining for the visitors. We were able to achieve this self-evidence with the scaffolding. For one thing, it was used for its actual purpose—namely to reach high wall surfaces—for another it became a shelf for the lamps, and completely new, spatial usages were created.

For example, the structural framework for a work of art: for the entire duration of the fair, the Austrian street artist Knarf applied a twelve-by-six metre painting to a wall within the scaffolding structure—by hand, of course. The only requirement of the client was to incorporate the claim "from Belgium with love". Brands can describe themselves as creative or do creative things, and doing them makes much more sense...

Through the work of art that was completed during the trade fair, the stand was constantly changing. How did this dynamic presentation come about and how did it develop? What were the challenges?

The biggest challenge was to find a street artist who paints with a paintbrush. Understandably, the exhibition office was not so enthused about the idea of sprayers. No, seriously: The actual challenge was to tell the whole story around this appearance: Wever & Ducré commissioned Knarf to create a first teaser for the brand at the Art Basel in Miami, by presenting a very similar work in a public space. Photos of this artistic intervention were then also used on the cover of the company's current catalogue. In this way, it became a narrative in images and media—before, during and after the fair. This is exactly in line with our ideas because we understand trade fair stands as a communication tool that should be more than just a "pretty photo". If the strategy works, the social networks offer fantastic opportunities to reach people in exactly the right spot—even a long time after the few days of the trade fair. We didn't invent this approach, but we are certainly making use of it!

⟶ **Bernd Steinhuber**, born 1972, initially studied architecture at the University of Applied Sciences Graz, before teaming up with Martin Lesjak, Andreas Reiter and Peter Schwaiger in 1999 to found the architects' office INNOCAD in Graz. He has had his own studio since 2009 where his work is divided up between products, graphics, (interior) architecture.

> www.berndsteinhuber.com

Atelier Bernd Steinhuber, Vienna
XAL GmbH, Graz
Light + Building 2016, Frankfurt a. Main

STRAHLKRAFT

Der österreichische Leuchtenhersteller XAL demonstrierte auf der Light + Building 2016, was technisches Licht heute leisten kann: Smart, vernetzt, miniaturisiert und flexibel werden Räume den jeweilgen Nutzeranforderungen entsprechend inszeniert. Unter dem Motto „See the Light" gestaltete das Wiener Atelier Bernd Steinhuber dementsprechend einen mattschwarzen Monolith, der den Besuchern durch 428 kreisrunde Öffnungen Einblicke in die Zukunft des Lichts gewährte. Überdimensionale, sieben Meter hohe Eingangsportale aus Eichenholz sollten zudem Offenheit und Gastfreundschaft signalisieren. Im Zentrum des 726 Quadratmeter großen Messestands, abgeschirmt vom Messetrubel, tauchten die Gäste schließlich in das XAL-Lichttheater ein. Der großzügige, puristische Raum diente dank Bar und runden Sitz-Lounges dabei nicht nur als Ort der Kommunikation, sondern auch als Ort des Staunens: Vorprogrammierte Lichtszenen versetzten den Raum in wechselnde Stimmungen. Über 250 XAL-Leuchten und -Strahler, die über die gesamte Deckenfläche verteilt waren, inszenierten ein Wechselspiel aus ruhigen Lichtwellen und pointierten Akzenten – von dunklen bis hin zu strahlend hellen. Zu jeder vollen Stunde verwandelte die „360° SEE THE LIGHT SHOW" den Raum zudem in ein immersives Erlebnis: Die Vorhänge schlossen sich, das Licht ging aus und eine beeindruckende Show begann, mit der die Gäste zu zufälligen Schauspielern wurden und mit allen Sinnen Licht als Inspirationsquelle erleben konnten.

428 kreisrunde Öffnungen waren in die mattschwarze Alucobond-Fassade eingearbeitet. Sie dienten als Schaufenster und erlaubten den Besuchern Einblicke in die Zukunft des Lichts. Unmittelbar dahinter waren die Exponate direkt erleb- sowie (be-)greifbar.

428 circular openings were integrated in the matt-black Alucobond façade. They served as shop windows and allowed visitors a glimpse of the future of light. Directly behind that, the exhibits could be experienced and touched.

RADIANCE

At the Light + Building 2016, the Austrian lighting manufacturer XAL demonstrated what technical light can do these days: smart, connected, miniaturised and flexible—rooms can be precisely equipped to meet the requirements of the user. Under the slogan "See the Light", the Vienna-based Atelier Bernd Steinhuber designed a matt-black monolith that allowed visitors to look into the future of light through 428 circular openings. Oversized, seven-metre high entrance gates made of oak were intended to signal openness and hospitality. At the centre of the 726 m² booth, shielded from the hustle and bustle of the fair, the guests were finally submerged in the XAL light theatre. Thanks to the bar and round seating lounge, the generous, puristic room served as a place for communication. But it was also a place for amazement: programmed light scenes immersed the room in changing moods. More than 250 XAL lamps and spotlights spread over the entire ceiling produced an interplay of quiet light waves and expressive highlights—from dark to bright and radiant. Once an hour, on the hour the "360° SEE THE LIGHT SHOW" transformed the room into an immersive experience: the curtains closed, the lights were dimmed and an impressive show commenced in which the guests unwittingly became actors and were able to experience with all their senses light as a source of inspiration.

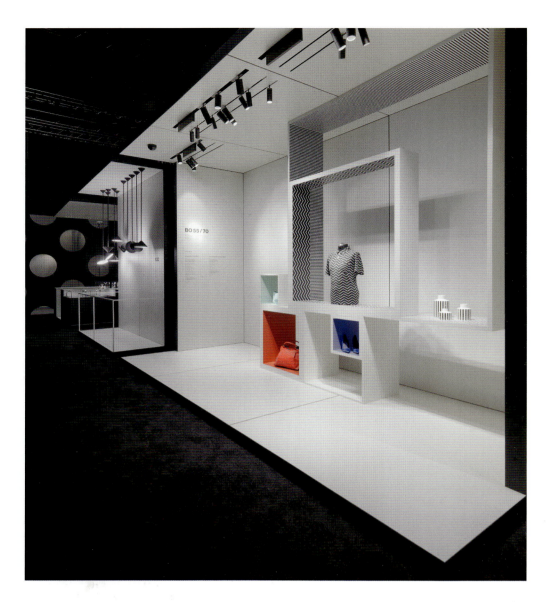
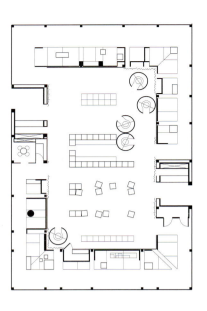

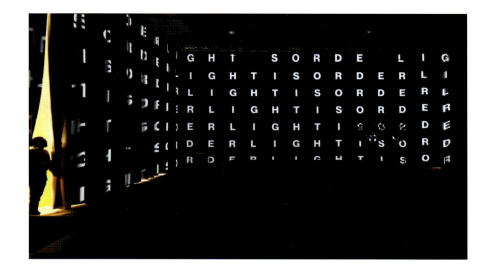

Stündlich wurde mit zehn Projektoren vier Minuten lang das Lichttheater in ein immersives Raumerlebnis verwandelt. Geometrische Formen und Lichtreflektionen waren dabei sowohl auf die sechs Meter hohe Innenfassade als auch auf die Besucher projiziert, die damit zu zufälligen Akteuren wurden.

Once an hour, the light theatre was plunged with the help of ten projectors into a 4-minute immersive spatial experience. Geometrical shapes and light reflections were projected both on the six-metre high interior façade and onto the visitors who thus became part of the show.

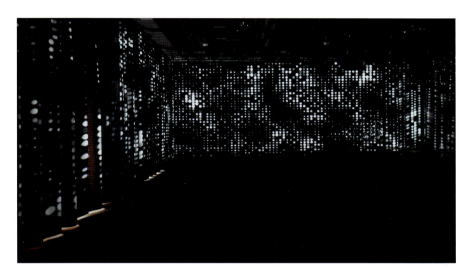

Size 726 m² | **Exhibitor** XAL GmbH, Graz | **Photos** Paul Ott, Graz | **Architecture / Design** Atelier Bernd Steinhuber, Vienna | **Graphics** Atelier Bernd Steinhuber with superplus, Vienna | **Lighting** XAL GmbH, Graz | **Construction** X-TEC GmbH, St. Margarethen a. d. Raab

BachmannKern & Partner, Solingen
OSRAM Opto Semiconductors GmbH, Regensburg
Light + Building 2016, Frankfurt a. Main

IN FORM GEFALTET

OSRAM Opto Semiconductors begrüßte die Besucher der Frankfurter Light + Building 2016 mit einem massiven, weißen Kubus. Jener war in asymmetrische Flächen zerschnitten sowie in ungleiche Winkel verdreht und gefaltet, sodass ein polygonaler Körper entstand, dessen Falze von Innen warm erleuchtet waren. Gestaltet wurde dieser Blickfang von BachmannKern & Partner, die sich dabei am neu entwickelten und auf der Messe erstmalig präsentierten „TEN°-Binning Feature" orientierten – einem erhöhten Farbraum von weißen LEDs. Mittels großflächiger Typografie wurde schon von weitem auf die drei Kernthemen „More Efficiency", „More Quality" und „More Flexibility" aufmerksam gemacht. Im Innenraum des Kubus erwartete die Besucher eine Bar mit Kommunikationsbereich sowie Produktinszenierungen zu jenen Kernthemen und der TEN°-Binning-Methode. Zentrales visuelles Element auf der 180 Quadratmeter großen Standfläche war jedoch die mediale Bespielung von Fußboden und LED-Videowand, die ineinander übergingen. Hier konnten die Besucher Filme und Animationen betrachten, wobei sie diese mit den eigenen Bewegungen auf dem drucksensitiven Fußboden selbst steuerten.

FOLDED INTO SHAPE

OSRAM Opto Semiconductors welcomed visitors to the Frankfurt Light + Building 2016 with a solid, white cube. This was cut up into asymmetrical areas and rotated and folded at unequal angles to produce a polygonal object whose folds were warmly lit from the inside. This eyecatcher was designed by BachmannKern & Partner, who were guided in their design by the newly developed "TEN° binning feature"—an enhanced colour space of white LEDs. By means of large-scale typography, attention was drawn from afar to the three core topics: "More Efficiency", "More Quality" and "More Flexibility". Inside the cube, visitors found a bar with communication zone as well as product presentations on these core topics and the TEN° binning method. However, the central visual of the 180 m² stand were the projections on the LED video wall and continued along the floor. Visitors could watch films and animations, or even control them themselves with their own movements on the pressure-sensitive floor.

Durch die ungewöhnliche Form und deren Beleuchtung erregte der gefaltete, polygonale Kubus weithin die Aufmerksamkeit der Besucher. Für diesen Effekt gestalteten BachmannKern & Partner im Inneren einen interaktiven LED-Screen an Wand und Boden.

The unusual form and illumination of the folded, polygonal cube attracted the attention of the visitors from a distance. To achieve this effect, BachmannKern & Partner created an interactive LED screen on the interior walls and floor.

Sich aus der Decke lösende, kreisrunde Scheiben inszenierten als Eyecatcher die 10°-Binning-Technologie, mit der weiße LEDs genauer selektiert werden können – erheblich näher an der physiologischen Farbwahrnehmung als bisher.

As an impressive spatial installation, circular discs emerging from the ceiling presented the 10° Binning technology which allows white LEDs to be selected more precisely—far closer to the physiological colour perception than was possible to date.

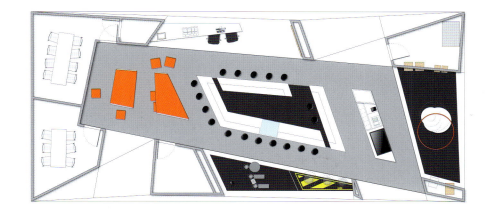

Size 180 m² | **Exhibitor** OSRAM Opto Semiconductors GmbH, Regensburg | **Photos** Frank Dora / photoprop, Wuppertal | **Architecture / Design / Graphics** BachmannKern & Partner, Solingen | **Lighting** OSRAM Opto Semiconductors GmbH, Regensburg | **Media** Innlights c/o TRENDCARD GmbH, Wuppertal | **Construction** Manuel de la Rosa GmbH, Rosbach

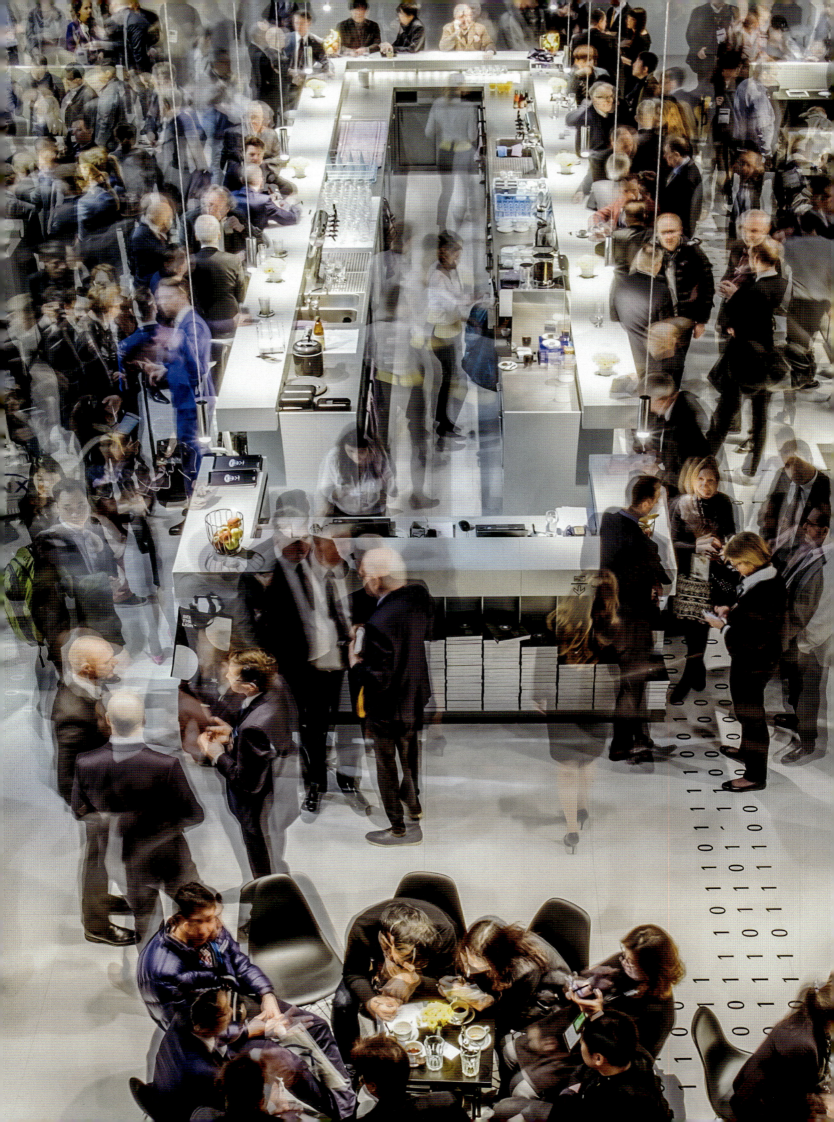

ERCO GmbH, Lüdenscheid
ERCO GmbH, Lüdenscheid
Light + Building 2016, Frankfurt a. Main

LICHT UND LINSEN

Auf dem 495 Quadratmeter großen Messestand präsentierte der Lüdenscheider Spezialist für Architekturbeleuchtung mit LED-Technologie ERCO auf der Light + Building 2016 sein Produktportfolio in den Bereichen Work, Culture, Shop und Community unter dem Motto „light digital", um die konsequente und frühe Umstellung des Unternehmens auf LED-Technologie aufzugreifen. Dabei führte der Messestand die Tradition bisheriger ERCO-Auftritte fort: Zwischen zwei raumhohen Bauten an den Schmalseiten entfaltete sich ein offener und großzügiger Bereich. Neu war die grafische Gestaltung einer geradlinigen Schwarz-Weiß-Ästhetik, welche die thematische Dualität zwischen technisch und kreativ orientierter Lichtplanung spiegelte. Während sich der in Weiß gehaltene Abschnitt aus Produkttischen und Mock-up-Raum technologischen Themen widmete, diente der in Schwarz gestaltete Bereich aus Präsentationstischen und einer Lounge mit Multimediawand als vielfältige Inspirationsquelle. Auch die Lichtfarben waren auf das dual angelegte Standkonzept abgestimmt: dynamisch und zukunftsgewandt anmutendes neutralweißes Licht für das Themengebiet „Technologie", angenehm warmweißes Licht für das Themengebiet „Anwendungen" – wobei beide Bereiche durch eine Bodengrafik wieder visuell miteinander verbunden waren.

LIGHT AND CANDY

On ERCO's 495 m² stand at the Light + Building 2016, the specialist from Lüdenscheid for architectural lighting with LED technology presented their product portfolio in the segments Work, Culture, Shop and Community. Under the tagline "light digital", they wanted to draw attention to company's rigorous and early changeover to LED technology. The booth continued the tradition of previous ERCO presentations: Between two floor-to-ceiling structures at the narrow sides of the stand there emerged an open and generously dimensioned space. What was new was the graphic design of a simple black-and-white aesthetic which reflected the thematic duality between technical and creative lighting planning. While the white zone consisting of product tables and mock-up room was devoted to technical topics, the black zone consisting of presentation tables and a lounge with multimedia wall was designed as a diverse source of inspiration. The light colours were also aligned with the dual stand concept: neutral white light gave the "Technology" themed area a dynamic and forward-looking feel, while the "Applications" area was bathed in pleasantly warm-white light. The two areas were, however, visually reunited by floor graphics.

Die thematische Dualität zwischen technisch und kreativ orientierter Lichtplanung wurde durch eine geteilte Lichtstimmung unterstrichen. Neutrales Weiß beleuchtete den Technik-, warmes Weiß den Anwendungsbereich.

The thematic duality between technical and creatively oriented lighting planning was underlined by separate light moods. Neutral white light illuminated the technology section, warm white light the application section.

An der Außenseite des Messestands wurden mithilfe von wandhohen Glaszylindern – gefüllt mit Schokolinsen – die acht Anwendungsbereiche von ERCO evaluiert. Je nach Arbeitsbereich der Besucher leerten sich die Behälter und zurück blieb ein Säulendiagramm mit dem Ergebnis der Befragung.

On the outer edge of the booth, tall glass cylinders—each filled with sugar-coated chocolate candy—were used to evaluate the eight application areas of ERCO. The containers were emptied as visitors took sweets from the cylinder representing their sphere of work. What was left was a bar chart visualising the results of the survey.

Size 495 m² | **Exhibitor** ERCO GmbH, Lüdenscheid | **Photos** Sebastian Mayer / AEIOU, Berlin | **Architecture / Design / Lighting** ERCO GmbH, Lüdenscheid | **Graphics** Oliver Zink / zink-projects communication GmbH, Cologne | **Media** Axel Groß / Electric Gobo, Berlin | **Construction** b+s exhibitions GmbH, Dusseldorf

Martin et Karczinski GmbH, Munich
Occhio GmbH, Munich
Light + Building 2016, Frankfurt a. Main

UNIVERSUM DES LICHTS

Alle zwei Jahre interpretiert Occhio, Marktführer im Bereich hochwertiger Designleuchten, auf der Weltleitmesse für Licht und Gebäudetechnik, der Light + Building, seinen Markenkern „light is evolution" neu. Der von der Münchner Agentur Martin et Karczinski entwickelte Auftritt 2016 stand ganz unter dem Motto „THE UNIVERSE". Planeten, die im Occhio Universum schweben, stehen dabei für Innovationen in Sachen Produkt, Design und Technologie – und somit für die Zukunft des Lichts bei Occhio. Insgesamt elf Planeten thematisieren die Zukunftsvisionen von Occhio und führen den Besucher anhand digitaler „space stations" über den eindrucksvollen, mehr als 400 Quadratmeter großen Stand. Fünf dieser Himmelskörper repräsentieren das zukünftige und umfassend erweiterte Produktportfolio, sechs weitere stellen besondere Features von Occhio vor, zum Beispiel die Occhio air App für die Bluetooth-basierte Steuerung von Leuchten oder die von Occhio entwickelte innovative Hochvolt-LED. So erschließt sich das einzigartige Universum an Anwendungsmöglichkeiten von Occhio für den Endverbraucher und den professionellen Anwender.

„THE UNIVERSE" transportiert die übergreifende Philosophie Occhios. Gleichzeitig steht jeder Planet des Universums für Innovationen in Produkt, Design und Technologie. Konsequenterweise zeigt sich Axel Meise, Firmengründer und CEO, im Raumanzug.

"THE UNIVERSE" transports the overarching philosophy of Occhio. At the same time, each planet in the universe stands for innovation in products, design and technology. Logically, Axel Meise, the founder of the firm and CEO, appeared in a spacesuit.

UNIVERSE OF LIGHT

Every two years, Occhio, market leader in the field of high-quality design lights, reinterprets its brand core "light is evolution" anew at the world's leading fair for light and building technology, Light + Building. The appearance at the 2016 fair developed by Munich-based agency Martin et Karczinski was themed "THE UNIVERSE". The planets floating in the Occhio universe stand for innovation in product, design and technology—and thus for the future of light at Occhio. A total of eleven planets elaborated the future visions of Occhio, leading the visitors by means of digital "space stations" round the impressive booth with a footprint of 400 m². Five of the heavenly spheres represented the company's future, greatly extended product portfolio, the other six planets presented the special features of Occhio, for example the air app for the Bluetooth-based control of lights or the innovative high-voltage LED developed by Occhio. In this way, the unique universe showed potential applications of Occhio for both the end consumer and for professional users.

Auf über 400 Quadratmetern konnten die Besucher an elf Planeten Innovationen von Occhio erkunden, an digitalen „space stations" Einblick in die einzigartigen Möglichkeiten des Umgangs mit Licht gewinnen und auf der umlaufenden Balustrade in aller Ruhe entspannen.

On more than 400 m², visitors could explore Occhio's innovations on eleven planets, gain an insight into the unique possibilities of light at digital "space stations" and relax in peace and quiet on the balustrade that ran round the stand.

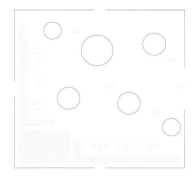
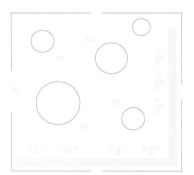

Size 400 m² | **Exhibitor** Occhio GmbH, Munich | **Photos** Robert Sprang / rsfotografie, Egling; Nadine Ingold / INGOLD PHOTOGRAPHY, Munich | **Architecture / Design** Martin et Karczinski GmbH, Munich; Drändle 70I30 GmbH, Munich | **Media** LurexX optical GmbH, Pfaffenhofen a. d. Ilm; winhard 3d, Munich; Sunday Digital GmbH, Munich | **Construction** Steffen Jastrob Schreiner & Messemontage, Langenfeld

Meiré und Meiré GmbH & Co. KG, Cologne
BÄRO GmbH & Co. KG, Cologne
Light + Building 2016, Frankfurt a. Main

LICHT UND SCHATTEN

Unter dem Motto „There are all sorts of lights. Because there are all sorts of products" entwickelte die Kölner Agentur Meiré und Meiré für BÄRO ein 220 Quadratmeter großes Messekonzept, bei dem sowohl das Design verschiedener Leuchtenserien als auch deren Lichtwirkung betont wurden. Stellvertretend für Licht und Schatten verwendeten die Gestalter hierfür die Farben Schwarz und Weiß und ergänzten diese durch symbolhafte Materialien: So deutete gebürsteter Edelstahl auf die anspruchsvolle Technologie und hochwertigen Materialeigenschaften der Produkte hin, während der warme Farbton des Eichenholzes die klaren, fast harten Konturen der Standarchitektur um eine weiche Komponente ergänzte. Die Produkte selbst wurden in ihren jeweiligen Charakteristika auf dem Stand verteilt präsentiert. Begehbare Lichtvitrinen gaben den Besuchern der Light + Building 2016 zudem die Möglichkeit, die Wirkung unterschiedlicher Lichtfarben – die so bezeichnende Namen trugen wie „GoldenBread", „Sun", „BeColor", „Fish&Seafood" oder „FreshMeat" – zu erkennen und sie dabei direkt miteinander zu vergleichen.

LIGHT AND SHADOW

Under the slogan "There are all sorts of lights. Because there are all sorts of products", the Cologne-based agency Meiré und Meiré developed a 220 m² trade fair concept for BÄRO which emphasised both the design of the various luminaire ranges as well as their light effect. To represent light and shadow, the designers used the colours black and white, supplemented by symbolic materials: Brushed stainless steel, for instance, was used to indicate the sophisticated technology and the high-quality material properties of the products, while the warm colour of oak wood added a soft component to the otherwise clear, almost hard contours of the stand architecture. The products themselves were grouped around the stand based on their respective characteristics. Walk-in light cabinets also gave visitors to the Light + Building 2016 the opportunity to recognise the effect of different light colours, bearing telling names such as "GoldenBread", "Sun", "BeColor", "Fish&Seafood" or "FreshMeat", and to compare them with one another.

Gestalter von Leuchten – Gestalter von Licht: Der Messeauftritt von BÄRO auf der Light + Building 2016 brachte die beiden Kernkompetenzen des Herstellers zum Ausdruck und präsentierte ihn als kompetenten Partner für Beleuchtungsprojekte im Handel.

Designers of luminaires—designers of light: The trade fair appearance of BÄRO at the Light + Building 2016 expressed the two core competences of the manufacturer and presented the company as a competent partner for commercial lighting projects.

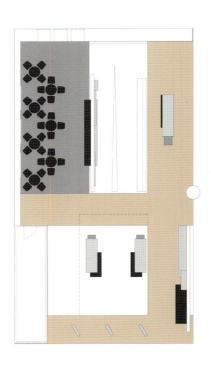

Die Wirkung von Licht und Schatten und der damit einhergehende veränderte Raumeindruck waren zentrales Gestaltungsthema des Messestands und wurden unter anderem an einer Reliefwand mithilfe zahlreicher Prismen und Pyramiden demonstriert.

The effect of light and shadow and the changed spatial impression this creates was the central design theme of the booth and was demonstrated, among other ways, in a relief wall with the help of numerous prisms and pyramids.

Size 220 m² | **Exhibitor** BÄRO GmbH & Co. KG, Cologne | **Photos** Boris Golz, Arnsberg | **Architecture / Design** Meiré und Meiré GmbH & Co. KG, Cologne | **Lighting** BÄRO GmbH & Co. KG, Cologne | **Construction** kubix GmbH zur Entwicklung und Produktion temporärer Bauten a. o., Berlin

OCKERTUNDPARTNER, Stuttgart
Nimbus Group GmbH, Stuttgart
Light + Building 2016, Frankfurt a. Main

KABELLOS GLÜCKLICH

Geflochtene schwarze Seile mit einer Gesamtlänge von 13 Kilometern umgaben den Stand der Stuttgarter Nimbus Group auf der Light + Building 2016 und versinnbildlichten damit von der Decke hängende Kabel. Da der 196 Quadratmeter große Auftritt einen Solitär darstellte, konnte dieses umlaufende Filterelement an allen vier Seiten von den Besuchern problemlos durchschritten werden, um die dahinterliegende neue Generation kabelloser Leuchten zu betrachten. Konzipiert von OCKERTUNDPARTNER wurde die Ausstellungsfläche durch einen Monolith mittig geteilt, der einen Infotresen zur Präsentationsfläche und eine Bar zum Kommunikationsbereich hin beinhaltete. Letzterer war mit kleinen Sitzgruppen möbliert und lag zu Messebeginn im Halbdunkeln – nur durch einige wenige kabellose Pendelleuchten inszeniert. Erst durch die Messegäste, die unterschiedliche Leuchten mit in den Besprechungsbereich mitnehmen konnten, entstanden flexible Lichtinseln und damit eine dynamische Choreografie auf dem Messestand.

LIGHT UNLEASHED

Plaited black ropes with a total length of 13 km surrounded the booth of the Stuttgart-based Nimbus Group at the Light + Building 2016 and symbolised cables hanging from the ceiling. As the 196 m² stand was a solitaire, visitors could easily pass through this all-round filter element to inspect the new generation of cable-free lights. Designed by OCKERTUNDPARTNER, the exhibition space was divided down the middle by a monolith which housed an information counter as presentation area and a bar as communication zone. The latter was furnished with small seating groups and at the beginning of the fair was only dimly lit by a few cable-free hanging lamps. It was not until fairgoers took various lights with them into the consultation section that flexible light islands evolved, creating a dynamic choreography on the stand.

Der Präsentationsbereich wurde durch etwa 200 Steh- und Wandleuchten auf weiß markierten Flächen erhellt, die nicht nur angeschaut, sondern explizit berührt und bewegt werden sollten.

The presentation area was illuminated by some 200 standard and wall lamps on areas marked out in white. Visitors were expressly encouraged to not just look at the lamps, but to touch and even move them about.

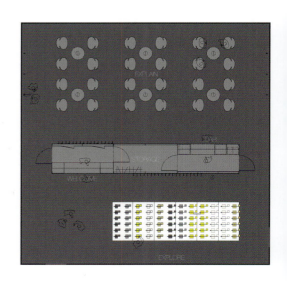

Der mit kleinen Sitzgruppen möblierte Besprechungsbereich lag zu Messebeginn noch im Halbdunkeln und wurde erst durch die Besucher nach und nach illuminiert. Einer dynamischen Choreografie folgend entstand so ein wechselndes Lichtspiel – abhängig von der Besucheranzahl und -bewegung auf dem Stand.

The consultation area furnished with small seating groups was only dimly lit at the start of the fair and was only gradually illuminated by the visitors. Following a dynamic choreography, the result was an ever changing play of lights—depending on the number of visitors and movement on the stand.

Size 196 m² | **Exhibitor** Nimbus Group GmbH, Stuttgart | **Photos** Frank Ockert / OCKERTUNDPARTNER, Stuttgart; Gordon Koelmel / FTGRF Fotodesign, Stuttgart | **Architecture / Design / Graphics** OCKERTUNDPARTNER, Stuttgart | **Lighting** Nimbus Group GmbH, Stuttgart | **Construction** Hospes Team GmbH, Leinfelden-Echterdingen

Schmidhuber Brand Experience GmbH, Munich
OSRAM GmbH, Munich
Light + Building 2016, Frankfurt a. Main

STADT, LICHT, NETZ

Unter dem Motto „Welcome to Smart City" transformierte der Lichtspezialist OSRAM sein breites und innovatives Portfolio auf der Light + Building 2016 in Frankfurt in echte Emotionen. Intelligente Lichtlösungen adäquat im Raum darzustellen und konkret erfahrbar zu machen war dabei die Herausforderung, der sich die Münchner Gestalter von SCHMIDHUBER stellen mussten. Um das Thema der digitalen Vernetzung in den Vordergrund zu stellen, entwickelten sie die „Smart City" – eine Stadt, in der Digitalisierung und Vernetzung Realität geworden sind, die durch Menschen zum Leben erwacht und mit ihren Bewohnern interagiert. So wurde eine urbane und moderne Erlebniswelt erschaffen, in der Licht mit all seinen Facetten und Entfaltungen spürbar wurde. Dabei war auf dem 1.500 Quadratmeter großen Messestand nicht nur alles miteinander vernetzt, auch die Besucher wurden mit eingebunden. Sie konnten mit den Exponaten interagieren, Virtual Reality erleben oder über Apps Einfluss auf Farbgebungen und -stimmungen nehmen.

CITY, LIGHT, NETWORK

At the Light and Building 2015 in Frankfurt the light specialist OSRAM translated their broad and innovative portfolio into genuine emotions under the slogan "Welcome to Smart City". Finding an adequate way of spatially presenting intelligent light solutions and allowing them to be directly experienced was the challenge that Munich-based designers from SCHMIDHUBER had to master. In order to place the focus on digital connectivity, they developed the "Smart City"—a city in which digitalisation and connectivity have become reality and which is brought to life by people and which interacts with its residents. The result was an urban and modern themed world in which light could be perceived in all its facets and evolvements. Not only were all the items located on the 1,500 m² stand connected to one another; even the visitors were integrated. They could interact with the exhibits, experience virtual reality or use apps to influence colour schemes and moods.

Vernetzung wurde zum Erlebnis: Die „Smart City" lud nicht nur zum virtuellen Schaufensterbummel ein, über die sichtbaren Bereiche hinaus demonstrierte sie auch die technologischen Möglichkeiten der modernen Welt.

Connectivity became an experience: The "Smart City" not only invited visitors to virtual window shopping. Beyond the visible areas, it demonstrated the technological possibilities of the modern world.

In den verschiedenen, lebensnah gestalteten Bereichen – wie Baumarkt, Bar, Salon oder Wohnraum – konnten sich die Besucher über alle Produkte informieren – von der intelligenten Hausbeleuchtung bis zu WLAN-Hotspots und Ladestationen für Elektromobile in Lichtmasten.

In the various, realistically designed areas—such as property market, bar, salon or living room—visitors could obtain information about all the products—from intelligent house lighting through to WLAN hotspots and charging stations for electric cars in light towers.

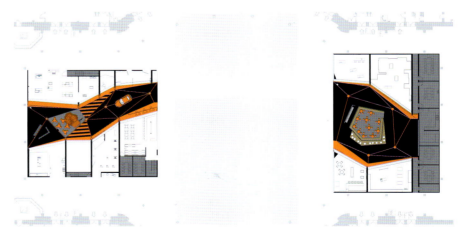

Size 1,500 m² | **Exhibitor** OSRAM GmbH, Munich | **Photos** Jean-Luc Valentin, Frankfurt a. Main | **Architecture / Design** Schmidhuber Brand Experience GmbH, Munich | **General Contractor** prio Event Management GmbH, Berlin | **Lighting** TLD Planungsgruppe GmbH, Taufkirchen | **Construction** bluepool GmbH, Leinfelden-Echterdingen

PRECIOSA

VASKU & KLUG, Vienna
Preciosa Lighting, Kamenický Šenov
Euroluce 2015, Milan

LICHT-SCHIMMER

Auf der Euroluce 2015 – Bestandteil des Salone del Mobile Milano – inszenierten die Wiener Gestalter VASKU & KLUG den Messeauftritt des tschechischen Kronleuchterherstellers Preciosa Lighting. Dabei legten sie den Fokus weniger auf das Produktportfolio, sondern vielmehr auf die Firmenphilosophie – stellvertretend für das Selbstverständnis einer weltweit für Glas- und Kristallkunst bekannten Region. Dementsprechend betraten die Besucher einen stimmungsvollen Raum mit dunklen bis schwarzen Materialien, in dem in gedimmter Beleuchtung die Ästhetik sowie das Kunsthandwerk der Produkte ausgestellt wurden. Zentrales Element des 300 Quadratmeter großen Auftritts bildete ein Brunnen, über dem zwei klassische Kronleuchter jeweils flankiert von ihrer Neuinterpretation zu schweben schienen. VASKU & KLUG schufen damit ein symbolisches Bild um die weissagenden Fähigkeiten von Brunnen: Wie der Blick auf die Wasseroberfläche den Blick auf die Zukunft des eigenen Antlitzes preisgibt, so ließ auch der Blick von den Stirnseiten des Brunnens in der Ausstellung einen Blick auf die Zukunft des Kronleuchters erhaschen.

SHIMMER OF LIGHT

At the Euroluce 2015—part of the Salone del Mobile Milano—the Viennese designers VASKU & KLUG created the trade fair stand for the Czech chandelier manufacturer Preciosa Lighting. The focus was placed less on the product portfolio, and rather on the corporate philosophy—representative of the self-image of a region that is known the world over for glass and crystal artwork. The atmospheric room decorated with dark to black materials that the visitors entered was therefore such that in the dimmed light the aesthetics and the craftsmanship of the products took centre stage. The central element of the 300 m² stand was a well; above this two classical chandeliers appeared to be floating, flanked on each side by their new interpretations. VASKU & KLUG thus created a symbolic image referring to the prophetic capabilities of wells: just as by looking at the surface of the water reveals a view of the future of one's own countenance, so the view from the head of the well into the exhibition allowed a glimpse of the future of the chandelier.

Im Zentrum des Auftritts konnten die Besucher einen Brunnen sehen, in dessen Wasseroberfläche sich Neuinterpretationen klassischer Kronleuchter gemeinsam mit ihren historischen Vorbildern spiegelten und so Vergangenheit und Zukunft miteinander verbanden.

When visitors looked into the well at the centre of the booth they saw a reflection in the water surface of new interpretations of classic chandeliers alongside their historical models, thus combining past and future.

Die mystische Inszenierung tschechischer Glasmacherkunst wurde zur Grundstimmung des Messestands, der zu einem geheimnisvollen Lichttempel avancierte, indem er durch geometrische Lichtwände sowie expressive Leuchten auf dunklen Wänden ergänzt wurde.

The mystical staging of the Czech art of glass-making created the basic mood of the trade fair stand; supplemented by geometrical light walls and expressive luminaires against dark walls, the stand was transformed into a mysterious temple of light.

Size 300 m² | **Exhibitor** Preciosa Lighting, Kamenický Šenov | **Photos** VASKU & KLUG, Vienna | **Architecture / Design** VASKU & KLUG, Vienna | **Lighting** Preciosa Lighting, Kamenický Šenov | **Construction** System Standbau GmbH, Salzburg

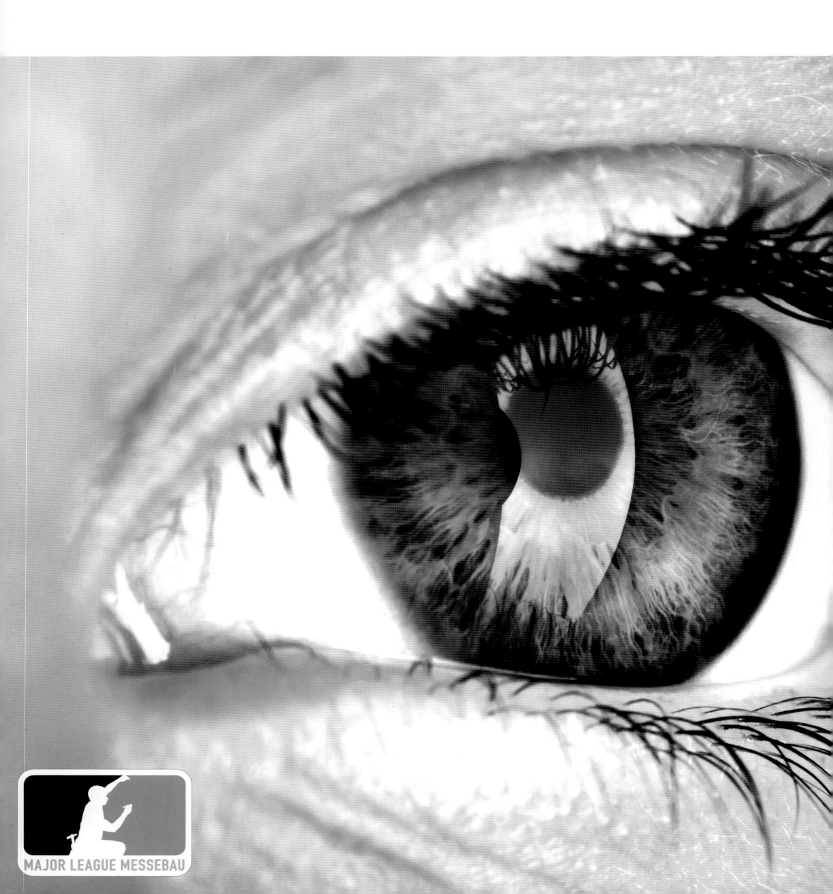

KLARTEXT GRAFIK MESSE EVENT GMBH

FIRMA

KLARTEXT GRAFIK
MESSE EVENT GMBH

LEISTUNGEN

Wir bauen Räume,
die Sie bewegen.

REFERENZEN

DAIMLER AG, Volkswagen AG,
MeyerSound, BASF SE

KONTAKT

www.klartextgmbh.de
info@klartextgmbh.de
Tel. +49 (0) 2154-8863-0

IMPRESSUM
IMPRINT

Herausgeber Editors
Sabine Marinescu, Janina Poesch
Redaktion Editing
Annerose Bach
Autoren Authors
Sabine Marinescu, Janina Poesch, Andreas Finger, Isabella Kusche
Übersetzung Translation
Beverley Locke
Layout Layout
We & Me Design Studio GbR | Jule Schubert, Franziska Strantz, Nils Krämer
Layout-Umsetzung Realisation
av edition GmbH, Stuttgart
Schriften Fonts
Avenir, Avenir LT Pro
Coverfoto Cover photo
Erik Chmil / CHMIL.FOTOGRAFIE. GbR, Cologne; hw.design gmbh, Munich; Munksjö Decor, Aalen
Lithografie Lithography
corinna rieber prepress, Marbach
Papier Paper
Core Silk, 150 g/m²
Druck Printing
Gorenjski tisk storitve, Kranj

av edition GmbH
Verlag für Architektur und Design
Senefelderstr. 109
70176 Stuttgart
Germany
Tel.: +49 (0)711 / 220 22 79-0
Fax: +49 (0)711 / 220 22 79-15
contact@avedition.com
www.avedition.com

Dank Acknowledgements
Verlag und Autoren danken den beteiligten Firmen, Architekten, Agenturen, Messebauern und Fotografen für die zur Verfügung gestellten Bilder und Materialien.
The publisher and authors wish to thank those companies, architects, agencies, stand construction firms and photographers who have provided images and material.

Copyright Copyright
© Copyright 2016 **av**edition GmbH, Stuttgart, Verlag für Architektur und Design
© Copyright für die Fotos bei den Unternehmen und Fotografen
© Copyright 2016 **av**edition GmbH, Stuttgart, Publishers for Architecture and Design
© Copyright of photos with individual companies and photographers

Alle Rechte, insbesondere das Recht der Vervielfältigung, Verbreitung und Übersetzung, vorbehalten. Kein Teil des Werkes darf in irgendeiner Form (durch Fotokopie, Mikrofilm oder ein anderes Verfahren) ohne schriftliche Genehmigung reproduziert oder unter Verwendung elektronischer Systeme verarbeitet werden.
This work is subject to copyright. All rights are reserved, whether the whole or part of the material is concerned, and specifically but not exclusively the right of translation, reprinting, reuse of illustrations, recitation, broadcasting, reproduction on microfilms or in other ways, and storage in databases or any other media. For use of any kind, the written permission of the copyright owner must be obtained.

ISBN 978-3-89986-257-7
Printed in Europe